Joomla! 1.5 Development Cookbook

Solve real world Joomla! 1.5 development problems with over 130 simple but incredibly useful recipes

James Kennard

BIRMINGHAM - MUMBAI

Joomla! 1.5 Development Cookbook

First published: September 2009

Production Reference: 1150909

Published by Packt Publishing Ltd.
32 Lincoln Road
Olton
Birmingham, B27 6PA, UK.

ISBN 978-1-847198-14-3

www.packtpub.com

Cover Image by Karl Moore (karl.moore@ukonline.co.uk)

Credits

Author
James Kennard

Reviewers
Rob Clayburn

Kevin Devine

Acquisition Editor
Douglas Paterson

Development Editor
Dhiraj Chandiramani

Technical Editors
Elizabeth Mathew

Ishita Dhabalia

Aditi Srivastava

Copy Editor
Sneha Kulkarni

Editorial Team Leader
Gagandeep Singh

Project Team Leader
Lata Basantani

Project Coordinator
Srimoyee Ghoshal

Indexer
Rekha Nair

Proofreader
Sandra Hopper

Graphics
Nilesh Mohite

Production Coordinator
Shantanu Zagade

Cover Work
Shantanu Zagade

About the Author

James Kennard is an accomplished programmer with proven experience in many different types of organizations. He has worked as a private consultant, and has worked in the public and private sectors for the likes of Logica and the National Library of Wales. He has over six years of experience working with Joomla!, previously Mambo. As an active member of the Joomla! community, he maintains a popular open source helpdesk component and wrote the popular book *Mastering Joomla! 1.5 extension and framework development*, also available from Packt Publishing.

About the Reviewers

Rob Clayburn, along with running his company, Pollen 8 Design Ltd, is heavily involved as a project leader in Fabrik, an open source Joomla application builder, which allows users to rapidly prototype and create web applications.

As an avid and experienced web developer, Rob strives in all his projects to balance sound programming practices, intuitive UI design, and eye-catching graphics.

During his career, he has developed various web, mobile, and kiosk applications for clients ranging from a 3D kiosk game for The London Planetarium to various web applications, including a portfolio creator site and a geo-spatial social network.

Kevin Devine has been developing web sites using Joomla! since 2006 when he accepted a full-time position with PICnet. Based in Washington, D.C, PICnet is a web development company serving non-profit organizations across the United States. He also devotes time to the Joomla! project as a member of the Bug Squad, a co-maintainer of the 1.5.x release, and a member of the Joomla! Security Strike Team.

Table of Contents

Preface

This book has a "wealth" of solutions for problems that Joomla! developers face regularly. It provides step-by-step mini examples, which show how to overcome common design and implementation problems when creating Joomla! extensions. It will help you set up a sustainable collaborative development environment using the powerful free services offered by JoomlaCode.org.

This book can be used in different ways. It can be used by the pro Joomla! developer looking for a specific solution to a problem, and can also be used by a novice developer looking for an insight into an area of common problems, such as effectively handling errors in Joomla!. Readers who choose to read an entire chapter will first be given a brief overview of the topic in hand, and its role and importance when developing for Joomla!. The recipes contained within the chapters will introduce the reader to specific problems and provide hands-on solutions. It provides solutions for core design topics, including security, data access, users, sessions, and multilingual capabilities.

What this book covers

Chapter 1, Development using JoomlaCode.org and SVN, explores how to set up and use project hosting at `JoomlaCode.org` and explains how to use a `JoomlaCode.org` Subversion repository.

Chapter 2, Keeping Extensions Secure, demonstrates how we can secure extensions and explains some of the ramifications if we fail to do this.

Chapter 3, Working with the Database, teaches us how to interact with the Joomla! database using the handy JDatabase interface.

Chapter 4, The Session and the User, shows how we can interact with the current user, logged in or not, and how we can interact with their session.

Chapter 5, Multilingual Recipes, discusses how to overcome common problems with making international extensions, such as how to deal with UTF-8.

Chapter 6, Interaction and Styling, describes how to restyle pages using CSS and JavaScript, and how to improve the user experience by adding Ajax capabilities.

Chapter 7, Customizing the Document, shows how we can modify the server response by working with the global document object.

Chapter 8, Customizing the Backend, looks at how to tailor the backend for our extensions, for example how to add buttons to the toolbar.

Chapter 9, Keeping it Extensible and Modular, focuses on modularity and extensibility, showing how we can create versatile solutions that can be further extended by third parties.

Chapter 10, JObjects and Arrays, looks at common things we can do with JObjects and arrays using Joomla!.

Chapter 11, Error Handling and Reporting, will help us discover how to deal with errors and, for PHP 5 extensions, exceptions.

Chapter 12, Files and Folders, deals with the filesystem and how we can interact with the filesystem using the Joomla! framework.

What you need for this book

To use this book effectively you need access to a Joomla! 1.5 installation. In order to run Joomla! 1.5 you need the following software: PHP 4.3.10 or higher (4.4.7 or higher is recommended), MySQL 3.23 or higher and Apache 1.3 or higher or an equivalent web server.

Some of the information in this book pertains specifically to PHP 5. In these instances you will need access to PHP 5 (5.2.0 or higher is recommended).

Who this book is for

This book is for PHP developers who have prior experience of developing for Joomla! It does not introduce developing extensions for Joomla!, it is assumed that the reader has prior knowledge of the subject and is looking for a quick guide to solve common problems quickly, which commonly occur when developing for Joomla!. It does not matter if you are an accomplished Joomla! developer or just starting out. For each scenario that this book addresses, there is an introductory explanation of the problem and an easy-to-implement solution. For the more accomplished developers, recipes also include a discussion of the solution, explaining how it works and how it can be further enhanced or customized.

Conventions

In this book, you will find a number of styles of text that distinguish between different kinds of information. Here are some examples of these styles, and an explanation of their meaning.

Code words in text are shown as follows: "The JDatabase::nameQuote() method is used to safely represent identifiers and names."

A block of code is set as follows:

```
if (!JRequest::checkToken('REQUEST')) {
    // return 403 error
    JError::raiseError(403, JText::_('ALERTNOAUTH'));
    // belt and braces approach to guarantee the script stops
    jexit('Invalid Token');
}
```

When we wish to draw your attention to a particular part of a code block, the relevant lines or items are set in bold:

```
$script = <<<'SCRIPT'
var Account = new Class({
  options: {
    name: "Packt Publishing's Account",
    number: "0000001",
    $amount: 10
  },
  initialize: function(options){
    this.setOptions(options);
  }
});
```

Any command-line input or output is written as follows:

```
# cp /usr/src/asterisk-addons/configs/cdr_mysql.conf.sample
    /etc/asterisk/cdr_mysql.conf
```

New terms and **important words** are shown in bold. Words that you see on the screen, in menus or dialog boxes for example, appear in the text like this: "clicking the **Next** button moves you to the next screen".

Warnings or important notes appear in a box like this.

Tips and tricks appear like this.

Reader feedback

Feedback from our readers is always welcome. Let us know what you think about this book—what you liked or may have disliked. Reader feedback is important for us to develop titles that you really get the most out of.

To send us general feedback, simply send an email to `feedback@packtpub.com`, and mention the book title via the subject of your message.

If there is a book that you need and would like to see us publish, please send us a note in the **SUGGEST A TITLE** form on `www.packtpub.com` or email `suggest@packtpub.com`.

If there is a topic that you have expertise in and you are interested in either writing or contributing to a book on, see our author guide on `www.packtpub.com/authors`.

Customer support

Now that you are the proud owner of a Packt book, we have a number of things to help you to get the most from your purchase.

Downloading the example code for the book

Visit `http://www.packtpub.com/files/code/8143_Code.zip` to directly download the example code.

The downloadable files contain instructions on how to use them.

Errata

Although we have taken every care to ensure the accuracy of our content, mistakes do happen. If you find a mistake in one of our books—maybe a mistake in the text or the code—we would be grateful if you would report this to us. By doing so, you can save other readers from frustration, and help us to improve subsequent versions of this book. If you find any errata, please report them by visiting `http://www.packtpub.com/support`, selecting your book, clicking on the **let us know** link, and entering the details of your errata. Once your errata are verified, your submission will be accepted and the errata added to any list of existing errata. Any existing errata can be viewed by selecting your title from `http://www.packtpub.com/support`.

Piracy

Piracy of copyright material on the Internet is an ongoing problem across all media. At Packt, we take the protection of our copyright and licenses very seriously. If you come across any illegal copies of our works, in any form, on the Internet, please provide us with the location address or web site name immediately so that we can pursue a remedy.

Please contact us at copyright@packtpub.com with a link to the suspected pirated material.

We appreciate your help in protecting our authors, and our ability to bring you valuable content.

Questions

You can contact us at questions@packtpub.com if you are having a problem with any aspect of the book, and we will do our best to address it.

1

Development using JoomlaCode.org and SVN

This chapter contains the following recipes:

- ▶ Setting up a `JoomlaCode.org` project
- ▶ Managing members of a `JoomlaCode.org` project
- ▶ Setting up `JoomlaCode.org` Subversion
- ▶ Understanding the Subversion skeleton
- ▶ Understanding revisions in Subversion
- ▶ Understanding the Subversion process
- ▶ Checking out a Subversion repository using TortoiseSVN
- ▶ Editing a working copy using TortoiseSVN
- ▶ Inspecting changes using TortoiseSVN
- ▶ Updating a working copy and resolving conflicts using TortoiseSVN
- ▶ Committing changes using TortoiseSVN
- ▶ Exporting a working copy using TortoiseSVN

Introduction

In this chapter, we investigate how we can utilize the free `JoomlaCode.org` project hosting service. In particular, this chapter addresses how to use `JoomlaCode.org` **SVN (Subversion)** and how to work with **SVN** using the popular visual **TortoiseSVN** client for Windows.

`JoomlaCode.org` (`http://www.joomlacode.org`) provides a project management solution for open source Joomla! projects. The following list describes the tools that `JoomlaCode.org` provides us with:

- **Document Manager:** Simple document publishing (usually documentation)
- **File Release System (FRS):** Packages released by the project
- **Mailing Lists:** Multiple mailing list manager
- **News:** Latest project news
- **Public Forums:** Discussion forums for `JoomlaCode.org` users
- **Public Wiki:** Collaborative online documentation
- **Source Control Management (SCM):** Manage code base using **CVS**, **SVN**, or **Git** (in this book we focus on **SVN** exclusively)
- **Tracker:** Manager for tracking feature requests, bugs, and patches

The following diagram shows how these various tools can be thought of when used together. Note that this is not a concrete representation; how we utilize the tools that `JoomlaCode.org` provides us with is always the overriding factor.

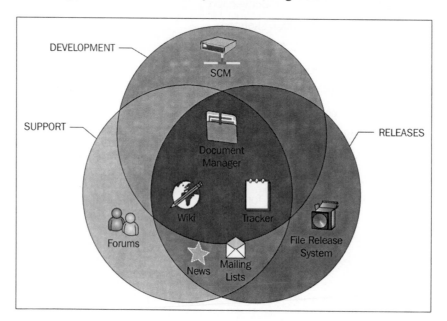

Don't let the tools dictate the processes

Software development isn't just about the tools we use. It is about the processes we undertake. We should use the tools that best fit our processes, as opposed to using the processes that happen to fit our tools.

Before we continue, we should take time to note that not all projects will successfully qualify for `JoomlaCode.org` project space. `JoomlaCode.org` only supports non-commercial open source Joomla! projects. Remember that non-commercial and open source are not mutually exclusive; it is possible to commercially release an open source product. If we are not creating a non-commercial open source project, there are other similar free and paid-for services; the following table compares four popular alternatives:

	Assembla (1)	Google Code	SourceForge	Unfuddle
Free Project Hosting	YES	YES	YES	YES
Commercial Project Hosting	YES	NO	NO	YES
Closed Source Project Hosting	YES	NO	NO	YES
Public Forums	YES (2)	YES (4)	YES	NO
SCM	Subversion, Git, Mercurial	Subversion	Subversion	Subversion, Git
Tracker	YES	YES	YES	YES
Document Manager	YES	YES (5)	YES (8)	NO (9)
News	YES (3)	YES (6)	YES	NO
FRS	NO	YES (5)	YES	NO
Mailing Lists	YES	YES (4)	YES	NO
Public Wiki	YES	YES	YES	NO (10)

(1)   Assembla intends to add a package to their catalog, specifi cally for Joomla! projects. This package will enable an enterprise-level commit-stage-release cycle in the development process. Assembla also provides an unusually high level of integration with other services; for example, we could hook into a `JoomlaCode.org` **Subversion** repository.

(2)   Assembla Messages Tool can be used to this effect.

(3)   Assembla does not offer a **News** tab. However, Assembla will display a *stream* of all project activity, and a **Messages** tab.

(4)   Google Code integrates with Google Groups. Google Groups provides public forums and mailing lists.

(5) Google Code provides downloads which can be used as an FRS and Document Manager.

(6) Google Code integrates with Blogger, and a blog can be used to this effect.

(7) SourceForge is very similar to JoomlaCode.org. (The underlying systems are much the same, GForge, used by `JoomlaCode.org`, is a fork of the SourceForge system.)

(8) SourceForge Documentation Plugin can be used to this effect.

(9) Unfuddle does not specifically provide a Document Manager, but files can be attached to tickets, messages, and notebooks.

(10) Unfuddle does not provide a public wiki, but does provide notebooks that can be used like a private wiki.

SVN is an **SCM** tool, and **SCM** is part of **SCM**... Confusing, isn't it! Let's try that again: **Subversion** is a **Source Control Management** tool, **Source Control Management** is part of **Software Configuration Management**. Which just goes to show the computer industry really does love its acronyms just a little too much! Even the IETF likes to have some fun with this once in a while `http://tools.ietf.org/html/rfc5513`.

`JoomlaCode.org` can be thought of as a system that provides Software Configuration Management. And as part of that package, we get Source Control Management tools. The topic of Software Configuration Management is beyond the scope of this book, and we will not be discussing it further.

Source Control Management is an integral part of modern software development. We need Source Control Management in our projects because it:

▸ Allows concurrent collaborative development of source code (working copies)

▸ Tracks all changes made to the source code (revisions)

▸ Provides states to which we can return at any time (revisions)

▸ Allows parallel development of various functionality (branches)

▸ Can be used to manage releases (tags)

▸ Can be used to maintain older versions (releases)

▸ Provides a common vocabulary for discussing Source Control Management

Source Control Management does require a good level of understanding if it is to be used effectively. This book covers the basic usage and theory of using Subversion.

Subversion client freedom

Although in this book we work exclusively with the popular TortoiseSVN visual Windows Subversion client, it is possible to use several clients on the same working copy. Therefore, we do not need to worry about restricting ourselves to a specific client. For example, I use TortoiseSVN, CollabNet's command line client, and the Netbeans SVN plugin, dependant on what I am doing.

Setting up a JoomlaCode.org project

This recipe describes how to set up our own `JoomlaCode.org` project so that we can start developing and managing our new extension. Use of `JoomlaCode.org` is not compulsory.

Getting ready

To set up a `JoomlaCode.org` project we must create a `JoomlaCode.org` user account. To register for a `JoomlaCode.org` user account, all we need to do is follow the **Register new account** link displayed in the top-right corner of the `JoomlaCode.org` web site.

The username we choose will be used for all activities that we initiate with `JoomlaCode.org`, for example using a `JoomlaCode.org` SVN repository.

`JoomlaCode.org` usernames must be lowercase. If you request a username with uppercase characters, these will be automatically replaced with the lowercase equivalent.

How to do it...

To create a new project we navigate to the **My Stuff** tab at the top of the page. This presents us with all sorts of information about our account. From the menu items on the lefthand side, select the **My Account** item. In the expanded menu there is an option to **Register Project**, shown as follows:

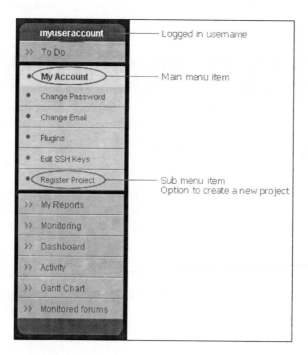

Once we select **Register Project**, we are presented with a form that allows us to define our project. The following table describes the purpose of the fields:

Field	Description
Project Full Name	Complete name of the project. This will generally be the name of the extension that we want to develop using JoomlaCode.org.
Project Purpose	What the project will be used for. This information is used exclusively to determine if the project should be approved for inclusion on JoomlaCode.org.
Project Public Description	Description of the project that is publicly viewable and searchable. This description is shown on the project home page and in the project listings. When a JoomlaCode.org user searches for a project, both the project name and description are searched.

Field	Description
Project UNIX Name	Restricted to alphanumeric characters, this field is used to uniquely identify the project. It is important to select a good UNIX name because the UNIX name of a project can never be altered. The UNIX name is used to identify the project home page, define the file repository location, and to access the GForge shell.
	The UNIX name must have the following properties:
	▶ Unique to `JoomlaCode.org`
	▶ Contain between 3 and 15 characters
	▶ Contain only lowercase characters
	▶ Contain only characters, numbers, and dashes
Homepage URL	If as part of the project we also maintain a web site external to `JoomlaCode.org`, we can specify this here.
Template Project	Template to use as a basis for the new project. Selecting **Empty Project** provides us with a clean slate.
Trove Categorization: Development Status	Maturity of the project. When creating a new project it is likely that the project will be in the early stages of development, for example, *Planning* or *Alpha*.
Trove Categorization: License	The License under which the project is released. Remember that `JoomlaCode.org` hosting is only available for open source projects.
Trove Categorization: Programming Language	The primary programming language in which the project is written. The majority of projects are PHP and at the time of writing 86% of `JoomlaCode.org` projects are defined as PHP projects.
Trove Categorization: Topic	The topic that best describes the project. The topics are organized in a way similar to **JED**. This is really intended to allow users to browse through the `JoomlaCode.org` projects. However, most users prefer to use **JED** because it is more complete and provides a greater level of feedback from users of extensions.
Trove Categorization: Intended Audience	The type of user for whom the project is intended to provide services. For example, a project that provides code libraries would be considered to be intended for developers, where as a project that generates tag clouds would be considered intended for end users.

After submitting the registration form the project is ready for approval by the `JoomlaCode.org` team. The approval process is administered manually, and so it may take some time before the project is approved. If there are any problems with the approval of the project, we will be contacted and given the opportunity to further explain the project.

Once the project has been approved, an approval confirmation email will be sent to us. The following screenshot shows the email received for the project **My JoomlaCode.org Project**, UNIX name **example-project**.

Project 'My JoomlaCode.org Project' has been approved

From: **noreply@joomlacode.org**
Sent: 12 January 2009 15:23:41
To:

```
The project you've submitted (My JoomlaCode.org Project) has been approved by the
system administrators.

You can visit your project in the following URL:
http://joomlacode.org/gf/project/example-project/
```

We should now have a project ready to go! It is generally a good idea to edit the project home page at this stage. To do this, press the **Edit project's homepage** button displayed on the home page itself.

My Project Homepage
Example project for the Packt Publishing book Joomla! 1.5 Cookbook.

Edit project's homepage

Activity

Request to join project

Description

Example project for the Packt Publishing book Joomla! 1.5 Cookbook.

Developer Info

James Kennard

Trove Categorization

- Development Status: 1 - Planning
- Intended Audience: Other Audience
- License: GNU General Public License (GPL)
- Programming Language: PHP
- Topic: Miscellaneous

There's more...

`JoomlaCode.org` projects are based on plugins. Each plugin provides us with a specific piece of functionality. When we look at the admin page for the project we find a list of plugins that we can enable and disable.

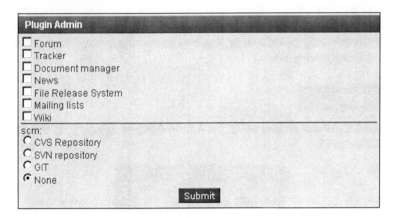

It is generally best to enable each plugin as and when we require it. Projects that enable all plugins but do not actually make use of them can be frustrating for users who are trying to find information about the project.

Getting Help

`JoomlaCode.org` uses GForge, and so the GForge documentation can prove helpful. Refer to `http://gforge.org/projects/gforge/` for more information.

See also

The following two recipes explain how to manage members of `JoomlaCode.org` projects and how to set up a `JoomlaCode.org` SVN repository.

Managing members of a JoomlaCode.org project

This recipe explains how, as an administrator of a `JoomlaCode.org` project, we can manage members of a project. The members are the `JoomlaCode.org` users who contribute to a project. The nature of the contributions does not necessarily have to be code development. For example, a member may contribute by regularly answering questions on the project forum and contributing to the project Wiki.

How to do it...

We manage members of our project using the **Admin Options** displayed to the righthand side of the project admin page.

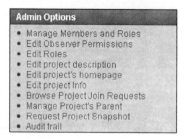

To add a new member, select the **Manage Members and Roles** option. On this page, we will see a list of users who are already members of the project and their role in the project. At the bottom of this list is an option to add a new member. In the example shown as follows, we are attempting to add the `JoomlaCode.org` user **webamoeba** to the project with the **Role** of **Admin**.

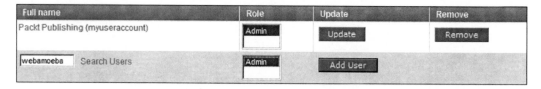

Once we're all done, the new user will appear in the members list.

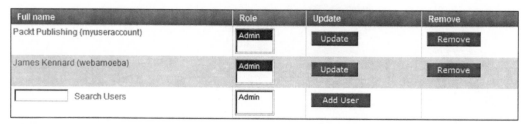

How it works...

Members of a project are always assigned a role. Roles define what a member can and cannot do. By default there is a single role, **Admin**. Allocating this role provides members of the project full administrative access to the project. Generally speaking, there should be only one or two members to whom this role is applied.

We can define additional roles and we can edit existing roles using the **Edit Roles** option in the **Admin Options** box. It is only possible to change permissions for plugins that are enabled in the project.

There's more...

In addition to manually specifying `JoomlaCode.org` users that we want to add as project members, users can request to join projects. Users can do so by pressing the **Request to join project** button displayed on the project home page and entering a short description of why they want to join the project. It is then up to us as a project administrator to accept or decline their request. To do this we use the **Browse Project Join Requests** link in the **Admin Options** box.

Only allow users you trust

It is not uncommon to receive requests to join a project by users who have misunderstood the meaning of member. Before allowing any user to join one of our projects, we should confirm exactly why they want to join and if we actually want them to!

Setting up JoomlaCode.org Subversion

This recipe describes how to set up Subversion for a `JoomlaCode.org` project.

SVN is not just for collaborative development

If we are the only developer for our project, Subversion can still be of use. Versioning, tagging, and branching are all invaluable functions irrespective of the number of developers.

How to do it...

Firstly we need to log in to our `JoomlaCode.org` project. From here we navigate to the **Admin** page. The **Plugin Admin** box displays the plugins that are active for our project; by default, none of the plugins will be activated. In the area named **scm**, change the radio button selection from **None**, to **SVN repository**. Once we submit our changes, **SVN** and **SVN Admin** will appear in the lefthand menu, as shown in the following screenshot:

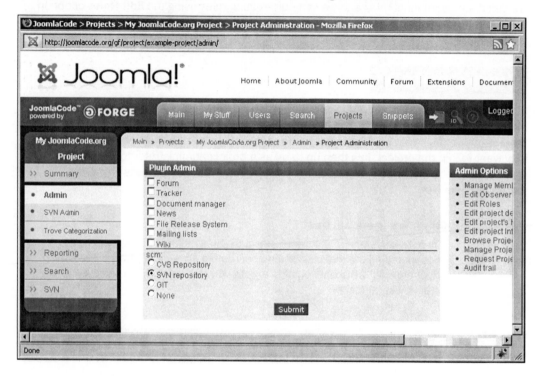

There is delay between enabling Subversion and the repository becoming active. As soon as the repository is active, we can start using and browsing it!

How it works...

When we create a **Subversion** repository, the repository will be populated with a skeleton structure. The following screenshot shows us what our new repository should look like:

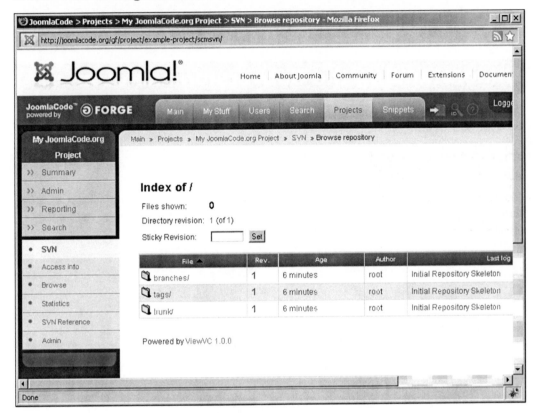

 This initial repository skeleton conforms to the suggested way of working with Subversion. The next recipe explains this skeleton in more detail.

As we can see, there is a normal looking filesystem tree structure, each item in the tree is of a specified revision and age. The last log entry shows the message that was created when the identified revision was committed; in this case, it is **Initial Repository Skeleton**.

See also

For information about setting up a project on `JoomlaCode.org`, please refer to the previous recipe *Setting up a JoomlaCode.org project*.

In the next recipe, *Understanding the Subversion skeleton*, we investigate the purpose of the skeleton folders that are initially created in the repository.

Understanding the Subversion skeleton

This recipe explains the purpose of the initial skeleton folders that are created in a new `JoomlaCode.org` Subversion repository.

How to do it...

Understanding the skeleton is vital when setting up a new repository. Getting it wrong early on in the set up process can lead to major problems later. There are three folders, each with a specific purpose. The following diagram describes the skeleton structure:

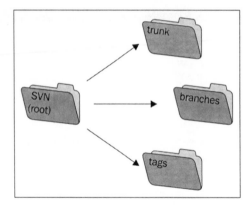

The folder that we will use the most is the `trunk` folder. This folder is the basis for all of current mainstream development activity. This is where the next release of the software will be developed.

The `branches` folder is similar; current development activity also occurs here. However, it is not for mainstream development, it is used for parallel development. Parallel development is development that is taking place at the same moment in time but is pursuing a different goal. For example, if part of the developer team is working on a new area of functionality, to shield that line of development from the mainstream development—and vice versa—a new branch may be created specifically for that line of development.

It is important to understand that `branches` are nearly always reincorporated with the `trunk` at a later date. A new folder is created in the branches folder for every line of parallel development.

The concept of the `tags` folder in Subversion isn't much different from tagging in the semantic web. Tagging is all about semantics, giving things meaning. We create a new tag whenever we create a new release. Tags are always static, that is to say, no more development ever occurs to a tag.

So if there is no development, what's the point? A release will always be associated with a repository revision. For example, if we released our software at version 1.0.0 when the repository was at revision number 165, we could simply extract revision 165 at a later date to rebuild version 1.0.0. But 165 can hardly be considered an easy to remember number. Also, it does not bear any direct relation to version 1.0.0. Creating a tag that contains a complete instance of version 1.0.0 makes it semantically easy to understand, for developers and non-developers alike.

How it works...

OK, let's consider a really basic repository. This project has only one file, `myonlyfile.php`. There are two releases 1.0.0 and 1.0.1, and the developers are currently working on version 1.0.2. One of the developers is in the process of adding ACL support, and they are doing this separately from the main thrust of development. The following figure shows what the repository will look like:

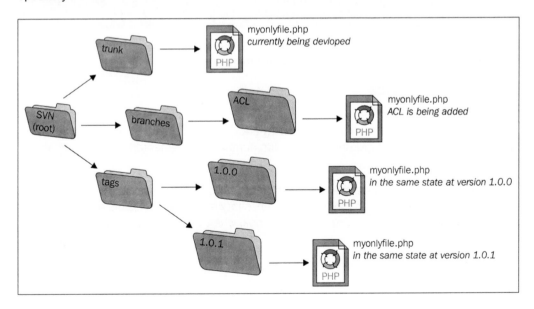

Sticking to tradition

We do not have to work to these standards, and we can remove the skeleton structure if we do not want to use it. Generally speaking, it is best to stick to this arrangement, or a similar structure, because developers who are familiar with Subversion will be able to understand the repository structure immediately.

There's more...

Another useful folder we can add to the skeleton is the `releases` folder. The purpose of a `releases` folder is to enable release maintenance, after earlier releases have been surpassed by a newer release.

For example, if after we have released version 2.0.0 and if 20% of our user base is still using version 1.n.n, we may want to continue to resolve bugs in the earlier release. To manage this, we create a folder for each major release, which has been surpassed, in a `releases` folder. We can then continue to patch these versions without interfering with the main development.

The Joomla! project itself uses this approach. At the time of writing, in the Joomla SVN there is a `releases` folder that contains `1.0` and `1.5`. Allowing continued maintenance of these versions whilst with the main development of 1.6 is addressed in the `trunk` folder.

Understanding revisions in Subversion

Part of what makes Subversion so useful is its ability to archive changes. This recipe looks at revisions and how they work in practice in a Subversion repository.

How to do it...

Revisions are expressed as a positive integer. Whenever a set of changes is committed to a repository, a new revision is created. The revision number is incremented every time changes are applied to the repository.

The revision number is global to the repository. In other words, it applies to all files, irrespective of which have been modified. The repository is always accessible as a whole at any given revision. For example, like pages in a book, when a new edition of a book is released all pages are of that edition.

The most recent revision is called the **HEAD revision**.

The following image illustrates how revisions and the skeleton described in the previous recipe correspond. Each circle represents a revision of the repository. The arrows represent the sources of the new revisions.

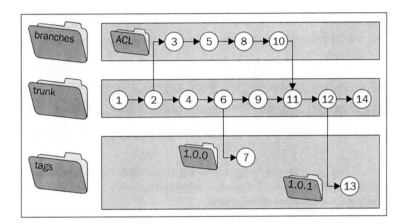

We can see that the `trunk` is continuously developed. We can see a branch created at revision 3 and reincorporated at revision 11. We can see two tags created at revisions 7 and 13 and that these are not modified after they have been created.

There's more...

Notice how the two tags are named 1.0.0 and 1.0.1. Revisions are a very technical (or if you prefer, nerdy or geeky or techie) way of referring to versions. Our tags have version names that are far easier to understand.

There is a standard form of versioning used by most software projects, which can be summarized as `major.minor.patch`. The impact of the changes dictates whether it is a major, minor, or patch update. For example, removing a bug would be a patch update, improving all of the views in a component would be considered a minor update, while adding some important extra functionality might be considered a major update.

Therefore, we can assert from our example that the changes made between version 1.0.0 and version 1.0.1 were a patch. Had we been using the revision number, we would not have been able to make any assertions.

See also

For information about setting up a project on `JoomlaCode.org`, please refer to first recipe in this chapter *Setting up a JoomlaCode.org project.*

In the next recipe, *Understanding the SVN process*, we will examine the theory behind the working practices of SVN.

Understanding the Subversion process

This recipe explains as a developer how to work with Subversion on a day-to-day basis.

 This recipe purposefully avoids referring to concrete examples. This recipe does, however, refer to Subversion commands, Subversion commands remain the same irrespective of the client.

How to do it...

When we work with Subversion we need a working copy. A **working copy** is an editable copy of all or part of the repository that is held on a client machine.

A working copy contains hidden metadata which is located in the hidden `.svn` folders. This metadata enables a Subversion client to understand the status of the working copy and to communicate with the server from which the working copy originated.

We obtain a working copy by checking out all or part of the repository. It is possible to check out any revision of the repository. In most instances we check the contents of the `trunk` folder and the HEAD revision (latest and greatest!).

Every working copy has a BASE revision. This is the revision that forms the basis of the working copy. In time we will find it necessary to update the BASE revision of our working copy.

As soon as we have a working copy we can start the iterative process of development!

Checking out is a one-off event used to obtain an initial working copy. The following diagram illustrates the iterative nature of working with Subversion once we have a working copy. We start in the **Edit Working Copy** position, and make our way around the circle until we end up back where we started.

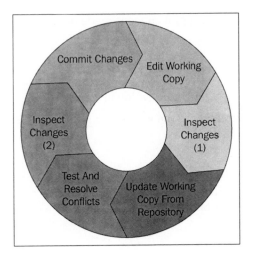

The following list describes each segment of the circle:

▶ **Edit Working Copy**
   ❑ Add new files and folders (svn add)
   ❑ Copy existing files and folders (svn copy)
   ❑ Move/Rename existing files and folders (svn move)
   ❑ Remove existing files and folders (svn delete)

▶ **Inspect Changes (1)**
   ❑ Compare working copy with the repository (svn diff)

▶ **Update Working Copy From Repository**
   ❑ Check for new revisions after the local working copy was last updated/checked out (svn status)
   ❑ Get the latest updates from the repository and merge them with the working copy (svn update)

- ▶ **Test And Resolve Conflicts**
    - ❏ Resolve conflicts introduced during the update (`svn resolve`)
    - ❏ Test the working copy to ensure that the update has not "broken" anything
    - ❏ Edit the working copy if changes made during the update require it

- ▶ **Inspect Changes (2)**
    - ❏ Compare working copy with the repository (`svn diff`)

- ▶ **Commit Changes** (create a new revision in the repository)
    - ❏ Apply the changes in the working copy to the repository (`svn commit`)

Commit only when ready

As a general rule of thumb, we should only try to commit changes to an SVN repository once we have finished making a contained definable set of changes.

Leave a digital paper trail

When we commit changes to the repository, we should always include a short concise message that describes the changes made. Doing so will pay dividends later should we need to inspect past changes.

The process is likely to differ in practice. For example, we may update our working copy several times and resolve conflicts several times before we come to commit any changes.

How it works...

Subversion uses the Copy-Edit-Merge paradigm to enable several developers to edit the same files at the same time. Unlike traditional file sharing, the Copy-Edit-Merge paradigm removes the risk of one user irrecoverably overwriting changes made by another user. This is achieved by forcing users to resolve conflicts between their own changes and other users' changes before they are allowed to write their changes back to the repository. And, of course, the repository maintains an archive of past revisions, so we can always step back over the changes made.

We can visualize the state of the repository and the working copies, as shown in the following illustration. Here we can see the Subversion server connected to the Internet. In this instance, there are three users, all with working copies. **User One** has checked out a branch named `ACL`. **User Two** and **User Three** have checked out the `trunk`. The base revisions are 10, 14, and 11 respectively.

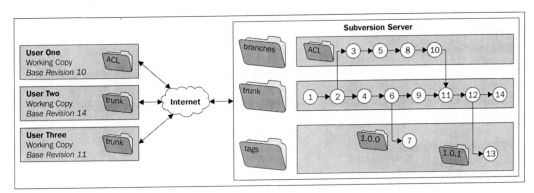

 Subversion servers do not keep a record of the various working copies. This means it is the responsibility of the developer to manage their working copy.

Locking in SVN

Subversion also supports the Lock-Edit-Release paradigm. This can sometimes be useful if we want to ensure that only one developer is editing a file at any one time.

There's more...

Subversion is an incredibly complex system. It is easy for new users of Subversion to underestimate its complexity, and as a result fail to maintain a repository correctly. The topic is far too big to cover in its entirety in this book. For more information, visit the official Subversion web site `http://subversion.tigris.org/`.

See also

To find out how to set up an SVN repository, refer to the recipe, *Setting up JoomlaCode.org SVN*. For information about applying the process described in this recipe, refer to all of the remaining recipes in this chapter.

Checking out a Subversion repository using TortoiseSVN

This recipe describes how to check out a Subversion repository using TortoiseSVN.

Getting ready

The first step we need to take is to download the latest version of TortoiseSVN and install it on our local Windows machine http://tortoisesvn.net/downloads/. TortoiseSVN is only available as an MSI (Windows Installer). TortoiseSVN installation requires a reboot after installation.

How to do it...

To create a new working copy we use the context menu on the folder in which we want to create the working copy. This menu will provide us with the **SVN Checkout** option for the **My Working Copy** folder, as shown in the following screenshot:

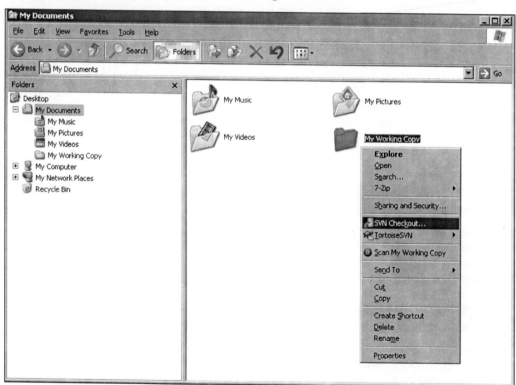

Selecting **SVN Checkout** prompts us with a dialog box; the following table describes the options in the dialog box:

Option	Description
URL of repository	Location of the repository, for `JoomlaCode.org` projects this is in the form `http://joomlacode.org/svn/project-unix-name/sub/location`, in most instances the optional sub location will be the `trunk` folder.
Checkout directory	Local directory into which we are checking out; this is automatically populated.
Checkout Depth	How much of the repository we want to check out. Generally this will be fully recursive, that is, all sub folders and files.
Omit externals	Also check out external repositories with which this repository links.
Revision	Revision of the repository to check out.

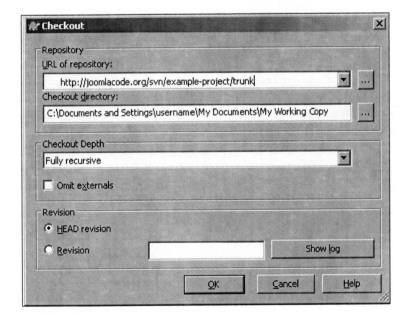

When we press the **OK** button, TortoiseSVN connects to the Subversion server and prompts for our `JoomlaCode.org` user credentials. It is possible to checkout anonymously; for this we enter the username **anonymous**, and leave the password field blank. The checkout process will then begin.

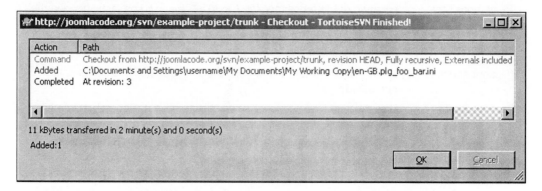

The transcript describes the actions taken during the checkout. This will generally take quite some time, depending on the size of repository. We can see from the transcript above that a total of one file was added to the working copy.

We now have a working copy ready and waiting!

There's more...

If we browse to our working copy, we will find the folders and files from the repository. At this stage all of these will be highlighted with a green-colored tick mark. This means that the file is part of the working copy and it is up-to-date. The following image shows the various icon overlays used by TortoiseSVN to indicate the status of files and folders in a working copy. Exact icons may vary.

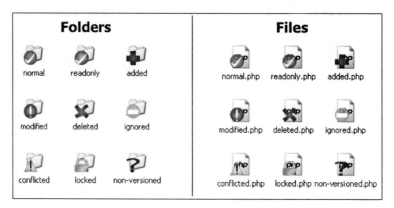

The status of folders is often inherited from a subfile or subfolder. For example, if a conflicted file exists deep in the tree, parent folders will be highlighted as conflicted. This makes it very easy to locate problems in the repository.

Hey! Teacher! Leave them .svn folders alone!

We should never make changes to the hidden .svn folders. These folders contain the metadata required by Subversion clients. If we do experience problems with a working copy, we should use cleanup, as explained in the *Committing changes using TortoiseSVN* recipe later in this chapter.

See also

For an explanation of the role of checkout refer to the *Understanding the Subversion process* recipe, earlier in this chapter.

Editing a working copy using TortoiseSVN

This recipe describes how we make changes to a working copy.

Getting ready

All you *right-handers* out there need to warm up your middle finger on your right hand. All you *lefties* need to warm up your middle finger on your left hand. The context menu in Explorer is about to become your new best friend!

How to do it...

As soon as we have a working copy, we can begin editing a repository. Editing existing files is the most common action. We don't need to do anything special in order to do this; just pick your favorite IDE/editor and work normally.

Adding new files and folders is just as easy; we simply create them as we would normally. However, because it is possible for a working copy to contain unversioned files—files that are not part of the repository—we must inform TortoiseSVN about new files and folders.

To do this, we can do one of two things. We can tell TortoiseSVN before we come to commit the changes by using the context menu **TortoieSVN | Add** command. Alternatively, we can select unversioned files and folders when we come to commit our changes.

Deleting is achieved slightly differently to normal. We delete files and folders using the **TortoiseSVN | Delete** context menu command. If we delete files and folders in the normal way, when we update our working copy, the removed files and folders will be restored!

Renaming should always be done using the **TortoiseSVN | Rename** command. If we do not use this, TortoiseSVN will misinterpret a renaming as a deletion of the original file or folder, and the creation of a new file or folder.

Moving files and folders is achieved using the **TortoiseSVN | Relocate** command. When we move files or folders, we can only move them to a folder that is versioned. That is to say, the new parent location in the tree must already exist in the repository. We can, alternatively, drag the file or folder using the mouse context button to the new location. Doing this provides us with a number of options, which are as follows:

- ▸ **SVN Move versioned files here:** Moves to new location
- ▸ **SVN Move and rename version files here:** Moves to new location and prompts for a new name
- ▸ **SVN Copy versioned files here:** Copies to the new location
- ▸ **SVN Copy and rename versioned file here:** Copies to the new location and prompts for a new name

See also

For an explanation of the role of editing a working copy, refer to the *Understanding the SVN process* recipe, earlier in this chapter.

Inspecting changes using TortoiseSVN

This recipe explains how to inspect changes made to files in a **working copy** using the TortoiseSVN tool TortoiseMerge.

How to do it...

Imagine we want to document language strings introduced in our **working copy**. To do this, we would use the context menu **TortoiseSVN | Diff** command. This allows us to compare our working copy with the base revision. In the example shown in the following screenshot, we can see that the new language string BAR has been added.

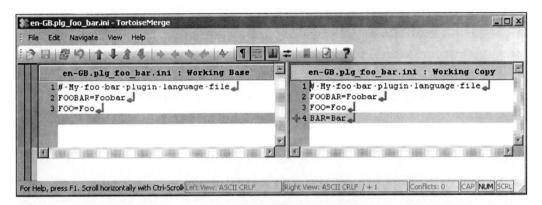

We can obtain a status list of files and folders using the context menu **TortoiseSVN | Check for modifications** command. This tool provides us with two useful options—view a list of changes between our working copy and the base revision; and view a list of changes between our working copy and the HEAD revision.

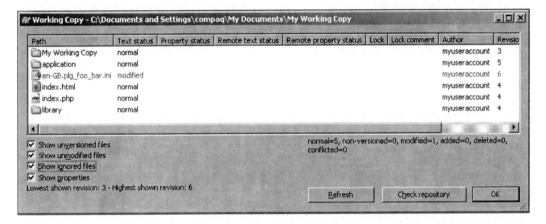

The ability to inspect changes can be especially useful if we are attempting to track down a bug. For example, if it is known that a bug was introduced in revision 70, we can compare revision 70 with its predecessor, revision 69.

See also

For an explanation of the role of inspecting changes made in a working copy, refer to the *Understanding the Subversion process* recipe, earlier in this chapter.

To learn about applying changes to the repository, refer to the *Committing changes to a Subversion repository using TortoiseSVN* recipe, later in this chapter.

Updating a working copy and resolving conflicts using TortoiseSVN

This recipe explains how to update a working copy and how to resolve any conflicts that arise as the result of an update.

How to do it...

It is possible to update a part or all of a working copy. For continuity, it is generally best always to update the entire working copy. To perform an update, we use the context menu for the part of the working copy we want to update. TortoiseSVN provides us with two update options. They are:

- ▸ **SVN Update:** Update working copy to the HEAD revision (latest repository revision)
- ▸ **TortoiseSVN | Update to revision:** Update working copy to the specified revision

During the update process, it is not uncommon to encounter conflicts. In the event that a conflict does arise, we will receive an error message identifying the conflict. Conflicts must be addressed as soon as reasonably practicable.

When we browse to the conflicted file, we will see the file highlighted as conflicted and three other helper files, `originalname.ext.mine`, `originalname.ext.rX`, and `originalname.ext.rY`. These files respectively contain the working copy that we had when we tried to update, the base revision, and the HEAD revision. The conflicted file contains a mixture of the changes.

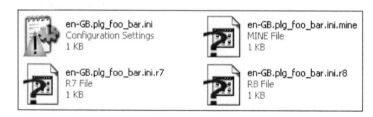

The TortoiseMerge tool can be used to resolve conflicts; we access this tool using the context menu **TortoiseSVN | Edit Conflicts** command. The following example shows a conflict in which the language strings LOREM and IPSUM have been appended to a file, and are now conflicting.

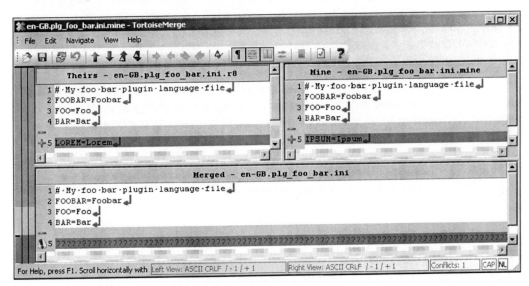

TortoiseMerge displays three of the four files—`originalname.ext.rY` (Theirs), `originalname.ext.mine` (Mine), and `originalname.ext` (Merged). We can select which of the changes we want to use from the `Theirs` and `Mine` panes. We can also directly edit the `Merged` pane. In this instance, we would likely take the changes from `Theirs` (using the right arrow in the toolbar) and manually copy the changes from `Mine`.

Once we have resolved the conflict, we can save the file and mark as resolved using the button on the toolbar, or the context menu **TortoiseSVN | Resolved** command. This will remove the helper files and allow us to continue development of our working copy. More importantly, it will mean that we are now in a position to successfully commit our changes.

Files can contain more than one conflict. In these instances, we can navigate through the conflicts using the up and down arrows in the toolbar.

How it works...

When we update our working copy, the changes in the repository are merged with our working copy. It is this merging of changes that enables Subversion to allow several users to work on the same file at once. Sometimes, however, Subversion will not be able to successfully merge the changes as demonstrated. For example, if two developers edit the same file by inserting new content, and that new content is inserted at the same location, Subversion will not be able to determine how to merge the sources.

This is where human intervention is required. It may be that the two developers have added content that does the same thing; therefore, one of those sets of changes needs to be discarded. On the other hand, the changes may need to be manually combined.

 A common source of conflicts when using Subversion to develop Joomla! extensions, are the INI language files, because new language strings are nearly always added to the end of the file.

See also

For an explanation of the role of updating a working copy, refer to the *Understanding the Subversion process* recipe, earlier in this chapter.

To learn about applying changes to the repository based on a working copy, refer to the next recipe, *Committing changes using TortoiseSVN*.

Committing changes using TortoiseSVN

This recipe describes how we commit changes to a Subversion repository.

How to do it...

To commit changes we make to our working copy, we use the context menu **TortoiseSVN | Commit** command. As with an update, a commit does not have to include the entire working copy.

The **Commit** dialog box allows us to select the files and folders—including unversioned files and folders—that have changed in our working copy that we want to include in the commit. We can also include a message. It is good practice to always include a message that briefly describes the changes that the new commit applies to the repository.

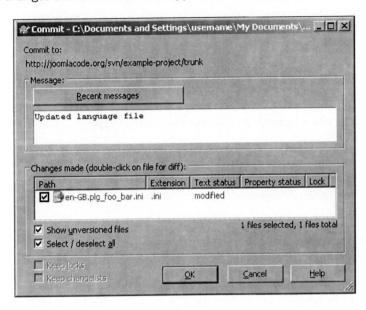

When we are happy with the selected changes that we want to apply, we simply click on the **OK** button. We will now be presented with a transcript dialog that will log the actions taken during the commit.

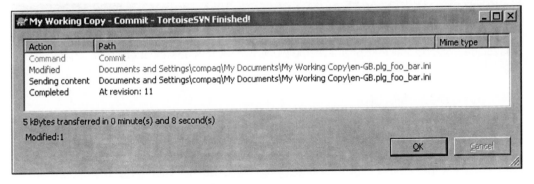

There's more...

Sometimes a commit will fail. This will usually be the result of inconsistencies in the working copy as the result of earlier failed Subversion actions. There is a quick and easy solution! Cleanup is an automated process that "cleans up" our working copy. To cleanup a working copy using TortoiseSVN, use the context menu **TortoiseSVN | Clean up**.

If using the TortoiseSVN `cleanup` command does not resolve the problem, try using the command-line client. This can prove more reliable. The command-line client `cleanup` command does not provide any output.

```
$> svn cleanup H:\path\to\working\copy
```

To get a copy of the SVN command-line client visit `http://www.collab.net/downloads/subversion/`.

See also

For an explanation of the role of committing changes from a working copy, refer to the *Understanding the Subversion process* recipe, earlier in this chapter. To learn how to apply other users' changes to your working copy, refer to the previous recipe *Updating a working copy and resolving conflicts using TortoiseSVN*.

Exporting a working copy using TortoiseSVN

This recipe explains how to export files in a working copy to a new location. This can be especially helpful when we come to package a release.

How to do it...

There are two very useful options that dragging folders outside of a repository using the mouse context button provides us with. There are two export options that enable us to export the contents of the working copy without copying the Subversion metadata. The options are:

- **SVN Export to here**: Exports the versioned files and folders to the new location (without the `.svn` metadata)
- **SVN Export all to here**: Exports all of the files and folders to the new location (without the `.svn` metadata)

2

Keeping Extensions Secure

This chapter contains the following recipes:

- ▶ Writing SQL safe queries
- ▶ Writing SQL-safe LIKE string comparison queries
- ▶ Using the token
- ▶ Making a filename safe
- ▶ Making a directory path safe
- ▶ Making a path safe
- ▶ Safely retrieving request data
- ▶ Getting a value from an array

Introduction

There's no such thing as a completely secure system. No matter how many precautions we take and how many times we verify our design and implementation, we will never be able to guarantee that we have created a truly secure Joomla! extension. Why not? This is because it is not possible to be prepared for every potential vulnerability.

This chapter explains how to avoid some of the more common mistakes that lead to security vulnerabilities, but not how to circumvent all known security vulnerabilities. When it comes to dealing with system security, it is always best to *err on the side of caution*. But just because we cannot guarantee complete security doesn't mean that we shouldn't aim for complete security.

Common Weakness Enumeration (CWE) is a project dedicated to generating a formal categorization and identification system of security vulnerabilities. CWE published a list of the top 25 security weaknesses, which were selected on the basis of their frequency and consequences. This list includes some of the most publicized security weaknesses, such as code injection (`CWE-94`) and XSS (`CWE-79`). When considering the security of our extensions, this list can prove useful. For information about common programming mistakes that lead to security vulnerabilities, refer to `http://cwe.mitre.org/top25/`.

This chapter includes references to the CWE weaknesses. These references are in the form of CWE IDs, that is, `CWE-n`. For information about a weakness, simply **Search By ID** on the CWE web site. These references are intended to help us better understand the weaknesses, the risks associated with the weaknesses, how the risks can be reduced using the Joomla! framework, and the suggested CWE mitigations.

Something we should consider is the ramifications of security flaws. Whichever way we look at this, the answer always involves financial loss. This is true even of non-profit organizations. If a web site is attacked and the attacker managed to completely obliterate all the data held on that web site, it will cost the owner's time to restore a backup or replace the data. OK, it may not seem like a financial loss because it's non profit. It is a wastage of time if the web site owner spends two hours to restore his or her data, as those two hours could have been used elsewhere.

For commercial web sites, the potential for financial loss is far more obvious. If we use a bank as an example, a security flaw could enable an attacker to transfer money from the bank to his or her own (probably untraceable) account. In 2004, the Internet bank Cahoot suffered a security flaw enabling any existing customer access to other customers' accounts. Cahoot did not suffer any obvious financial loss from the security flaw and they claimed there was no risk of financial loss. However, the customers' confidence in Cahoot was inevitably lost. This loss of confidence and bad press will certainly have affected Cahoot in some way. For example, some potential customers may have decided to open an account with a rival bank because of concerns over how secure their savings would, or would not, be with Cahoot. For more information, refer to `http://news.bbc.co.uk/1/hi/business/3984845.stm`.

From the perspective of an extension developer, we should reflect on our moral duty and our liability. *Disclaimers, especially for commercial software, do not relinquish us of legal responsibility.* We should always try to avoid any form of litigation, and I'm not suggesting that we run to Mexico or our closest safe haven. We should take a holistic approach to security. We need a complete view of how the system works and of the various elements that need to be secure. Security should be built into our extension from the requirements gathering stage through to the ongoing system maintenance.

How we do that depends on how we are managing our project and what the security implications of our extension are. For example, a shopping cart component with credit card processing facilities will require far greater attention to security than a content plugin that converts the occurrences of `:)` to smiley face images. Irrespective of the way we choose to manage the risks of weaknesses, we should always document how we are circumventing security threats. Doing so will make it easier to maintain our extension without introducing vulnerabilities. Documentation also provides us with proof of prudent risk management, which can be useful should we ever be accused of failing to adequately manage the security risks associated with our software.

This is all starting to sound like a lot of work! This brings us back to the ramifications of vulnerabilities. If on the one hand, it costs us one extra month of development time to produce a piece of near-secure software. And on the other hand, it costs us two months to patch a non-secure piece of software and an incalculable amount of damage to our reputation. It is clear which route we should favor!

> Packt Publishing offers a book that deals specifically with Joomla! security. For more information, refer to http://www.packtpub.com/joomla-web-security-guide/.

Writing SQL safe queries

SQL injection is probably the most high profile of all malicious web attacks. The effects of an SQL injection attack can be devastating and wide ranging. Whereas some of the more strategic attacks may simply be aimed at gaining access, others may intend on bringing about total disruption and even destruction. Some of the most prestigious organizations in the world have found themselves dealing with the effects of SQL injection attacks. For example, in August 2007 the United Nations web site was defaced as a result of an SQL injection vulnerability. More information can be found at http://news.bbc.co.uk/1/hi/technology/6943385.stm.

Dealing with the effects of an SQL injection attack is one thing, but preventing them is quite another. This recipe explains how we can ensure that our queries are safe from attack by utilizing the Joomla! framework. For more information about SQL injection, refer to CWE-89.

Getting ready

The first thing we need is the database handler. There is nothing special here, just the usual Joomla! code as follows:

```
$db =& JFactory::getDBO();
```

How to do it...

There are two aspects of a query that require special attention:

- Identifiers and names
- Literal values

The JDatabase::nameQuote() method is used to safely represent identifiers and names. We will start with an easy example, a name that consists of a single identifier.

```
$name = $db->nameQuote('columnIdentifier');
```

We must take care when dealing with multiple-part names (that is, names that include more than one identifier separated by a period). If we attempt to do the same thing with the name tableIdentifier.columnIdentifier, we won't get the expected result! Instead, we would have to do the following:

```
// prepare identifiers
$tableIdentifier  = $db->nameQuote('tableIdentifier');
$columnIdentifier = $db->nameQuote('columnIdentifier');

// create name
$name = "$tableIdentifier.$columnIdentifier";
```

Avoid hardcoding encapsulation

Instead of using the JDatabase::nameQuote() method, it can be tempting to do this: $sql = 'SELECT * FROM `#__foobar_groups` AS `group`'. This is OK as it works. But the query is now tightly coupled with the database system, making it difficult to employ an alternative database system.

Now we will take a look at how to deal with literal values. Let's start with strings. In MySQL, strings are encapsulated in double or single quotes. This makes the process of dealing with strings seem extremely simple. Unfortunately, this would be an oversight. Strings can contain any character, including the type of quotes we use to encapsulate them. Therefore, it is also necessary to escape strings. We do all of this using the JDatabase::Quote() method as follows:

```
$tableIdentifier  = $db->nameQuote('tableIdentifier');
$columnIdentifier = $db->nameQuote('columnIdentifier');

$sql = "SELECT * FROM $tableIdentifier "
     . "WHERE $columnIdentifier "
     . ' = ' . $db->Quote("How's the recipe\book going?");
```

The JDatabase::Quote() method essentially does the following. *The exact output will depend on the database handler. However, most databases escape and encapsulate strings in pretty much the same way.*

Original	Quoted
How's the recipe\book going?	'How\'s the recipe\\book going?'

Dealing with the `LIKE` clauses requires slightly different string handling. For more information, refer to the next recipe, _Writing SQL safe_ `LIKE` _string comparison queries._

The other type of literal value we often use in the queries is numbers. In MySQL, there are two types of literal numbers—integers (whole numbers) and floats (decimal numbers). The following examples show how we can cast unsafe values or use the PHP `*val()` functions to make these values safe for use in a query:

```
// integer
$safeNumber = (int)$unsafeValue;
$safeNumber = intval($unsafeValue);

// floating-point
$safeNumber = (float)$unsafeValue;
$safeNumber = floatval($unsafeValue);
```

In most instances, `$unsafeValue` will have been extracted from the request data; for example, `index.php?option=com_foobar&int=unsafeInt&flt=unsafeFlt`. In these instances, we can use `JRequest` to do the work for us as follows:

```
// integer
$safeInt = JRequest::getInt('int');
$safeInt = JRequest::getVar('int', 0, 'DEFAULT', 'INT');
$safeInt = JRequest::getVar('int', 0, 'DEFAULT', 'INTEGER');

// floating-point
$safeFlt = JRequest::getFloat('float');
$safeFlt = JRequest::getVar('float', 0, 'DEFAULT', 'FLOAT');
$safeFlt = JRequest::getVar('float', 0, 'DEFAULT', 'DOUBLE');
```

For more information about using `JRequest` and the various methods shown above, refer to the _Safely retrieving request data_ recipe, later in the chapter.

The final and the most complex option is to use `JFilterInput`. This class allows us to use the same sort of principles as with `JRequest` as shown here:

```
// get filter instance
$filter = JFilterInput::getInstance();

// integer
$safeInt = $filter->clean($unsafeValue, 'INT');
$safeInt = $filter->clean($unsafeValue, 'INTEGER');

// floating-point
$safeFlt = $filter->clean($unsafeValue, 'FLOAT');
$safeFlt = $filter->clean($unsafeValue, 'DOUBLE');
```

> **Quoting numbers**
>
> As an extra line of defense, we can also treat a number as a string. For example, we could use `$db->Quote((int)$unsafeValue)`. Although numbers do not require encapsulation, it is acceptable to quote a number.

How it works...

An **identifier** identifies a database, table, or a column. A **literal value** is an expression that cannot be broken down any further. Therefore, they are literally equal to themselves, for example `1 == 1`. To make identifiers and literal values safe, we encapsulate them in special characters defined by the server. For example, when we are dealing with MySQL identifiers, we encapsulate the identifiers in grave accents such as `` `identifier` ``. Of course, we don't need to know this because `JDatabase` deals with this for us!

A **name** consists of one or more identifiers separated by a period. Names that contain more than one identifier are known as multiple-part names. Multiple-part names provide the ability to drill down, for example `myTable.myColumn`. The `JDatabase::nameQuote()` method cannot handle multiple-part names. Hence, each identifier in a name must be handled separately.

In most database systems, encapsulating identifiers is not technically required, and MySQL is no exception. However, there are occasions when failure to do so will prevent a query from working. SQL has reserved keywords. If any of our identifiers are also reserved words, we must encapsulate them. This tends to be especially noticeable when using aliases. For example, `SELECT * FROM #__foobar_groups AS group` will fail because `group` is a keyword. We can easily overcome this in Joomla! as follows:

```
$sql = 'SELECT * FROM ' . $db->nameQuote('#__foobar_groups')
                        . ' AS ' . $db->nameQuote('group');
```

There's more...

In MySQL, there are six different types of literal values. Absent from this list are date and time. This is because the date and time values are expressed as strings. For example, November 2nd, 1815 would be expressed as the literal value `'1815-11-02'`. The six types of literal values are as follows:

- String
- Number
- NULL
- Hexadecimal
- Boolean
- Bit field

The type of the value makes a difference as to how we should handle it. We have already addressed strings and numbers. The following subsections describe how to safely handle the remaining literal types.

NULL

A NULL value represents the absence of data. This is not the same as an empty value. For example, a string with no characters is not a NULL value. NULL values should always be written as NULL or \N. We should never use raw input when we express a NULL value in a query.

```
$safeValue = ($unsafeValue == 'NULL') ? 'NULL' : 'NOT NULL';
```

Hexadecimal

It is unusual to use hexadecimal literal values in Joomla! extensions. It is no surprise that there are no special tricks for dealing with hexadecimal values in the Joomla! framework. An example of when we might want to use hexadecimal is recording colors such as red, FF0000. The following example shows how we can sanitize some hexadecimal data. There are three normal ways of representing hexadecimal data—X'value', x'value', and 0xvalue. The following example uses the standard SQL notation, x'value':

```
$matches = array();
$pattern = "~^([Xx]\'|0x)([0-9A-F]+)\'?$~";

$safeHex = $defaultSafeHexValue;
if (preg_match($pattern, $unsafeValue, $matches)) {
    $safeHex = "x'" . $matches[2] . "'";
}
```

Boolean

Boolean values are very straightforward. They are represented as the raw strings TRUE and FALSE. We should always use a PHP expression to determine a Boolean value.

```
$boolean = ($unsafeValue) ? 'TRUE' : 'FALSE' ;
```

Bit field

Binary values are also unusual in Joomla! extensions. Values of this type can be useful for storing bit patterns (essentially flags). Again, there are no special tricks for dealing with these types of literal values. To overcome this we can improvise, as shown in the following example. There are two ways of representing binary values—b'value' and 0bvalue:

```
$matches = array();
$pattern = "~^(b\'|0b)([01]+)\'?$~";
$safeBin = $defaultSafeBinValue;
if (preg_match($pattern, $unsafeValue, $matches)) {
    $safeBin = "b'" . $matches[2] . "'";
}
```

Binary representation is only available in MySQL from version 5.0.3 onwards.

Writing SQL-safe LIKE string comparison queries

Performing searches on a database using strings takes a bit more thought than normal. String-based searches use special characters to enable special searching capabilities that are not present when using basic operators, such as =. Therefore, we must treat comparison strings slightly differently to normal strings (described in the previous recipe).

Failure to properly manage the risks associated with constructing an SQL query with a LIKE clause can lead to an SQL injection weakness. For more information about SQL injection, refer to CWE-89.

Getting ready

The first thing we need is the database handler. Nothing special here, just the usual Joomla! code as follows:

```
$db =& JFactory::getDBO();
```

How to do it...

Searching in Joomla! is commonly achieved using the string comparison function, LIKE. This function compares two strings character by character. When we use the function, we can include the special characters % and _. These represent *zero-to-many characters* and *one character* respectively. Of course, including special characters means that we have to pay special attention if we want to use the special characters in their unadulterated form. As with special characters in a normal string, we escape the characters with backslashes.

It is standard practice in Joomla! to simply surround a search string with % characters. This will attempt to find an exact match to the string somewhere within the string being searched.

There are two steps to this process, escaping and encapsulating. We can escape the comparison string by using the JDatabase::getEscaped() method, and we can encapsulate the escaped string using the JDatabase::Quote() method.

```
// prepare search
$escaped = $db->getEscaped($searchFor, true);
$quoted  = $db->Quote('%' . $escaped . '%', false);
// write the SQL
$like = $db->nameQuote('columnName') . ' LIKE ' . $quoted;
```

How it works...

Normally when we use the `JDatabase::Quote()` method, the string we pass in is automatically escaped. However, that escaping does not allow for the extra characters `%` and `_`. To overcome this, we take care of the escaping of characters ourselves. This means when we use the `JDatabase::Quote()` method, we must ensure that we do not escape the string a second time! When the optional second Boolean parameter is specified as `false`, it is used to prevent escaping, as shown in the example.

Luckily, Joomla! provides us with the `JDatabase::getEscaped()` method specifically for escaping strings. This method also accepts a second optional Boolean parameter. This parameter is used to determine if the extra characters, `%` and `_`, should also be escaped.

After we have escaped the string and before we quote it, we encapsulate the string in `%` characters. It is vital that we add these at the correct point in time. If we add these too early, they will be escaped; and if we add them too late, they will cause the query to fail. We can easily summarize this process by inspecting the variables:

Variable	Value
`$searchFor`	We are 25% through the_chapter
`$escaped`	We are 25\% through the_chapter
`$quoted`	'%We are 25\% through the_chapter%'
`$like`	'columnName' LIKE '%We are 25\% through the_chapter%'

It is possible to make the search a little more flexible by replacing spaces with `%` characters. The following code sample shows how we can achieve this:

```
// split the search into an array of words
$words = preg_split('~[\s,\.]+~', $searchFor);

// iterate over the words
for ($i = 0; $i < count($words); $i ++) {
    $words[$i] = $db->getEscaped($words[$i], true);
}
// implode and quote the words
$quotedSearch = implode('%', $words);
$quotedSearch = $db->Quote('%' . $quotedSearch . '%', false);

// write the SQL
$like = $db->nameQuote('columnName') . ' LIKE ' . $quoted;
```

This time we end up with the following values:

Variable	Value
`$searchFor`	We are 25% through the_chapter
`$words`	array('We', 'are', '25%', 'through', 'the_chapter')
`$words`	array('We', 'are', '25\%', 'through', 'the_chapter')
`$quotedSearch`	We%are%25\%%through%the_chapter
`$quotedSearch`	'%We%are%25\%%through%the_chapter%'
`$like`	'columnName' LIKE '%We%are%25\%%through%the_chapter%'

Trailing spaces

The `LIKE` function can also be useful if we want to compare two strings and one or more of those strings contains trailing spaces. The = operator always ignores trailing spaces, for example `'J!'` is considered equivalent to `'J!  '`. The `LIKE` function, on the other hand, would consider the strings to be different.

See also

For information about safely dealing with other values in queries, refer to the previous recipe, *Writing SQL safe queries*.

Using the token

Tokens provide an additional layer of security, typically for use with logged-in users. It is generally quite easy to assume that once a user is logged in, all the requests he or she makes are legitimate. And assuming the login itself was legitimate, why wouldn't all of the requests also be legitimate? Once a user has logged into a system, it is not technically the user who gains access to the system; it is the client machine itself! Therefore, if the client machine has been compromised in any way, there may be some unexpected skullduggery occurring without the user's knowledge. For web applications such as Joomla!, this threat is primarily from **Cross-Site Request Forgery (CSRF)** CWE-352.

Consider the following scenario. A user has a browser with tabbed windows. In one tab, they have logged into a Joomla! web site and in another tab they have unwittingly browsed to a compromised web site. The compromised web site contains JavaScript, or another client-side language, which is able to take advantage of the fact that privileges have been granted to the browser.

It is unsurprising to discover that financial institutions are the most commonly targeted because a successful attack could bring the attacker significant financial gain. We must not become careless in instances where we are creating extensions that would provide limited or no tangible gain for an attacker. In 2006, a CSRF vulnerability was discovered in Google that enabled an attacker to change a user's language preferences. You can read more about this at `http://isc.sans.org/diary.html?date=2006-10-01`.

So, where do tokens come in? A token is a value, normally an alphanumeric string, which can be used to verify the authenticity of a request. The server generates a token, and that token is sent to the client. When the client makes any subsequent requests, the same token must be returned. If it is not, it indicates that the origin of the request is not quite what it seems.

Getting ready

Joomla! has a built-in token system that we can use to easily add an extra layer of security. This makes it very easy to protect ourselves against CSRF attacks. To use the built-in token system, we use the static classes `JUtility`, `JRequest`, and `JHTML`.

How to do it...

In Joomla!, we pass a token using the token value as the name. The value of this is then set to 1, for example `index.php?tokenValue=1`. There is a good reason for using the value of the token as the name of the query value. It is more secure. Systems that use a name such as `token` and simply set the value of this to the token value, that is `index. php?token=tokenValue`, are less secure because it is very easy to extract the value of the token. With this in mind, the following example shows how to include the token in a URL:

```
// get the value of the token
$token = JUtility::getToken();

// build the URL with the token embedded
$url = 'index.php?option=com_foobar&controller=foo&task=bar'
                                            .'&'.$token.'=1';

$url = JRoute::_($url);
```

It is unusual to use the token in this way. Generally, we only use the token when dealing with forms because forms are used to make the most important requests. As a general rule of thumb, we should use the token for requests that will result in changes to data or in execution of secure transactions (such as a bank transfer). The following example shows a shortcut we can use to add the token to a form:

```
// import JHTML
jimport('joomla.html.html');

// insert a hidden token to the form field
echo JHTML::_('form.token');
```

We're almost there. There's just one thing left to do—validate the token once a request is received. Joomla! provides us with a quick and easy way to do this. The `JRequest::` `checkToken()` method compares the token value against the request and provides a Boolean response. For this reason, it is up to us to act on that response.

```
// check the token (POST request)
JRequest::checkToken() or jexit('Invalid Token');
```

 The `jexit()` function is equivalent to the `exit()` and `die()` PHP functions. We should always use `jexit()` in preference to `exit()` and `die()` because it gives Joomla! the opportunity to tidy up any resources.

By default, the `JRequest::checkToken()` method looks specifically at the `POST` request data. We can override this by providing the name of the request hash we want to check, for example `GET` or `REQUEST`.

```
// check the token (whatever the request method)
JRequest::checkToken('REQUEST') or jexit('Invalid Token');
```

In the previous examples, we take the hard-line approach of invoking `jexit()` in case the comparison fails. This is generally the best policy. However, there are other options such as using `JError` to return an HTTP error.

```
// check the token (POST request)
if (!JRequest::checkToken('REQUEST')) {
    // return 403 error
    JError::raiseError(403, JText::_('ALERTNOAUTH'));

    // belt and braces approach to guarantee the script stops
    jexit('Invalid Token');
}
```

There's more...

Joomla! uses the same token throughout the life of a session. Although this is not a flaw. it does not conform to the suggested solution indicated by the CWE. The CWE suggests that creating a new token for each and every form will be more secure. Admittedly, the CWE appears to favor the *double-submitted cookie* solution as opposed to the state-recorded token solution, as implemented in Joomla!. It can still be useful to change the token, especially for systems that require very high levels of security.

There is one problem with this. If a user has multiple pages from the site open in different windows or tabs, frequently changing the tokens in these pages may render them outdated. Therefore, we should carefully consider whether or not we need to reset the token before doing so.

The token is reset as follows:

```
// the old token
$oldToken = JUtility::getToken();

// the new token
$newToken = JUtility::getToken(true);
```

Easy! However, there is one more issue to consider. If we are going to reset the token, we should do so only if forms that don't use the token have already been generated in the same page. It is best to generate a new token only when creating components, because components are always rendered first.

There is an additional option we can incorporate in an attempt to prevent the CSRF attacks. However, this solution is not foolproof and can be circumvented. It can also potentially cause problems for legitimate clients.

HTTP request headers include a referrer, which is the URL from which the requested URL was obtained. Unfortunately, this header is not required by the HTTP specification. Some browsers don't send this information, some proxies and gateways strip this information, and it is also possible to spoof this information. Put simply, this is not a reliable solution and should, therefore, be used only as a supplement alongside a token.

The following example shows how we could safely include referrer validation. *This example will not block any requests that do not include the referrer in the headers of the HTTP request.*

```
// check the token (POST request)
JRequest::checkToken() or jexit('Invalid Token');

// get referrer
$referer = JRequest::getString('HTTP_REFERER', null, 'SERVER');

// check referrer was included in the request
if ($referer != null && $referer != '') {
    // referrer is present in request, validate referrer!
    if (JURI::isInternal($referer)) {
        // invalid referrer
        jexit('Invalid Referrer');
    }
}
```

For more information about the HTTP protocol, refer to `http://www.w3.org/Protocols/rfc2616/rfc2616-sec14.html#sec14.36`.

Making a filename safe

Joomla! extensions can contain many files and interacting with them is a typical process. In instances where a filename is generated dynamically, for example from user input, we need to be especially attentive. Unsafe filenames can lead to security vulnerabilities such as code injection. Joomla! provides us with an easy way to ensure that filenames are safe.

For more information about external control of filenames, refer to CWE-73.

How to do it...

The static JFile class, which is a part of the joomla.filesystem library, provides us with all sorts of useful methods for working with files. To use the class, we must import it as follows:

```
jimport('joomla.filesystem.file');
```

This bit is nice and easy. We use the JFile::makeSafe() method and pass the name of the file we want to sanitize. This method returns a string that can be used to interact safely with a file.

```
// make the filename safe
$safeFilename = JFile::makeSafe($unsafeFilename);
```

How it works...

So, what exactly does the JFile::makeSafe() method do to guarantee a safe filename? It strips out any characters or character sequences that are seen as posing potential security risks. The following list describes the rules that are used by the JFile::makeSafe() method. *Any characters that do not meet the criteria are stripped from the string.*

- ▸ Only consists of alphanumeric characters, periods, underscores, dashes, and spaces
- ▸ Periods do not occur together (is not attempting filesystem traversal, CWE-22)
- ▸ Does not start with a period (is not a hidden *nix file)

The following table shows some examples of input and output strings from the JFile::makeSafe() method:

Original	Safe	Stripped
.htaccess	htaccess	Leading period
some%20file.html	some20file.html	% character
../../traversed.file	traversed.file	/ character and consecutive periods
spaced out.file	spaced out.file	
dotty...to..the.dot	dottytothe.dot	Consecutive periods

There's more...

Depending on how we are using the filename, we may also want to check the file extension. For this, we use the `JFile::getExt()` method as shown here:

```
switch (JFile::getExt($filename)) {
    case 'jpeg':
    case 'jpg':
        echo 'File is a JPEG';
        break;
    case 'gif':
        echo 'File is a GIF';
        break;
    default:
        echo 'File is not a JPEG or a GIF';
}
```

Verify file type by content

A file extension cannot be used as a reliable mechanism to determine a file type. We can attempt to determine the MIME (Multipurpose Internet Mail Extensions) type of a file using the deprecated PHP function `mime_content_type()`, or the PECL (PHP Extensions Community Library) *File Information* module. For more information, refer to `http://php.net/manual/function.mime-content-type.php` and `http://php.net/manual/book.fileinfo.php`.

Along with determining the extension of a filename, we can also strip the extension.

```
$filenameWithoutExtension = JFile::stripExt($filename);
```

This can be useful if we want to specify the extension ourselves. For example, if we are dealing with JPEGs, the extension can be `.jpeg` or `.jpg`.

```
$filename = JFile::stripExt($filename) . '.jpeg';
```

Depending on what we intend to do with the filename, it can also be useful to check that the file exists before continuing. We are probably used to working with the PHP functions `file_exists()` and `is_file()`. But when we use Joomla!, we should use the `JFile::exists()` method instead.

```
if (JFile::exists($filename)) {
    echo "<img src=\"$filename\" alt=\"image\">";
} else {
    echo JText::_("No Image File");
}
```

See also

The following two recipes, *Making a directory path safe* and *Making a path safe*, investigate how to safely deal with directories and paths.

Making a directory path safe

When we poke around in the server filesystem, we want to make sure that we know what we are doing. If we are dealing with directories, Joomla! provides us with some easy ways to make sure that those directories are being safely referenced. Failure to properly sanitize directory paths can lead to major security vulnerabilities. For example, if we were attempting to remove a directory, a security vulnerability could allow the deletion of the completely wrong resource! For more information about external control of paths, refer to CWE-73.

 A directory path is a URL to a directory. A directory path does not include a file. To safely manage a path to a file, refer to the next recipe, *Making a path safe*.

How to do it...

The static `JFolder` class, which is a part of the `joomla.filesystem` library, provides us with all sorts of useful methods for working with folders. To use the class, we must import it.

```
jimport('joomla.filesystem.folder');
```

This bit is nice and easy. We use the `JFolder::makeSafe()` method and pass the name of the folder we want to sanitize. This method returns a string that can be used to interact safely with a folder.

```
// make the directory path safe
$safeDirPath = JFolder::makeSafe($unsafeDirPath);
```

The one downside of `JFolder::makeSafe()` is that it assumes that the directory separators are correctly defined in the original string. For example, while running on a *nix system, if the string contained Windows-style backslashes instead of *nix style forward slashes, those slashes would be stripped. We can use the static `JPath` class to overcome this, as follows:

```
// import JPath and JFolder
jimport('joomla.filesystem.path');
jimport('joomla.filesystem.folder');
// clean the path
```

```
$cleanDirPath = JPath::clean($unsafeDirPath);

// make the directory path safe
$safeDirPath = JFolder::makeSafe($cleanDirPath);
```

This time we have included the `JPath::clean()` method prior to making the path safe. For more information about `JPath`, refer to the next recipe, _Making a path safe_.

> **Directory separators**
>
> The correct way to add directory separators in Joomla! is to use the DS constant. For example, the path to `bar` from `foo` is expressed as `'foo' . DS . 'bar'`.

How it works...

What exactly does the `JFolder::makeSafe()` method do to guarantee that the directory path is safe? It strips out any characters or character sequences that are seen as posing potential security risks. The following list describes the characters that are considered safe:

- Alphanumeric (a-z, A-Z, and 0-9)
- Colon
- Dash
- Directory separators—the exact character sequence will depend on the environment
- Space
- Underscore

The following table shows some examples of input and output strings from the `JFolder::makeSafe()` and `JPath::clean()` methods running on a Windows system (DS == '\'). This is intended to show why using the two together can be preferable. If we choose to use the two together, order of usage is important. We should always use the `JPath::clean()` method first and the `JFolder::makeSafe()` method next. Although, as the fourth example shows, sometimes it can be worth cleaning a second time, which means clean, make safe, and clean.

Original	Clean	Safe	Clean and safe
\\foo\bar	\foo\bar	\\foo\bar	\foo\bar
//foo/bar	\foo\bar	foobar	\foo\bar
\foo%20bar	\foo%20bar	\foo20bar	\foo20bar
\foo bar/..\	\foo bar\..\	\foo bar\	\foo bar\\
/foo"	\foo"	foodel	\foodel
del *.*	del *.*		

See also

For information about safely dealing with files, refer to the previous recipe, *Making a filename safe*. For information about dealing with paths, please refer to the next recipe, *Making a path safe*.

Making a path safe

This recipe is similar to the previous two recipes, *Making a filename safe* and *Making a directory path safe*. This recipe differs in that it is for a complete path, normally to a file. There is a whole raft of security issues associated with processing paths. The following list identifies some of the more common issues we need to be aware of:

- CWE-22: Path traversal
- CWE-73: External control of filename or path
- CWE-98: Insufficient control of filename for include/require statement in PHP program (aka 'PHP file inclusion')
- CWE-434: Unrestricted file upload

All of these vulnerabilities can have serious consequences, which should not be overlooked. For example, a malicious user could upload a destructively tailored script file and then execute it. Luckily, Joomla! provides us with some easy ways to reduce the risks associated with these potential weaknesses.

Getting ready

Before we delve into some of the complex ways of safely dealing with paths, let's start small. If we browse a basic installation of Joomla!, we will discover a large number of empty `index.html` files. These files prevent directory listings. Most web servers automatically generate directory listings if we visit a directory in which there are no index files. We should always add a copy of the empty `index.html` file to every directory in our extension.

 The use of empty `index.html` files provides a form of *security through obscurity*. This is only intended to be a very basic safeguard and should never be relied on for complete protection. For more information, refer to CWE-656.

The second thing we should do is ensure that all of our PHP files can only be executed if the `_JEXEC` constant has been defined. This is used to make sure that the file has been executed from within Joomla!, that is, make sure it is not being used as a standalone script or is included from a script other than Joomla!

```
// Check file executed from within Joomla!
defined('_JEXEC') or die('Restricted access');
```

How to do it...

If we are retrieving a path value from a request variable, we can use the PATH type. This type is not entirely what it seems, as a PATH type cannot be an absolute path and cannot reference hidden files and folders. This means it cannot start with any form of directory separator, as it would in a *nix environment, or a drive identifier, as it would in a Windows environment. It also means that none of the folder names or the optional filename can start with a period (a *nix hidden file/folder). If a value does not reach these criteria, the return value will be null. Therefore, it is very important to consider the suitability of the PATH type before opting to use it.

```
// get the value of myPath from the request
$myPath = JRequest::getVar('myPath', 'default', 'REQUEST', 'PATH');
```

 On its own, the PATH type does not really constitute a security measure. For example, it does not protect against the path traversal CWE-22.

Once we have our path variable, it is time to clean it. Cleaning is done in Joomla! using the static JPath class. Cleaning resolves any issues with directory separators. The exact process depends on the filesystem directory separator, for example a back or forward slash. The point is that if the directory separators in the string are incorrect, they are corrected as necessary.

```
// import the JPath class
jimport('joomla.filesystem.path');

// clean $myPath
$myPath = JPath::clean($myPath);
```

 Like the PATH type, a cleaned path does not really constitute a security measure. For example, it too does not protect against path traversal CWE-22.

OK, we've heard enough about not constituting a security measure. Now it's time to overcome that problem. The static JPath class includes the JPath::check() method, which checks for path traversal and also that the path is within the Joomla! installation. The only constraint is that the method can only deal with absolute paths. Remember the PATH type used in JRequest can only cope with relative paths. Therefore, if we use the PATH type, we must convert it to an absolute path before using the JPath::check() method.

```
// check for path traversal and snooping
JPath::check($myPath);
```

The odd thing about this method is that we don't really do anything with the result! There is a very good reason for this. If the check fails, Joomla! will exit and display a suitable error message. In some instances, this may not be appropriate. Unfortunately, there is nothing we can do to prevent this. Therefore, if we want to avoid this we will have to check the path ourselves. Generally speaking, if a path fails the check, it is likely that an attack has been attempted. For that reason, exiting Joomla! is probably the most suitable response.

However, the `JPath::check()` method does have one serious limitation. It only checks for snooping outside of the Joomla! root directory. We can manually check that we are only looking in a specified area in the Joomla! installation.

```
// create path which must be the root of the directory
$safePath = JPATH_COMPONENT . DS . 'safeFolder' . DS;

// check for snooping outside of $safePath
if (strpos($myPath, $safePath) !== 0) {
    JError::raiseError(20, 'Snooping out of bounds');
    jexit();
}

// check for file traversal
jimport('joomla.filesystem.path');
JPath::check($directory);
```

Essentially, this only ensures that the start of the `$myPath` string is equivalent to `$safePath`. We deal with failures in the same way as the `JPath::check()` method. Notice that we still use the `JPath::check()` method because we can still effectively use this method to check for file traversal.

See also

The previous two recipes, *Making a filename safe* and *Making a directory path safe*, discuss how to work safely with filenames and paths.

We can also use filesystem permissions to secure files and folders. For more information, refer to the Chapter 12 recipe, *Changing file and folder permissions*.

Safely retrieving request data

Almost 99% of the time, security vulnerabilities in PHP applications such as Joomla! are caused by inadequate input parsing and validation CWE-20. We access request data in Joomla! using the static `JRequest` class. Built into this class is the ability to cast values to specific types and to mask data.

We cannot rely solely on `JRequest` to ensure that incoming data is safe. This is where validation comes into play. Input data always has definable constraints. For example, we might define an entity identifier as a positive integer no less than 1 and no greater than 4294967295 (the maximum value for an unsigned MySQL `INT`). If we can define the constraints, we can also check that the input adheres to the constraints.

Validating strings tend to be more complex. This is because strings are highly versatile and can contain many different characters. One thing we should always bear in mind when dealing with string validation is the effect of different character encodings. Joomla! 1.5 is UTF-8 compliant. **UTF-8** is a Unicode variable-size multibyte character encoding that enables the encoding of many different alphabets and symbols that would otherwise be unavailable. As PHP is not UTF-8 aware, we should always use the static `JString` methods instead of the PHP string functions when dealing with UTF-8 strings.

Getting ready

Prior to doing anything, it is worth defining and documenting the boundaries of all the input that we use in our extension. This may include value ranges and formats. This can be a lengthy task, but it will help to ensure that our extension is secure.

How to do it...

The most important thing we must do when accessing request data is to use `JRequest`. Even if we just want the raw values, `JRequest` forms an important part of the Joomla! framework. Even before we get a chance to execute any code in our extension, `JRequest` will have already performed vital security work in an attempt to prevent global variable injection, `CWE-471`.

So where do we begin? We start with the simple `JRequest::getVar()` method. This method is used to safely get at the request data. There are five parameters, of which only the first is required. The following example shows how we use the first three of these parameters:

```
// gets the value of name
$value = JRequest::getVar('nameOfVar');

// gets the value of name,
// if name is not specified returns defaultValue
$value = JRequest::getVar('nameOfVar', 'defaultValue');

// gets the value of name,
// if name is not specified returns defaultValue
// name is retrieved from the GET request data
$value = JRequest::getVar('nameOfVar', 'defaultValue', 'GET');
```

The third parameter can be any of the following values:

Value	Description
COOKIE	HTTP Cookies
ENV	Environment variables
FILES	Uploaded file details
GET	HTTP GET variables
POST	HTTP POST variables
REQUEST	Combination of GET, POST, and COOKIE; this is the default
SERVER	Server and environment variables

In most instances, REQUEST (the default) should be sufficient. The only time we need to use GET and POST explicitly is when we are expecting a request to use a specific HTTP method. For added security, we can restrict a request to a certain HTTP method using the static JRequest::getMethod() method, as shown in the following example:

```
if (JRequest::getMethod() != 'GET') {
    jexit('UNEXPECTED REQUEST METHOD');
}
```

There's more...

The following two subsections discuss the last two parameters, $type and $mask. It is in the last two parameters where the security benefits of JRequest become very apparent.

Casting

Strictly speaking, casting is not an accurate description of the fourth JRequest::getVar() parameter. The types that we can cast to are not the types that we would use to describe a variable. For example, WORD is not a PHP or Joomla! type, but it is an available option.

The following example extracts an integer representation of the GET request value, nameOfVar:

```
// gets the value of nameOfVar,
// if nameOfVar is not specified returns 0
// name is retrieved from the GET request data
// casts the return value as an integer
$int = JRequest::getVar('nameOfVar', 0, 'GET', 'INT');
```

Hey presto! We have a safe value that we know is an integer. Had we not included the parameter to cast the value, we would not have been able to guarantee that $int was in fact an integer. Of course, we could have used the PHP intval() function or cast the value ourselves using (int). Not all of the types we can cast to are as simple as an integer; for example, ALNUM is used to strip non-alphanumeric characters from a string value.

JRequest also provides alias methods that allow us to achieve the same thing, but with less code. For example, we can quickly extract an integer. The following example is the same as the previous example:

```
$int = JRequest::getInt('nameOfVar', 0);
```

The following table describes all of the types we can cast to using JRequest. Note that only the most commonly used types have alias methods.

Type	Description	Alias
DEFAULT	Aggressive cleaning occurs to remove all detected code elements	
ALNUM	Alphanumeric string; strips all non-ASCII letters and numbers	
ARRAY	Force array cast	
BASE64	Base64 string; strips all non Base64 characters, which is useful for passing encoded data in a URL, for example a return URL	
BOOL or BOOLEAN	Force Boolean cast	getBool()
CMD	Command; strips all non-alphanumeric, underscore, period, and dash characters, which is ideal for values such as task	getCmd()
FLOAT or DOUBLE	Floating point number	getFloat()
INT or INTEGER	Whole number	getInt()
PATH	Filesystem path; used to identify a resource in a filesystem, for example the path to an image to use as a logo (relative paths only)	
STRING	String; often used with a mask to clean the data	getString()
USERNAME	Username; strips characters unsuitable for use in a username, including non-printing characters (for example a backspace), angled brackets, double and single quotation marks, percent signs, and ampersands	
WORD	Word; strips all non-alpha and underscore characters	getWord()

 By default, the most aggressive mask is applied. This will remove code, such as HTML and JavaScript, from the data. The next section describes how we use masks.

Masking strings

The fifth `JRequest::getVar()` parameter defines a mask. Masks are used in `JRequest` to define what is and isn't allowed in a string value. By default no masking is applied, which means that very aggressive security measures are taken to ensure that the incoming data is as safe as possible. While this is useful, it is not always appropriate. For example, the core component `com_content` allows users to enter HTML data in an article. Without a mask, this information would be stripped from the request data.

There are three constants we can use to easily define the mask we want to apply. These are `JREQUEST_NOTRIM`, `JREQUEST_ALLOWRAW`, and `JREQUEST_ALLOWHTML`. The following example shows how we can use these:

```
// using getVar
$string = JRequest::getVar('nameOfVar', 'default', 'REQUEST',
                            'STRING', JREQUEST_ALLOWRAW);
// using getString alias
$string = JRequest::getString('nameOfVar', 'default', 'REQUEST',
                                          JREQUEST_ALLOWRAW);
```

The following examples show how the output varies depending on the mask that we apply:

#	Original input value
1	`<p>Paragraph <a onClick="alert('foobar');">link</a></p>`
2	`CSS <link type="text/css", href="http://somewhere/nasty.css" />`
3	`   space at front of input`
4	`&ltp&gtPara&lt/p&gt`

#	Output value (No mask)
1	`Paragraph link`
2	`CSS`
3	`space at front of input`
4	`&ltp&gtPara&lt/p&gt`

#	Output value (mask `JREQUEST_NOTRIM`)
1	`Paragraph link`
2	`CSS`
3	`   space at front of input`
4	`&ltp&gtPara&lt/p&gt`

#	Output value (mask `JREQUEST_ALLOWHTML`)
1	`<p>Paragraph <a>link</a></p>`
2	`CSS`
3	`space at front of input`
4	`&ltp&gtPara&lt/p&gt`

#	Output value (mask `JREQUEST_ALLOWRAW`)
1	`<p>Paragraph <a onClick="alert('foobar');">link</a></p>`
2	`CSS <link type="text/css", href="http://somewhere/nasty.css" />`
3	`space at front of input`
4	`&ltp&gtPara&lt/p&gt`

`JRequest` uses the `JFilterInput` class to perform casting. For more information about casting, refer to the `JFilterInput::clean()` method in the official Joomla! API documentation at `http://api.joomla.org/`.

Masks are defined using flags. These flags are represented as integers, and bitwise logic is used to determine what the combined flags mean for the mask. There are three flags we can use—`trim`, `raw`, and `html`. The `trim` flag determines if leading and trailing whitespace should be removed. The `raw` flag determines if we should leave the input alone. The `html` flag determines if HTML is allowed in the input. *The `raw` flag can be considered greedy because it overrides* `html`.

The following table describes the mask values we might want to use:

Constant	Value	Allow `html`	Allow `raw`	Prevent `trim`
	0			
`JREQUEST_NOTRIM`	1			YES
`JREQUEST_ALLOWRAW`	2		YES	
	3		YES	YES
`JREQUEST_ALLOWHTML`	4	YES		
	5	YES		YES

Joomla! provides us with three handy constants so that we do not have to remember the values. But as you have probably already realized, there are six possible values and only three constants! The first value of 0 does not require a constant because it is the default. The values 3 and 4 can be safely obtained using the constants and the PHP | (inclusive or) bitwise operator. *We should use only the constants to define a mask. This ensures that we retain a loosely coupled relationship with the mask.*

```
// allow raw and do not trim
$mask = JREQUEST_ALLOWRAW | JREQUEST_NOTRIM;

// allow html and do not trim
$mask = JREQUEST_ALLOWHTML | JREQUEST_NOTRIM;
```

As we can combine the constants, we can also add the following possibilities. Remember that JREQUEST_ALLOWRAW is greedy. Therefore, combining it with JREQUEST_HTML is pointless.

#	Output value (mask JREQUEST_ALLOWHTML | JREQUEST_NOTRIM)
1	`<p>Paragraph <a>link</a></p>`
2	`CSS`
3	`  space at front of input`
4	`&ltp&gtPara&lt/p&gt`

#	Output value (mask JREQUEST_ALLOWRAW | JREQUEST_NOTRIM)
1	`<p>Paragraph <a onClick="alert('foobar');">link</a></p>`
2	`CSS <link type="text/css", href="http://somewhere/nasty.css" />`
3	`  space at front of input`
4	`&ltp&gtPara&lt/p&gt`

No mask

If we don't want to modify the data in any way, we should use the expression JREQUEST_ALLOWRAW | JREQUEST_NOTRIM to define the mask. *Do not confuse 0 with no mask; 0 represents the strictest mask.*

Getting a value from an array

This is the most insignificant sounding of all the recipes in this chapter! We all know how to get a value from an array. It's simple. We just drop in the index of the element we want and abracadabra! We've got our value. The problem is that if there's no security involved in this process, we end up with a raw value.

So why would we need additional security when accessing a value in an array? One good example is processing of form-based multiple-select boxes. In these instances, `JRequest` cannot help us to any great extent—instead, we need to add in our security after we have retrieved the array from the request data.

How to do it...

To find out how to safely extract data from an array, refer to *Getting a value from an array* recipe in Chapter 10, *JObjects and Arrays*.

3
Working with the Database

This chapter contains the following recipes:

- ▶ Executing a query
- ▶ Loading the first cell from the result of a query
- ▶ Loading the first record from a query
- ▶ Loading more than one record from a query
- ▶ Handling DBO errors
- ▶ Creating a `JTable`
- ▶ Creating a new record using a `JTable`
- ▶ Updating a record using a `JTable`
- ▶ Reading an existing record using a `JTable`
- ▶ Deleting a record using a `JTable`
- ▶ Checking a record in and out (record locking) using a `JTable`
- ▶ Modifying record ordering using a `JTable`
- ▶ Publishing and unpublishing a record using a `JTable`
- ▶ Incrementing a record hit counter using a `JTable`

Introduction

In Joomla!, the majority of data is held in the database. This is true of core extensions and many third-party extensions. Joomla! is often described as a PHP MySQL application. While it is true that Joomla! uses MySQL, the Joomla! architecture does allow the use of other database systems. Currently, Joomla! 1.5 only officially supports MySQL databases.

A Joomla! database uses a prefix for all table names. As this prefix is defined on a per-installation basis, when we reference tables we need to use the current installation's prefix. Luckily, we don't have to work this out ourselves. Imagine that the prefix is `jos` and we have a table named `jos_mycomponent_foobars`. We use the `#_` string to denote the prefix. Therefore, we express the table name as:

```
#__mycomponent_foobars
```

The object we most commonly use to interact with the database is the global **DBO (Database Object)**. We retrieve this using `JFactory`. Note that we must use `=&` when assigning the object to a variable. If we don't do this and use a PHP version prior to PHP 5, we will inadvertently create a copy of the DBO.

```
$db =& JFactory::getDBO();
```

Security and SQL

Writing SQL queries requires some thought because it is easy to accidentally introduce security vulnerabilities. For information about writing queries safely, refer to the SQL recipes in Chapter 2.

For the purpose of this chapter, we will use an example table to demonstrate how each recipe applies in the real world. Obviously, we won't want to use the entire table for every recipe. Therefore, we will deal with explicitly defined datasets as applicable.

#__mycomponent_foobars

Field	Type	NOT NULL	Auto increment	Unsigned	Description
id	int(11)	YES	YES	YES	Primary Key
foo	varchar(100)	YES			General text field that does not allow NULL values
bar	varchar(100)				General text field that does allow NULL values
checked_ out	int(11)	YES		YES	User to whom the record is checked out
checked_ out_time	datetime	YES			Time at which the record was checked out

Field	Type	NOT NULL	Auto increment	Unsigned	Description
ordering	int(11)	YES		YES	Position where the record should be located within a group of records
published	tinyint(1)	YES		YES	Record is or isn't publicly visible
hits	int(11)	YES		YES	Number of times the record has been viewed
catid	int(11)			YES	Foreign key that relates to a categorization table
params	text	YES			Additional parameters

In addition to the table definition, we will use the following example data:

id	foo	bar	checked_out	checked_out_time	order-ing	publi-shed	hits	catid	params
100		NULL	0	0000-00-00 00:00:00	4	1	13	1	
101	Lorem	NULL	0	0000-00-00 00:00:00	3	1	43	1	
102	ipsum	NULL	0	0000-00-00 00:00:00	1	1	72	1	
103	dolor	NULL	62	2009-03-11 11:18:32	2	1	55	1	
104	sit	NULL	0	0000-00-00 00:00:00	1	0	0	2	
105	amet	NULL	0	0000-00-00 00:00:00	2	1	49	2	

If you want to create this table for testing purposes, please refer to the code downloads available from the Packt Publishing web site (http://www.packtpub.com/files/code/ 8143_Code.zip) where you can download the code samples that accompany the book.

Use of the params field is not explained in this chapter. This field is used to extend the database beyond its original design. For more information refer to the JParameter and JElement recipes in Chapter 9, _Keeping it Extensible and Modular_.

One of the more powerful classes that Joomla! provides us with is the abstract JTable class. The abstract JTable class enables us to rapidly develop an interface for each of our database tables. In addition to the usual things that we would expect to find in this type of class, we get a whole bunch of methods that we can use to effortlessly implement common Joomla! table functionality such as record locking. The following list describes the built-in functionality that a concrete JTable provides us with:

- **Binding**: Copy data from an array or object to the JTable object
- **XMLify**: Present record as XML
- **Managing records**: Create, read, update, and delete records

> ▸ **Validating**: Checks that the record data conforms to a set of predefined rules
> ▸ **Locking**: Prevent more than one user from editing a record at any one time
> ▸ **Ordering**: User-defined ordering of records
> ▸ **Publishing**: Make a record visible or not invisible to the public
> ▸ **Hit counter**: Number of times a record has been viewed

In this chapter we show how to create concrete implementations of `JTable`. This chapter also explains how to use all of the functionality described in the list shown above.

Managing records refers to **CRUD**, which in turn refers to the activities Create, Read, Update, and Delete that encapsulate the life of an item in persistent storage. When we refer to CRUD in a `JTable`, the persistent storage facility is the database and the item is a record in one of the database tables or, more specifically, the table that the concrete `JTable` represents.

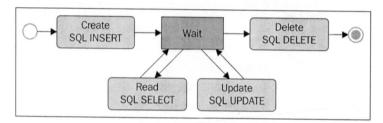

Sometimes it can be difficult to understand the purpose of `JTable` and how it fits into an MVC Joomla! component, given that we already have a model and access to the database via the DBO. To help put this into context, we need to think of `JTable` as another layer of abstraction between us and the database. Using a `JTable` removes us from the raw data by an extra step.

Executing a query

The most basic of all the `JDatabase` methods for executing a query is the `JDatabase::query()` method. We should only use this method when we are dealing with queries that do not return datasets because this method returns raw responses. For example, if we successfully executed a `SELECT` query, we would be rewarded with a result resource. We don't really want to be in a position where we need to manually interrogate a resource!

So when exactly do we use the `JDatabase::query()` method? In simple terms, we use it when the result is Boolean. That is to say, it will either be successful or unsuccessful. The following list identifies the data manipulation query types that we would expect to use with this method:

- DELETE
- INSERT
- RENAME
- REPLACE
- UPDATE

Getting ready

In order to execute a query, we need an instance of the Joomla! DBO.

```
$db =& JFactory::getDBO();
```

How to do it...

The first step is to create the query we want to execute. The following example creates a basic DELETE query that removes all records from the #__mycomponent_foobars table where the value of ordering is greater than 4:

```
// prepare names
$tableName  = $db->nameQuote('#__mycomponent_foobars');
$columnName = $db->nameQuote('ordering');

// build DELETE query
$sql = "DELETE FROM $tableName " .
       . "WHERE $columnName > 4 ";
```

Before we execute the query, we must tell the DBO what the query is! Sounds simple, and it is, but it is very easy to forget this all-important step:

```
$db->setQuery($sql);
```

Finally, we come to the actual execution of the query.

```
if ($db->query()) {
    // on success
} else {
    // on fail
}
```

Because we know the result will be always be `true` or `false` when executing a `DELETE` query, it is safe to use the return value to check for success or failure. Check out the *Handling DBO errors* recipe later in this chapter.

There's more...

A useful method after the successful completion of a query is `JDatabase::getAffectedRows()`. This method returns the number of records that were affected by the last executed query.

```
// on success
$affectRowCount = $db->getAffectedRows();

// show confirmation
echo JText::sprintf('DELETED %u RECORDS', $affectRowCount);
```

See also

The next three recipes, *Loading the first cell from the result of a query, Loading the first record from a query*, and *Loading more than one record from a query*, explain how to execute `SELECT` queries and get the returned data.

Loading the first cell from the result of a query

Sometimes our queries are very simple, only retrieving a single value. An example would be getting the number of records that match some given criteria using the `COUNT()` function, or getting the value of one column in a record where the record identifier is known. In these instances, there is no need to go though complex datasets to get the value. `JDatabase` provides us with a quick and easy way to retrieve the first value in the first record of the dataset.

Getting ready

In order to retrieve a single value, we need an instance of the Joomla! DBO.

```
$db =& JFactory::getDBO();
```

How to do it...

The first step is to prepare the query. The following example determines the number of records in the #__mycomponent_foobars table using the aggregate COUNT() function. *This is a good example of when we would only be retrieving a single value from the database.*

```
// prepare names
$tableName = $db->nameQuote('#__mycomponent_foobars');

// build COUNT query
$sql = "SELECT COUNT(*) FROM $tableName";
```

Before we execute the query, we must tell the DBO what the query is!

```
$db->setQuery($sql);
```

Finally, we come to the actual execution of the query.

```
$total = $db->loadResult();
```

Based on our example table defined in the chapter introduction, the value of $total will be string(1) "6". Notice that although MySQL considers the value to be an integer, it is represented as a string.

How it works...

In the example, the query is only extracting a single value. So what happens if the query actually retrieves a more complex dataset? Consider the following query:

```
SELECT *
FROM `#__mycomponent_foobars`
WHERE `id` > 103;
```

This provides the following dataset:

104	sit	NULL	0	0000-00-00 00:00:00	1	0	0	2
105	amet	NULL	0	0000-00-00 00:00:00	2	1	49	2

Using the JDatabase::loadResult() method here will return the value in the upper left corner, in this instance 104.

OK, it's not rocket science. In fact, it is quite easy to see how this works. However, there is a caveat we need to be aware of. We will use a data subset from the `#__mycomponent_foobars` table as an example.

id	foo	bar
100		NULL
101	Lorem	NULL
102	ipsum	NULL
103	dolor	NULL
104	sit	NULL
105	amet	NULL

Executing an aggregate `COUNT()` query here gives us the value 6 (as a string), a nice and easy value to understand. Executing the same query again, but this time where `bar IS NOT NULL`, gives us the value 0 (also as a string)—still very straightforward. If we retrieve the `MAX()` value of `id`, we get the value `105`. If we retrieve the value of `foo` for the record `100`, we get an empty string. If we retrieve the value of `bar` for any of the records, we get the value `NULL`.

So what? It works like a charm! However, if the query fails for any reason, we also get the value `NULL`. Depending on the context of the query, this result could be ambiguous. With a `COUNT()` query, it is easy to understand because we know the value will be an integer (although represented as a string). When retrieving a value from a column that allows `NULL` values such as `bar`, the meaning of a `NULL` response becomes unclear.

See also

The *Handling DBO errors* recipe explains how to check for errors after executing a query.

Loading the first record from a query

Retrieving one record from a query is not unusual. For example, if we created a component that handles recipes, we only need to retrieve one record when a user wants to retrieve a recipe. It can be easy to overlook this because of the fact that we are used to navigating our way through datasets, for example `$record = array_shift($dataset)`. Doing this the Joomla! way is even easier!

There are actually three ways of doing this. Which way to use depends on the format that we want the record to be in. It can be an array, an associative array, or an object. The following diagram shows a record as represented by the database. Beneath this are the three formats in which we can retrieve the record using `JDatabase`:

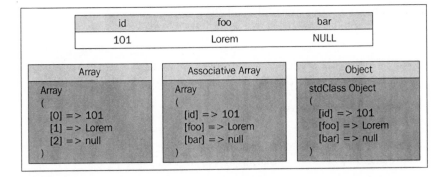

The value of `bar` in the database is `NULL`. This equates directly to the PHP value `null`. It should not be confused with a null string, that is, a string with no characters. The object representation is a `stdClass` object. This is a basic built-in PHP class that has no predefined members.

Use a JTable instead

It can be beneficial to use a `JTable` in instances where we are retrieving a single record from a single table, and we do not need to use any SQL functions, and we know the value of the primary key. A `JTable` provides us with an easy-to-use interface for tables in the database. For more information, refer to the *Creating a JTable* recipe later in this chapter.

Getting ready

In order to retrieve a single record, we need an instance of the Joomla! DBO.

```
$db =& JFactory::getDBO();
```

How to do it...

The first step is to prepare the query. The following example gets the record in the `#__mycomponent_foobars` example table with the ID `101`:

```
// prepare names
$tableName = $db->nameQuote('#__mycomponent_foobars');
$idColumn  = $db->nameQuote('id');
$fooColumn = $db->nameQuote('foo');
$barColumn = $db->nameQuote('bar');
// build COUNT query
$sql = "SELECT $idColumn, $fooColumn, $barColumn "
    . "FROM $tableName "
    . "WHERE $idColumn = 101";
```

Before we execute the query, we must tell the DBO what the query is!

```
$db->setQuery($sql);
```

Finally, we come to the actual execution of the query. As we have already mentioned, there are three ways to do this. They are as follows:

```
// get record as an array
$array = $db->loadRow();

// get record as an associative array
$associativeArray = $db->loadAssoc();

// get record as an object (stdClass)
$object = $db->loadObject();
```

So what does each of these actually give us? If we look back at the diagram in the recipe introduction, we have our answer! We get an array, associative array, and an object, all of which represent the record with the ID `101`.

Basic arrays use a position-orientated index, that is, the first field is at position `0`. This means that to use them, we must have prior knowledge of the position of the field in the dataset. Although this isn't necessarily a problem, it can easily lead to simple errors and maintenance issues. For example, if we add a new column to a table, we may have to change a substantial amount of our code.

On the other hand, associative arrays and objects reference values based on the name of the field. This makes associative arrays and objects less susceptible to changes in the database, and makes the representation semantically understandable. Therefore, it is generally best to use associative arrays and/or objects.

There's more...

For security reasons, it can sometimes be wise to check that the query has only returned a single row. In some instances, a malicious user might be able to trick an extension into loading more than one row. A prime example of when it is good practice to check the number of rows is when interrogating the user's table. We don't want to give away any data by mistake!

We can check the number of rows that have been retrieved using the `JDatabase::getNumRows()` method. This method returns the number of rows that were retrieved by the last query.

```
if ($db->getNumRows() > 1) {
    // uh oh, something fishy going on!
}
```

Beware of LIMIT when counting rows

The `JDatabase::getNumRows()` method returns the number of returned rows. If we limit the number of results using `LIMIT`, the maximum number of rows will be equal to `LIMIT`. If we want the total potential number of rows, we should use the aggregate `COUNT()` function.

See also

The *Handling DBO errors* recipe explains how to check for errors after executing a query.

Loading more than one record from a query

Whichever way we choose to retrieve multiple records from the database, we will always end up with an array of records. How each record is represented in the array can vary. When we use `JDatabase`, there are three ways in which a row may be represented. Rows can be arrays, associative arrays, or objects. The following diagram shows some records as represented by the database. Beneath these are the three formats in which we can retrieve the records using `JDatabase`:

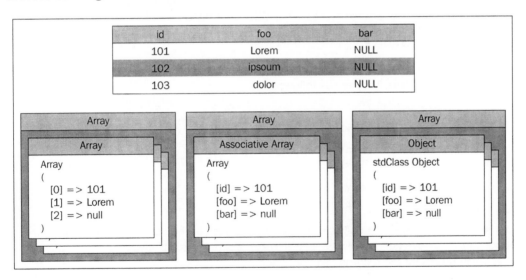

The value of `bar` in the database is `NULL`. This equates directly to the PHP value `null`. It should not be confused with a null string, that is, a string with no characters. The object representation is a `stdClass` object. This is a basic built-in PHP class that has no predefined members.

Getting ready

In order to retrieve an array of records, we need an instance of the Joomla! DBO.

```
$db =& JFactory::getDBO();
```

How to do it...

The first step is to prepare the query. The following example query gets the records with the IDs 101, 102, and 103:

```
// prepare names
$tableName = $db->nameQuote('#__table_name');
$idColumn  = $db->nameQuote('id');
$fooColumn = $db->nameQuote('foo');
$barColumn = $db->nameQuote('bar');

// build query
$sql = "SELECT $idColumn, $fooColumn, $barColumn "
    . "FROM $tableName "
    . "WHERE $idColumn >= 101 AND "
    . "      $idColumn <= 103 ";
```

Before we execute the query, we must tell the DBO what the query is!

```
$db->setQuery($sql);
```

Finally, we come to the actual execution of the query. We have already mentioned that there are three ways to do this. They are as follows:

```
// get rows as arrays
$arrays = $db->loadRowList();

// get rows as associative arrays
$associativeArrays = $db->loadAssocList();

// get rows as objects (stdClass)
$objects = $db->loadObjectList();
```

So what do each of these actually give us? If we look back at the diagram in the recipe introduction, we have our answer! We get an array of arrays, associative arrays, and objects, all of which represent the records 101, 102, and 103.

Basic arrays use a position-orientated index, that is, the first field is at position 0. This means that to use these we must have prior knowledge of the position of the field in the dataset. Although this isn't necessarily a problem, it can easily lead to simple errors and maintenance issues. For example, if we add a new column to a table, we may have to change a substantial amount of our code.

Associative arrays and objects, on the other hand, reference values based on the name of the field. This makes associative arrays and objects less susceptible to changes in the database and makes the representation semantically understandable. Therefore, it is generally best to use associative arrays and/or objects.

There's more...

The array in which the results are returned is by default an ordinary array, that is, numerically indexed in the order in which the rows were extracted from the database. However, there is an interesting option that allows us to use a more complex index. In instances where the rows have a single distinguishable key value, we can use the key as the array index. For example, given the key values 101, 102, and 103, the keys in the array can match these. This is shown below:

```
Array
(
    [101] => Array ( [0] => 101 [1] => Lorem [2] => null )
    [102] => Array ( [0] => 102 [1] => ipsum [2] => null )
    [103] => Array ( [0] => 103 [1] => dolor [2] => null )
)
```

To achieve this, we must provide the JDatabase::load*List() method with the optional first parameter. This parameter tells the method which column represents the key. For JDatabase::loadRowList(), this value must be an integer—the index of the column in the dataset. For the other two methods, this value must be a string—the name of the column in the dataset.

```
// get rows as arrays
$arrays = $db->loadRowList(0);
// get rows as associative arrays
$associativeArrays = $db->loadAssocList('id');
// get rows as objects (stdClass)
$objects = $db->loadObjectList('id');
```

See also

The next recipe, *Handling DBO errors*, explains how to check for errors after executing a query.

Handling DBO errors

Things don't always go according to a plan. The way in which we execute a query makes a difference to how we can check for errors. For example, using the JDatabase::query() method we can expect a Boolean response of false when something goes wrong. Although this is an acceptable way of checking for errors, there is a more generic mechanism.

The problem with checking the return value is we need to be aware of how each method that executes a query represents a failure in the return value. The other problem with this is that Joomla! can potentially support database systems other than MySQL. Adapters for other database systems might report failures in slightly different ways. Luckily, we have another way to check for errors that reduces the coupling between our code and the DBO handler.

How to do it...

The `JDatabase::getErrorNum()` method returns the error number generated by the last query. If no errors occurred, the method returns 0. Therefore, we check for errors by checking the error number.

```
if ($db->getErrorNum() == 0) {
    // no errors occurred
} else {
    // errors occurred
}
```

How it works...

The error numbers that are returned by the `JDatabase::getErrorNum()` method are the native database system errors. The problem with this is that different database systems use different error codes, for example the MySQL error code for *no such table* is 1146, but in SQL Server the error code is 208. For this reason, by and large the `JDatabase::getErrorNum()` method is used only to check for the existence of an error.

There's more...

In addition to retrieving an error code, we can retrieve an error message. Just like the error codes, the error messages are native to the database system. Although the DBO is technically a `JObject`, we do not use the normal `JObject::getError()` method to get the last error message. Instead, we use the `JDatabase::getErrorMsg()` method.

```
// on fail
$error = $db->getErrorMsg();

// display error
JError::raiseWarning(500, $error);
```

There is an alterative. The `JDatabase::stderr()` method produces a more verbose error message.

```
// on fail
$error = $db->stderr();

// display error
JError::raiseError(500, $error);
```

A downside of retrieving the error messages in this way is that they are not translated into the current language. In general, these error messages are only used when the error is fatal and we are raising a 500 internal server error, as in the previous example.

Using the `JDatabase::stderr()` method, we can also output the offending SQL. To do this, we provide the optional Boolean parameter `$showSQL` as `true`, which by default is `false`. *It is not recommended to show the offending SQL on live servers because it may give away important information that a malicious user could attempt to use to exploit the system.*

Creating a JTable

This recipe explains how to create a `JTable` for the `#__mycomponent_foobars` example table described in the chapter introduction. For the purposes of this recipe, we will only use the first three fields: `id`, `foo`, and `bar`.

Getting ready

If we are building a `JTable` class in a component, we must first create a `tables` folder (if it doesn't already exist). This folder is located in the root of the component's administration folder. For example, for the `mycomponent` component this would be `administrator/components/com_mycomponent/tables`.

In the unlikely event that we are building a `JTable` class for a different type of extension, there is no predefined location for `JTable` classes. If we want to make use of the static `JTable::getInstance()` method when using concrete `JTable` classes in an alternative location, it is necessary to tell `JTable` in which folder we added `JTable` subclasses. *Note that it is possible to add several paths.*

```
JTable::addIncludePath($pathToSomeJTables);
```

How to do it...

Naming conventions are important when creating concrete `JTable` classes. The file in which a class is defined should be named after the table it represents (singular, not plural). The class should be named `Table` followed by the table it represents (singular, not plural). For example, the `JTable` class for `#__mycomponent_foobars` would be located in `foobar.php` and would be named `TableFoobar`.

In a basic implementation of a `JTable` class, we normally override two methods: `__construct()` and `check()`. We also add class instance variables for each field in the table.

We must not add any public class instance variables that do not relate to a field in the table. If we want to add additional class instance variables, they must be prefixed with an underscore to denote that they are protected.

The following example class is designed to work with the cutdown version of the `#__mycomponent_foobars` table:

```
/**
 * Handles database table #__mycomponent_foobars
 */
class TableFoobar extends JTable
{
    /** @var int */
    var $id = null;

    /** @var string */
    var $foo = '';

    /** @var string */
    var $bar = '';

    /**
     * Create a new TableFoobar
     */
    function __construct(&$db) {
        parent::__construct('#__mycomponent_foobars', 'id', $db);
    }
    /**
     * Is the data valid?
     */
    function check() {
        // check for valid id (int or null)
        if (!preg_match('~^\d+$~', $this->id) || $this->id !== null) {
            $this->setError(JText::_('ID IS INVALID'));
            return false;
        }
        // check for valid foo
        if (JString::trim($this->foo) == '') {
            $this->setError(JText::_('FOOBAR MUST HAVE FOO'));
            return false;
        }
        // all OK, data is valid!
        return true;
    }
}
```

Once we have a concrete `JTable` implementation, we can use the class. How we access it depends on where we are attempting to use the class from. If we are creating an MVC component (probably the most common scenario), we use the `JModel::getTable()` method. *In most cases, we only use this method from within a model. Nevertheless, it is a public method and thus it's possible to use it externally.*

```
class SomeModel extends JModel {
    ...
    function someMethod() {
        $table =& $this->getModel('Foobar');
        ...
    }
}
```

Alternatively, we can directly use the `JTable::getInstance()` method.

```
$table =& JTable::getInstance('Foobar', 'Table');
```

Notice how we provide a second parameter. This is the table prefix, the default value is `JTable`. This is the prefix used for the core Joomla! implementations of `JTable`, such as `JTableUser`.

How it works...

The concrete `JTable` constructor passes the name of the table with which we want to work, the name of the primary key, and the DBO to the parent `JTable` constructor. The `check()` method overrides the parent method and is used to validate the data in the class instance variables.

We are not required to override the `check()` method. In rare cases where no rules apply to the data, there is no need to override the method. Although the `check()` method is intended solely to determine the validity of the data, it can be OK to modify the data within this method as long as the modifications are relatively simple. An example would be copying a title value to an alias value when an alias value is not provided.

It's important that we understand the role of the `check()` method. This method is intended for use prior to making any changes to the table itself, that is, creating or updating a record. Creating and updating records is done using either the `JTable::save()` method or the `JTable::store()` method. If we use the `JTable::save()` method, it is not necessary to manually invoke the `check()` method because this is done for us.

See also

The next four recipes explain how to create, read, update, and delete records using a `JTable`.

Creating a new record using a JTable

This recipe explains how to create a new record in a database using a `JTable` object. In this example, we will use the `JTable` class defined in the previous recipe. For the purposes of this recipe, we will assume that the data we want to use to create the new record is coming from a `POST`ed form.

Getting ready

The first thing we need is a `JTable` object. Refer to the previous recipe for information about getting an instance of a `JTable`.

How to do it...

The first step is to get the data from which we want to create the new record. This data will be bound to the `JTable` object. This means that the values are copied from the array to the table. It does not matter if the data to which we are binding contains arbitrary data, as this will be ignored by the `JTable` object. In the following example, we get the complete `POST` hash. Note that because we are using `JRequest::get()` to get this hash, the input will automatically be sanitized (more on this is given later in the chapter).

```
// values to use to create new record
$post = JRequest::get('POST');
```

We must make sure that the value of `id` (the primary key) is not set in such a way that it will interfere with the creation of the new record. Therefore, we set `id` to `false`. This ensures that we definitely create a record as opposed to updating an existing record.

```
// do not provide an ID
$post['id'] = false;
```

The final step is to save the new record using the `JTable::save()` method. The `JTable::save()` method returns a Boolean value that denotes success or failure.

```
if (!$table->save($post)) {
    // uh oh failed to save
}
```

If the `JTable::save()` method fails, we can try using the `JTable::getError()` method to get a textual description of what went wrong. It is worth noting that we won't always be able to get an error message. The `JTable::save()` method executes a number of other methods, for example `JTable::checkin()`. If `checkin` fails, no error message is set!

How it works...

The `JTable::save()` method is the all-inclusive package deal. It does all of the following:

- Binds with a source array or object using the `JTable::bind()` method
- Validates the data using the `JTable::check()` method
- Stores the data using the `JTable::store()` method
- Checks in the record using the `JTable::checkin()` method
- Orders the records using the `JTable::reorder()` method

Like a package holiday, the problem with this all-inclusive deal is that we don't get a great deal of control over the process. Due to these restrictions, the `JTable::save()` method isn't always appropriate. If we look at some of the core components, we'll notice that they opt not to use the `JTable::save()` method. Instead, they complete all of the above themselves. For more information, refer to the next section.

There's more...

Sometimes we may want a bit more control over the data with which we are binding. For example, if we have a `text` field in which we want to allow storage of HTML, using the sanitized `$post` variable would be unsuitable because HTML will have been stripped from the values. To achieve this, we must handle the field in which we want to allow HTML separately.

```
// allow raw untrimmed value for foo
$post['foo'] = JRequest::getString('foo', '', 'POST',
                            JREQUEST_ALLOWRAW | JREQUEST_NOTRIM);
```

This approach can also be useful when dealing with values that we know should be of a certain type. For example, if we know a value should be an integer, we might want to use the `JRequest::getInt()` method to guarantee that the value is indeed an integer. For more information about working with `JRequest`, refer to the Chapter 2 recipe, *Safely retrieving request data*.

No need for binding

Rather than using an array or object to bind with, we can set each data element using the `JTable::set()` method. If we do this, when we use the `JTable::save()` method, we must provide an empty array or object with which to bind.

In the *How it works* section, we saw that the third thing the `JTable::save()` method does is execute the `JTable::store()` method. This is the method that really gets stuck in and actually makes the changes to the database. The trouble with the `JTable::save()` method is that it does not provide us with a great deal of control.

As an example, the `JTable::store()` method has a parameter we can use to determine if we want to update the `null` values. When we use the `JTable::save()` method, it is assumed that we don't want to update the `null` values. This is something which might be vital for a table that does allow `null` values in some fields. *Note that the* `JTable::bind()` *method cannot bind with* `null` *values.*

Usage of the `JTable::reorder()` method is also restrictive. It assumes that the ordering in the table is based on grouping a field and cannot apply to the entire table.

The error messages that are set are also unreliable. If any one of these methods fails, the `JTable::save()` method will fail. But we get little feedback as to when the failure occurred in the process, and in some instances an error message won't even be set in the object to describe the failure!

The following example shows a more comprehensive solution. To simplify the example, each point of failure is denoted by a `// failed` comment. Ideally, at a point of failure the process will stop and the failure will be dealt with.

```php
// values to use to create new record
$post = JRequest::get('POST');

// do not provide an ID
$post['id'] = false;

// allow raw untrimmed value for foo
$post['foo'] = JRequest::getString('foo', '', 'POST', JREQUEST_
ALLOWRAW | JREQUEST_NOTRIM);

// bind $post with $table
if (!$table->bind($post)) {
    // failed
}
// check the data is valid
if (!$table->check()) {
    // failed
}
// store the data in the database table and update nulls
if (!$table->store(true)) {
    // failed
}
// check the record in
if (!$table->checkin()) {
    // failed
}
// reorder the entire table (not grouped in any way)
if (!$table->reorder()) {
    // failed
}
```

See also

The previous recipe, *Creating a JTable*, explains how to create a concrete `JTable` class.

The next two recipes explain how to update and read data using a concrete `JTable`.

Updating a record using a JTable

This recipe explains how to update an existing record in a database using a `JTable` object. In this example we will use the `JTable` class defined in the last but one recipe.

Getting ready

The first thing we need is a `JTable` object. Refer to the last but one recipe for information about getting an instance of a `JTable`.

How to do it...

As you have probably guessed, updating a record doesn't differ a great deal from creating a record. In fact, it is identical except that we provide the value of the record's primary key in the process.

```
// values to use to update an existing record
// $post contains the ID of the record we are updating
$post = JRequest::get('POST');

if (!$table->save($post)) {
    // uh oh failed to save
}
```

Given that creating and updating a record are very similar, we tend not to handle creating and updating of records separately. In an MVC component, creating and updating a record often occur in one method named `edit()`.

How it works...

For more information, refer to the previous recipe's *How it works* section.

There's more...

For more information, refer to the previous recipe's *There's more* section.

Reading an existing record using a JTable

This recipe explains how to read an existing record in a database using a JTable object. In this example we will use the JTable class defined in the *Creating a JTable* recipe.

Getting ready

The first thing we need is a JTable object. Refer to the *Creating a JTable* recipe for information about getting an instance of a JTable.

How to do it...

To read a record from the table, we use the JTable::load() method. This method loads the record into the class instance variables. The first and only parameter this method accepts is the value of the primary key of the record we want to read. This method returns a Boolean value, so we can also check for success or failure.

```
if ($table->load(JRequest::getInt('id'))) {
    // success!
}
```

 Sometimes the ID of the record we want to load might already be set in the object. In these instances it is not necessary to include the value of the record's primary key.

Reading the data is all very well, but where does it go and how do we access it? As we already know, concrete implementations of JTable include public instance variables that relate directly to fields in the table that the concrete JTable represents. Thus, once we have loaded a record, we can use the JTable::get() method to access the loaded record data.

```
$someField = $table->get('someField');
```

Deleting a record using a JTable

This recipe explains how to delete an existing record in a database using a JTable object. In this example we will use the JTable class defined in the *Creating a JTable* recipe.

Getting ready

The first thing we need is a JTable object. Refer to the *Creating a JTable* recipe for information about getting an instance of a JTable.

How to do it...

The key principle here is to not get sentimentally attached. No really, it is unhealthy to get attached to data! On a more serious note, to delete a record we use the `JTable::delete()` method. If we have already loaded the record, we can use this method without any parameters and it will delete the current record. On the other hand, if we have not loaded the record, we can provide this method with the value of the primary key of the record we want to delete.

```
if ($table->delete(JRequest::getInt('id'))) {
    // successfully deleted
}
```

Deleting a record when the table has dependencies

The `canDelete()` method can be used to determine if there are any dependencies that need to be removed first. To use this method, we must provide the primary key value of the record we want to check and an array defining the table associations.

Checking a record in and out (record locking) using a JTable

This recipe explains how to use a `JTable` to manually implement a form of record locking. Note that this type of record locking is controlled by Joomla!, and not by the database server, and thus can be circumvented.

Getting ready

The first thing we need is a `JTable` object. Refer to the *Creating a JTable* recipe earlier in this chapter for information about getting an instance of a `JTable`.

We can only lock records if our table has the `checked_out` and `checked_out_time` fields. These fields define who has checked out a record and at what time they checked it out. These fields are defined in MySQL as `INT UNSIGNED` and `DATETIME` respectively. Our `#__mycomponent_foobars` example table has the capacity to implement the `JTable` style record locking.

How to do it...

We check out records when we allow editing. For example, when a user edits an article in the content component, the record is checked out to prevent any other users from editing the article simultaneously. Prior to checking out a record, it is necessary to ensure that the record is not already checked out by another user.

```
// get current user
$user =& JFactory::getUser();
// load the record
$table->load($id);
// check if record is already checked out
if ($table->isCheckedOut($user->get('id'))) {
    // someone beat us to it!
}
```

If a record is already checked out, the normal action is to redirect the browser to a page where the item can be viewed and display a message explaining that the item is already being edited.

Assuming the record is not already checked out, the next step is to check out the record ourselves. We do this using the `JTable::checkout()` method.

```
// check out the current record
$table->checkout($user->get('id'));
```

Once we are finished with the record, we can check the record back in. This will typically occur when the user saves the changes to the record or cancels the record editing. We do this using the `JTable::checkin()` method.

```
// check the current record in
$table->checkin();
```

There's more...

The example in the *How to do it* section shows the normal usage of the `JTable::isCheckedOut()` method when dealing with a single record. It is possible if we do not want to load the record into the `JTable` (useful when dealing with a list of items where we want to show if each item is checked in or out) to provide the value of the `checked_out` field as a second parameter. The method can also be used statically.

```
// get current user
$user =& JFactory::getUser();
// check if is checked out
if (JTable::isCheckedOut($user->get('id'), $checkedOut)) {
    // record is checked out by another user
}
```

The `JTable::isCheckedOut()` method provides more than a basic comparison of values. It also checks that the current user for whom the record is checked out is still logged in.

It is possible to use the `JTable::checkin()` and `JTable::checkout()` method when the record we want to check in or out is not currently loaded. To do this, we must provide the methods with the optional `$oid` parameter. This parameter defines which record we want to check in or out. For example, to check out we use this:

```
// check out a record identified by $oid
$table->checkout($user->get('id'), $oid);
```

And to check in we use this:

```
// check in a record identified by $oid
$table->checkin($oid);
```

Modifying record ordering using a JTable

This recipe explains how to use a `JTable` to define the ordering of records. A prime example of this is the Joomla! menus which, as an administrator, we can reorder as we please. The following example shows how ordering is used in the menu administration area. Notice the **Order** column.

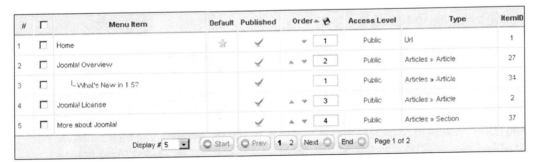

Getting ready

The first thing we need is a `JTable` object. Refer to the *Creating a JTable* recipe earlier in this chapter for information about getting an instance of a `JTable`.

We can only allow users to order records based on a numeric index if our table has the `ordering` field. This field is defined in MySQL as `INT UNSIGNED` as per the `#__mycomponent_foobars` example table described at the start of this chapter.

Ordering can be grouped. This means that we can use other fields in the table to define which ordering group a record belongs to. In most instances, this will be based on a single field. In our #__mycomponent_foobars example table defined in the chapter introduction, the grouping is based around the catid field. If we refer to the example data in the chapter introduction, we can see how grouping affects the ordering values.

How to do it...

There are three useful JTable methods for dealing with ordering. The first one we will look at is the JTable::getNextOrder() method, which is used to determine the next available space. We normally use this when adding a new record to the end of the order. The following example retrieves the next available space where grouping is used on the catid field and the category we are interested in is defined by $catid:

```
// prepare grouping
$db =& JFactory::getDBO();
$group = $db->nameQuote('catid') . ' = ' . intval($catid);

// get next space
$next = $table->getNextOrder($group);
```

Sometimes the ordering becomes inconsistent. For example, there may be spaces in the order and/or order positions might be used more than once. We can use the JTable::reorder() method to rectify any inconsistencies. This is often done after deleting a record, and sometimes after adding a record instead of using the JTable::getNextOrder() method to predetermine the position in the order.

```
// prepare grouping
$db =& JFactory::getDBO();
$group = $db->nameQuote('catid') . ' = ' . intval($catid);

// get next space
$next = $table->reorder($group);
```

As was shown in the menu administration screenshot, it is common to allow basic up and down movement of records (green arrows in the **Order** column). The third method, JTable::move(), allows us to do this. Move up is expressed as -1 and move down is expressed as +1.

```
// prepare grouping
$db =& JFactory::getDBO();
$group = $db->nameQuote('catid') . ' = ' . intval($catid);
// move current record up one
$table->move(-1, $group);
```

There is one other, less common, way to use this method. If we express the move as 0, we can update the ordering field of the current record by setting the ordering position we want. This is not a comprehensive solution as it does not (if required) shift the existing records.

We won't always want to group orders. This is especially true in instances where there is no logical separation of records. In these instances we can omit the $group parameter entirely.

Publishing and unpublishing a record using a JTable

This recipe explains how to use a JTable to publish and unpublish records. The core Joomla! content component is a primary example of where publishing is used to define the visibility of a table record.

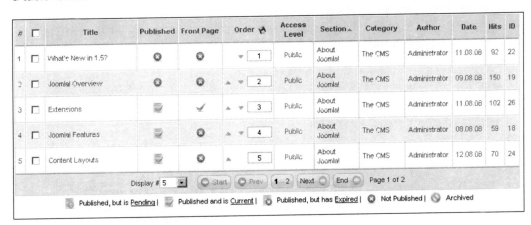

#		Title	Published	Front Page	Order ⇲	Access Level	Section ⯅	Category	Author	Date	Hits	ID
1	☐	What's New in 1.5?	⊗	⊗	▼ 1	Public	About Joomla!	The CMS	Administrator	11.08.08	92	22
2	☐	Joomla! Overview	⊗	⊗	▲ ▼ 2	Public	About Joomla!	The CMS	Administrator	09.08.08	150	19
3	☐	Extensions	✔	✔	▲ ▼ 3	Public	About Joomla!	The CMS	Administrator	11.08.08	102	26
4	☐	Joomla! Features	✔	⊗	▲ ▼ 4	Public	About Joomla!	The CMS	Administrator	08.08.08	59	18
5	☐	Content Layouts	✔	⊗	▲ 5	Public	About Joomla!	The CMS	Administrator	12.08.08	70	24

Display # 5 ▾   ◉ Start ◉ Prev **1** 2 Next ◉ End ◉   Page 1 of 2

🔲 Published, but is <u>Pending</u> | ✔ Published and is <u>Current</u> | ⊗ Published, but has <u>Expired</u> | ⊗ Not Published | 🚫 Archived

Getting ready

The first thing we need is a JTable object. Refer to the *Creating a JTable* recipe earlier in this chapter for information about getting an instance of a JTable.

In Joomla!, publishing is the act of setting a flag to determine whether or not a record is visible to the public. *The exact definition of public will depend on the table in question and potentially on other access rights.* We can only publish and unpublish records if our table has the published field. This field is defined in MySQL as TINYINT(1) UNSIGNED. Published is expressed as 1 and not published is expressed as 0.

How to do it...

In the following example, we publish a group of records based on the request data `cid`. In this instance, this is an array of integers that relate to the IDs of one or more records in the table we are dealing with. For more information about getting data from the request, refer to the Chapter 2 recipe, *Safely retrieving request data*.

```
// get array of records to publish
$cids = JRequest::getVar('cid', array(),'REQUEST', 'ARRAY');

// publish the records!
$table->publish($cids);
```

The `JTable::publish()` method is more intelligent than it appears. The second parameter allows us to determine if we are publishing or unpublishing (1 or 0). The third parameter allows us to specify a user ID so as to take notice of the checkout status of the records. This is important; if the table allows checking in and out we will not be allowed to change the published state of a record if the record is checked out. By providing our user ID, we widen the criteria to *if the record is checked out by another user*.

```
// get array of records to publish
$cids = JRequest::getVar('cid', array(),'REQUEST', 'ARRAY');

// get the current user
$user =& JFactory::getUser();

// unpublish the records!
$table->publish($cids, 0, $user->get('id'));
```

Perhaps a slightly unexpected feature of this method is the check in. If we are only publishing or unpublishing one record and the table has a `checked_out` field, the record will be checked in. On the other hand, if we have several records this will not happen at all.

Publish timeframe

Components such as the core content component favor specifying a time period during which an article is considered published. `JTable` does not have any way of explicitly dealing with this approach. However, it is relatively simple. It requires two `DATETIME` fields that define publish from and publish to dates (often named `publish_up` and `publish_down`).

Incrementing a record hit counter using a JTable

This recipe explains how to use a `JTable` to increment a record's hit counter. The core Joomla! content component is a leading example of where hits are used to track the popularity of records. In the following example, we can see that the **Joomla! Overview** article is the most popular with a total of **150** hits:

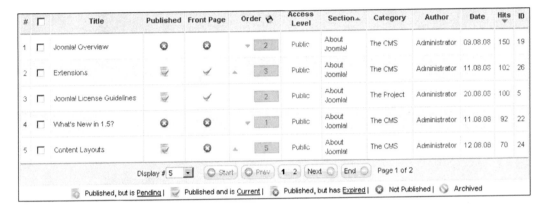

#		Title	Published	Front Page	Order ⚙	Access Level	Section▲	Category	Author	Date	Hits ▼	ID
1	☐	Joomla! Overview	⊗	⊗	▼ 2	Public	About Joomla!	The CMS	Administrator	09.08.08	150	19
2	☐	Extensions	✓	✓	▲ 3	Public	About Joomla!	The CMS	Administrator	11.08.08	102	26
3	☐	Joomla! License Guidelines	✓	✓	2	Public	About Joomla!	The Project	Administrator	20.08.08	100	5
4	☐	What's New in 1.5?	⊗	⊗	▼ 1	Public	About Joomla!	The CMS	Administrator	11.08.08	92	22
5	☐	Content Layouts	✓	⊗	▲ 5	Public	About Joomla!	The CMS	Administrator	12.08.08	70	24

Display # 5 ▾ | ◯ Start | ◯ Prev | **1** 2 | Next ◯ | End ◯ | Page 1 of 2

◯ Published, but is <u>Pending</u> | ✓ Published and is <u>Current</u> | ◯ Published, but has <u>Expired</u> | ⊗ Not Published | ◯ Archived

Getting ready

The first thing we need is a `JTable` object. Refer to the *Creating a JTable* recipe earlier in this chapter for information about getting an instance of a `JTable`.

We can only publish and unpublish records if our table has the `hits` field. This field is defined in MySQL as `INT UNSIGNED`. Our `#__mycomponent_foobars` example table has the capacity to implement the `JTable` style record publishing.

How to do it...

Every time a user views a record, we simply call the `JTable::hit()` method as follows:

```
// increment number of hits for current record
$table->hit();
```

If the record we want to hit is not currently loaded, we can supply the method with the primary key value of the record.

```
// increment number of hits
$table->hit($id);
```

The `JTable::hit()` method includes an option for logging. Unfortunately, there is no implemented functionality associated with this.

4

The Session and the User

This chapter contains the following recipes:

Introduction

This chapter explains how to use Joomla! sessions and how to work with Joomla! users. When a user starts browsing a Joomla! web site, a PHP session is created. Hidden away in the session is user information, this information will either represent a known registered user or a guest.

We can interact with the session using the session handler, a `JSession` object. The first five recipes in this chapter explain how we can work with the session. The remaining nine recipes explain how to work with the user.

When we work with the session in Joomla!, we must not use the global PHP `$_SESSION` variable or any of the PHP session functions.

Getting the session handler

To interact with the session we use the session handler; this is a `JSession` object that is globally available via the static `JFactory` interface. It is imperative that we only use the global `JSession` object to interact with the PHP session. Directly using `$_SESSION` or any of the PHP session functions could have unintended consequences.

How to do it...

To retrieve the `JSession` object we use `JFactory`. As `JFactory` returns an object, we must use `=&` when assigning the object to a variable. If we do not and our server is running a PHP version prior to PHP 5, we will inadvertently create a copy of the global `JSession` object.

```
$session =& JFactory::getSession();
```

How it works...

If we look at the `JSession` class, we will notice that there is a `getInstance()` method. It is tempting to think of this as synonymous with the `JFactory::getSession()` method. There is, however, an important difference, the `JSession::getInstance()` method requires configuration parameters. The `JFactory::getSession()` method accepts configuration parameters, but they are not required.

The first time the `JFactory::getSession()` method is executed, it is done by the `JApplication` object (often referred to as `mainframe`). This creates the session handler. It is the application and `JFactory` that deal with the configuration of the session. Subsequent usage of the `JFactory::getSession()` method will not require the creation of the object, and thus simply returns the existing object. The following sequence diagram shows how this process works the first time it is executed by the `JApplication` object:

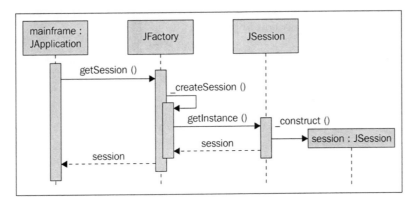

When the `JFactory::getSession()` method is subsequently executed, because `session` will already exist, the `_createSession()` method is not executed.

 The diagram is a simplification of the process; additional complexity has not been included because it is outside the scope of this recipe.

See also

For information about setting and retrieving values in the session, refer to the next two recipes, *Adding data to the session* and *Getting session data*.

Adding data to the session

Data that is set in the session is maintained between client requests. For example, we could display announcements at the top of all our pages and include an option to hide the announcements. Once a user opts to hide the announcements, by setting a value in the session, we would be able to 'remember' this throughout the user's visit.

To put this into context, we would set a session value `hideAnnouncements` to `true` when a user opts to hide announcements. In subsequent requests, we will be able to retrieve the value of `hideAnnouncements` from the session and its state will remain the same.

In Joomla!, session data is maintained using a `JSession` object, which we can retrieve using `JFactory`. This recipe explains how to set data in the session using this object instead of using the global PHP `$_SESSION` variable.

Getting ready

We must get the session handler, a `JSession` object. For more information, refer to the first recipe in this chapter, *Getting the session handler*.

```
$session =& JFactory::getSession();
```

How to do it...

The `JSession::set()` method is used to set a value in the session. The first parameter is the name of the value we want to set; the second is the value itself.

```
$session->set('hideAnnouncements', $value);
```

The `JSession::set()` method returns the previous value. If no value was previously set, the return value will be `null`.

```
// set the new value and retrieve the old
$oldValue = $session->set('hideAnnouncements', $value);

echo 'Hide Announcement was ' . ($oldValue ? 'true' : 'false');
echo 'Hide Announcement is now ' . ($value ? 'true' : 'false');
```

Lastly, we can remove data from the session by setting the value to `null`.

```
// remove something
$session->set('hideAnnouncements', null);
```

How it works...

The session contains a namespace-style data structure. Namespaces are required by `JSession` and by default all values are set in the `default` namespace. To set a value in a different namespace, we use the optional `JSession::set()` third parameter.

```
$session->set('something', $value, 'mynamespace');
```

Sessions aren't just restricted to storing basic values such as strings and integers. The `JUser` object is a case in point—every session includes an instance of `JUser` that represents the user the session belongs to. If we add objects to the session, we must be careful. All session data is serialized. To successfully unserialize an object, the class must already be known when the session is restored. For example, the `JObject` class is safe to serialize because it is loaded prior to restoring the session.

```
$value = new JObject();
$session->set('aJObject', $value);
```

If we attempt to do this with a class that is not loaded when the session is restored, we will end up with an object of type `__PHP_Incomplete_Class`. To overcome this, we can serialize the object ourselves.

```
// serialize the object in the session
$session->set('anObject', serialize($anObject));
```

To retrieve this, we must unserialize the object after we have loaded the class. If we do not do this, we will end up with a string that looks something like this **O:7:"MyClass":1:{s:1:"x";s:10:" some value";}**.

```
// load the class
include_once(JPATH_COMPONENT . DS . 'myclass.php');

// unserialize the object from the session
$value = unserialize($session->get('anObject'));
```

There's more...

There is an alternative way of setting data in the session. User state data is also part of the session, but this data allows us to save session data using more complex hierarchical namespaces, for example `com_myextension.foo.bar.baz`. To access this session data, we use the application object instead of the session handler.

```
// get the application
$app =& JFactory::getApplication();

// set some data
$app->setUserState('com_myextsion.foo.bar.baz, $value);
```

An advantage of using user state data is that we can combine this with request data. For more information refer to the next recipe, *Getting session data*.

 The `JApplication::setUserState()` method is documented as returning the old value. However, a bug prevents this from working; instead the new value is returned.

See also

For information about retrieving values from the session, refer to the next recipe, *Getting session data*.

Getting session data

Data that is set in the session is maintained between client requests. For example if during one request we set the session value of `hideAnnouncements` to `true`, as described in the previous recipe, in subsequent requests we will be able to retrieve the value of `hideAnnouncements` and its state will remain the same.

In Joomla!, session data is maintained using the global `JSession` object. This recipe explains how to get data from the session using this object instead of from the normal global PHP `$_SESSION` variable.

Getting ready

We must get the session handler, a `JSession` object. For more information, refer to the first recipe in this chapter, *Getting the session handler*.

```
$session =& JFactory::getSession();
```

How to do it...

We use the `JSession::get()` method to retrieve data from the session.

```
$value = $session->get('hideAnnouncements');
```

If the value we attempt to retrieve is not set in the session, the value `null` is returned. It is possible to specify a default value, which will be returned in instances where the value is not currently set in the session.

```
$defaultValue = false;
$value = $session->get('hideAnnouncements', $defaultValue);
```

How it works...

The session contains a namespace-style data structure. Namespaces are required by `JSession` and by default all values are retrieved from the `default` namespace. To get a value from a different namespace, we use the optional third `JSession::get()` parameter.

```
$value = $session->get('hideAnnouncements', $defaultValue,
                                            'mynamespace');
```

It is possible to store objects in the session. However, these require special attention when we extract them from the session. For more information about storing objects in the session, refer to the previous recipe, *Adding data to the session*.

There's more...

There is an alternative way of getting data from the session. User state data is also part of the session. The user state data allows us to store session data using more complex hierarchical namespaces, for example `com_myextension.foo.bar.baz`. To access user state data, we use the application object instead of the session handler.

```
// get the application (this is the same as $mainframe)
$app =& JFactory::getApplication();

// get some user state data
$value = $app->getUserState('com_myextsion.foo.bar.baz');
```

User state data is usually combined with request data. For example, if we know the request may include a value that we want to use to update the user state data, we use the `JApplication::getUserStateFromRequest()` method.

```
// get some user state data and update from request
$value = $app->getUserStateFromRequest(
    'com_myextsion.foo.bar.baz',
    'inputName',
    $defaultValue,
    'INTEGER'
);
```

The four parameters we provide this method with are the path to the value in the state data, the name of the request input from which we want to update the value, the default value (which is used if there is no value in the request), and the type of value. This method is used extensively for dealing with display state data, such as pagination.

```
// get global default pagination limit
$defaultListLimit = $app->getCfg('list_limit');
// get limit based on user state data / request data
$limit = $app->getUserStateFromRequest(
    'global.list.limit',
    'limit',
    $defaultListLimit,
    'INTEGER'
);
```

For information about setting values in the session, refer to the previous recipe, *Adding data to the session*.

Checking for session data

A little known, or at least little used ability of `JSession` is the capability to check whether or not a value has already been set in the session. This can be useful to determine the current state of an extension in the current session. For example, we may have a plugin that we want to behave differently the first time it is executed in a session.

Getting ready

We must have an instance of the session handler, which is a `JSession` object. For more information refer to the first recipe in this chapter, *Getting the session handler*.

```
$session =& JFactory::getSession();
```

How to do it...

The `JSession::has()` method determines if a value exists in the session. The method returns a Boolean response, `true` means that the session *has* the value, while `false` means the session *has not* got the value.

```
if ($session->has('someValue')) {
    // some value exists in the session :)
} else {
    // some value does not exist in the session :(
}
```

How it works...

The session contains a namespace style data structure. Namespaces are required by `JSession`, and by default, existence of a value is checked in the namespace `default`. To check for a value in a different namespace, we use the optional second parameter.

```
if ($session->has('someValue', 'mynamespace')) {
    // mynamespace some value exists in the session
} else {
    // mynamespace some value does not exist in the session
}
```

See also

For more information about dealing with session data, refer to the previous three recipes, *Getting the session handler*, *Adding data to the session*, and *Getting session data*.

Checking the session token

Every session contains a token. This is a random generated string that is used to prevent security weaknesses such as **Cross-Site Request Forgery (CSRF)**.

How to do it...

We can access the token directly in the session using the `JSession::getToken()` method.

```
$token = JSession::getToken();
```

Although this is acceptable, it does not really conform to the standard Joomla! way of dealing with tokens. For more information about how to use the token, refer to the Chapter 2 recipe, *Using the token*.

> The token value should be kept a closely guarded secret. It is crucial that we do not give away the value of the token, because it could be used to compromise the site.

Getting the user

A `JUser` object describes a user of the system. The user who initiated the request is always represented as a `JUser` object, even if the user is not logged in! This recipe explains how we retrieve the `JUser` object that represents the current user.

In instances where the user is not logged in, the `JUser` object represents an anonymous user. In Joomla! we refer to anonymous users as guests. The following diagram expresses the guest state of the global `JUser` object:

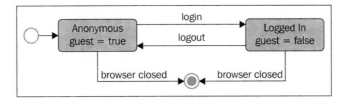

How to do it...

To retrieve the `JUser` object that represents the current user, we use `JFactory`. As `JFactory` returns an object we must use `=&` when assigning the object to a variable. If we do not and our server is running a PHP version prior to PHP 5, we will inadvertently create a copy of the global `JUser` object.

```
$user =& JFactory::getUser();
```

So now that we have the global `JUser` object, what do we do with it? We generally retrieve `JUser` objects when we want to find out something about a user. For example, we can use a `JUser` object to determine a user's email address (as described in the last recipe, *Sending an email to the user*). All of the remaining recipes in this chapter explain what we can do with `JUser` objects.

There's more...

Sometimes we may want to retrieve data that relates to other users. If we want to retrieve a different user (represented as a `JUser` object) when we call the static `JFactory::getUser()` method, we add the numeric ID or the username of the user we want to retrieve.

```
// retrieve a user based on ID
$aUser =& JFactory::getUser(100);
// retrieve a user based on username
$anotherUser =& JFactory::getUser('anotherusername');
```

Obviously, we wouldn't use hardcoded values. This is simply intended to make the usage of the method clearer, that is, a number to load based on ID, and an alphanumeric string to load based on a username.

Use ID whenever possible

As Joomla! uses the PHP `is_numeric()` function to determine if it is retrieving a user based on an ID or a username, if a username contained only numbers, the method could be tricked into retrieving a different user. For this reason we should use a user's ID whenever possible. If we only have the user's username, we can use the static `JUserHelper::getUserId()` method to manually retrieve their ID.

On the other hand, if we want to retrieve a number of users and we are executing a query that will retrieve data to which users are associated, we can `JOIN` with the `#__users` table. The following example shows a query in which the table `#__mytable` contains the foreign key `owner`, which relates to the primary key (`id`) of the `#__users` table:

```
SELECT `mytable`.*, `u`.`name` AS `owner`
FROM `#__mytable` AS `mytable`
LEFT JOIN `#__users` AS `u` ON `mytable`.`owner` = `u`.`id`
```

The following table describes some of the more useful #__users fields that are available to us:

Field	Type	Description
id	INTEGER	Unique identifier (PK) should always be used for foreign keys.
name	VARCHAR(255)	Actual name, for example, Fred Bloggs
username	VARCHAR(150)	Username for login credentials, for example fbloggs
email	VARCHAR(100)	Email address, for example fred.bloggs@example.org
sendemail	TINYINT(4)	Boolean value represented as 0 or 1. If true, the user is willing to accept system email notifications.

See also

The next recipe explains how to determine if the current user is or is not logged in.

Determining if the current user is a guest

Guests are users who are not logged into the site. Guests generally have very restricted access rights, which can significantly modify the way in which the logic of an extension flows. This recipe explains how to determine if the current user is a guest or a registered user.

Getting ready

To complete this recipe, we need the current user represented as a JUser object. For more information, refer to the previous recipe, *Getting the user*.

```
$user =& JFactory::getUser();
```

How to do it...

We use the JUser::get() method to retrieve the Boolean value of guest. If this value is true, the user is a guest, otherwise they are a registered user.

```
if ($user->get('guest') {
    // user is a guest
} else {
    // user is logged in user
}
```

How it works...

Whenever a user starts browsing an instance of Joomla! they always start off as a guest. We can, therefore, think of `JUser` objects as being guests by default. Once a user successfully logs in, the value of `guest` is set to `false`. Technically, the user's ID is also set at this point, and so it is possible to use the ID to determine if the user is a guest. However, this is not recommended. There is a useful diagram in the introduction to the previous recipe that explains this in more detail.

Getting the user's name and username

A user's name is their actual name, for example *Fred Bloggs*. A user's username is the name they use to log into the system, for example *fbloggs*. An important distinction between the two is that the username is unique while the name is not. As usernames are unique, when we display information about a user to another user, we tend to use usernames, for example in a thread on a forum. Conversely, when addressing a user directly we tend to use their name, for example in an email notification or a welcome message.

Getting ready

To complete this recipe, we need the `JUser` object that represents the current user. For more information, refer to the recipe *Getting the user* earlier in this chapter.

```
$user =& JFactory::getUser();
```

How to do it...

The following example extracts the user's username and name and outputs them:

```
// get username and name of user
$username = $user->get('username');
$name     = $user->get('name');

// output information about the user
echo "$username's real name is $name";
```

How it works...

The `JUser::get()` method retrieves public data from the `JUser` object. *Note that by public data we mean public in terms of object access, not legally public for everyone to see.* When dealing with a user that is logged in, their username and name is directly populated in the `JUser` object with data from the #__users table in the database (or from a comparable source, dependent on the user plugins).

There's more...

Sometimes a user may not be logged in, that is, they may be a guest. In these instances, we need to pay a little more attention because the username and name will both be set to `null`. The following example shows how combining this recipe with the previous recipe, *Determining if the current user is a guest*, we can better deal with usernames and names.

```
if ($user->get('guest') {
    // user is a guest
    $username = JText::_('ANONYMOUS');
    $name     = JText::_('ANONYMOUS');
} else {
    // user is a registered user
    $username = $user->get('username');
    $name     = $user->get('name');
}
```

 ANONYMOUS is not defined in any of the core language files, so we must define this, or a suitable equivalent, in our extension's language files. Refer to Chapter 5, *Multilingual Recipes*, for more information.

Getting the user's group ID and type

The following organized list describes the user groups in Joomla! 1.5 in a way in which we are all probably familiar. Each of these groups has an ID and a name; these are the group's ID and type respectively.

```
— Public Front end
  └─ Registered (18)
       └─ Author (19)
            └─ Editor (20)
                 └─ Publisher (21)

— Public Back end
  └─ Manager (23)
       └─ Administrator (25)
            └─ Super Administrator (25)
```

This recipe explains how to find the group ID and group type of the current user. Note that the hard coded group IDs should not generally be used for access control; for this it is best to take advantage of the `JAuthorization` class. For more information, refer to the Joomla! API site: `http://api.joomla.org/`.

Dynamic permissions

There is no administrative functionality that allows the modification of groups. It is, however, possible to programmatically modify groups and group permissions. Most of the time a Joomla! 1.5 extension will opt to implement its own permission management rather than use the incomplete Joomla! solution.

Joomla! 1.6, in development at the time of writing, promises a complete **GACL (Group Access Control List)** implementation.

Getting ready

To complete this recipe, we need the `JUser` object that represents the current user. For more information, refer to the *Getting the user* recipe covered earlier in this chapter.

```
$user =& JFactory::getUser();
```

How to do it...

The group ID is held in the `gid` field in the #__users table. We use the `JUser::get()` method to extract the user's group ID.

```
// determine group ID
$groupID = $user->get('gid');
```

The group type is held in the `usertype` field in the #__users table. Again, we use the `JUser::get()` method to extract the user's group ID.

```
$usertype = $user->get('usertype');
```

How it works...

Apart from the obvious format of the data, there is a subtle difference between the `gid` and `usertype` fields. The `gid` field is always populated, where as the `usertype` field is populated only if the user is not blocked. When dealing with the current user, the user will never be blocked, but when dealing with other users there is a possibility that the `usertype` field will not be populated. Therefore, we need to be careful that we select the most appropriate field, depending on the context of what we are doing.

The user groups that we have mentioned are maintained in the `#__core_acl_aro_groups` table, or as it can also be called, the *Access Control List Access Request Object Groups* table. This table holds a tree structure, as indicated in the introduction of the recipe. What is noticeable is that *Public Frontend* and *Public Backend* are both technically user groups. As this is a tree structure, we can use the left and right values to perform all sorts of neat tricks.

 The `#__core_acl_aro_groups` table employs the nested set model: `http://dev.mysql.com/tech-resources/articles/hierarchical-data.html`.

See also

The next recipe explains how to use the Public, Registered, and Special access levels.

Restricting a user's access using Public, Registered, and Special

In Joomla! we often define access based on three simple access levels. These levels relate to the user groups described in the previous recipe, *Getting the user's group ID and type*. This recipe explains how to use these access levels to restrict access to resources.

- ▶ Public (0)
- ▶ Registered (1)
- ▶ Special (2)

Getting ready

To complete this recipe, we need the `JUser` object that represents the current user. For more information, refer to the *Getting the user* recipe covered earlier in this chapter.

```
$user =& JFactory::getUser();
```

How to do it...

The `JUser::get()` method can be used to retrieve the user's `aid`. This is the access level number, as shown in braces in the recipe introduction.

```
// get access level
$aid = $user->get('aid');
```

For each resource we want to restrict access to, we must define the required access level. This is normally done in a database `TINYINT(3)` field named `access`. This can then be used to restrict the access using a database query (used when listing)...

```
// get the DBO
$db =& JFactory::getDBO();
// prepare access field name
$access = $db->nameQuote('access');
// restrict query by access level
$where = "WHERE $access <= " . intval($aid);
```

...or when viewing a single record. Note that `ALERTNOTAUTH` is a core translation string, which in en-GB is equivalent to `You are not authorised to view this resource`.

```
// make sure the user has the necessary access rights
if ($table->get('access') > $aid) {
    JError::raiseError(403, JText::_('ALERTNOTAUTH'));
    jexit();
}
```

How it works...

A good example of this in action is the content component. If we take a look at the article manager, we can see that there is an **Access Level** associated with each article that determines which users can access the article.

#	☐	Title	Published	Front Page	Order ▲ ☝	Access Level	Section ▲	Category	Author	Date	Hits	ID
1	☐	Example Pages	✓	✗	[1]	Public			Administrator	12.10.06	43	43
2	☐	What's New in 1.5?	✓	✗	▾ [1]	Registered	About Joomla!	The CMS	Administrator	11.10.06	92	22
3	☐	Joomla! Overview	✓	✗	▴ ▾ [2]	Public	About Joomla!	The CMS	Administrator	09.10.06	150	19
4	☐	Extensions	✓	✗	▴ ▾ [3]	Special	About Joomla!	The CMS	Administrator	11.10.06	102	26
5	☐	Joomla! Features	✓	✗	▴ [4]	Registered	About Joomla!	The CMS	Administrator	08.10.06	59	18

Display # 5 ▾ ⦿ Start ⦿ Prev **1** 2 3 4 5 6 7 8 9 Next ⦾ End ⦾ Page 1 of 9

These access levels are relatively primitive and we don't have any bona fide control over them. So how do they translate into concrete user groups? The following table describes the seven user groups and the guest group, and shows how these relate to the access levels:

User Group	User Group ID	Access Level	Access Level ID
None (Guest)	0	Public	0
Registered	18	Registered	1
Author	19	Special	2
Editor	20	Special	2
Publisher	21	Special	2
Manager	23	Special	2
Administrator	24	Special	2
Super Administrator	25	Special	2

See also

The previous recipe explains how to work with the user group ID and group type. This can also be useful for dealing with access control.

Getting the user's parameters

User parameters provide a mechanism for including additional user data without the need to modify the database. The core user parameters are defined in the XML files located in the `administrator\components\com_users\models` folder.

Getting ready

To complete this recipe, we need the `JUser` object that represents the current user. For more information, refer to the *Getting the user* recipe.

```
$user =& JFactory::getUser();
```

How to do it...

To retrieve a parameter we must first know the name of the parameter we want to retrieve. One example of a common parameter is `timezone`. This is an integer that defines the hours offset from **UTC (Coordinated Universal Time)**, also known as **GMT (Greenwich Mean Time)** and **Z (Zulu)**.

To retrieve a parameter, we can use the `JUser::getParam()` method.

```
$timezone = $user->getParam('timezone');
```

It is also possible to provide a default value. This is useful especially if the user we are dealing with is a guest because guest users do not have any parameters defined by default.

```
$timezone = $user->getParam('timezone', '0');
```

How it works...

A user's parameters are represented as a `JParameter` object. We do not have to interact directly with this object because `JUser` will do this for us.

A minor problem with this method is the default value. Technically the XML files define the default values, but by default these XML files are not loaded by the `JUser` class. Therefore, the XML defined default values are not employed. One way to overcome this is to interact directly with the `JParameter` object. The next section explains how to do this.

There's more...

The `JUser::getParamters()` method allows us to directly access the user's `JParameter` object. Note that we must use `=&` when assigning the return value to a variable. If we do not and we are using a PHP version prior to PHP 5, we will inadvertently create a copy of the returned `JParameter` object.

```
// get parameters with XML definition file loaded
$params =& $user->getParameters(true);
```

When we retrieve the `JParameter` object there are two optional parameters. The first parameter `$loadsetupfile` determines whether or not the XML file that defines the user's parameters should be loaded. Loading this file gives meaning to the data and also provides default values for defined data.

For information about the second optional parameter, refer to the recipe, *Extending and editing user parameters*.

To retrieve a value, we use the `JParameter::get()` method. We pass two parameters to this method—the name of the parameter we want the value of, and the default value to return if the parameter does not exist.

```
// get timezone (hours UTC offset)
$timezone = $params->get('timezone', '0');
```

See also

The next recipe, *Setting the user's parameters*, explains how to set a value in the user's parameters.

Setting the user's parameters

User parameters provide a mechanism for including additional user data without the need to modify the database. The parameters are defined in the XML files located in the `administrator\components\com_users\models` folder.

 User parameters are not restricted to the parameters defined in the XML files. It is perfectly acceptable to add additional parameters.

Getting ready

To complete this recipe, we need the `JUser` object that represents the current user. For more information, refer to the _Getting the user_ recipe.

```
$user =& JFactory::getUser();
```

How to do it...

To set the value of a parameter, we use the `JUser::setParam()` method. This method requires two parameters—the name of the parameter we want to set and the value to which we want to set the parameter. For example, we could change the user's editor preference to use no editor.

```
// set value of someparameter to some value
$user->setParam('editor', 'none');
```

There's more...

If we have retrieved the `JParamter` object directly from the user, we can alternatively use that object to set the user's parameters. For information about retrieving the user's parameters, refer to the previous recipe, _Getting the user's parameters_. To set data in the `JParameter` object, we use the `JParameter::set()` method.

```
// set value of someparameter to some value
$params->set('editor', 'none');
```

See also

The previous recipe explains how to get a value from the user's parameters.

Extending and editing user parameters

It is often desirable to store additional information about users. A common solution is to create another user table and implement a one-to-one relationship. However, this is problematic because a great deal of maintenance is required to preserve the integrity of that relationship.

This recipe explains how we can store additional user data without the problems associated with having two user tables.

 Note that the solution described here does not allow us to use the additional data for database querying purposes. This solution assumes we are creating a component extension.

Getting ready

To complete this recipe we need the `JUser` object that represents the current user. For more information, refer to the *Getting the user* recipe earlier in this chapter.

```
$user =& JFactory::getUser();
```

How to do it...

The first step is to define the new parameters in an XML metadata file. This is done using a normal `<params>` element. The following example defines one parameter, `myparameter`. This file is named `user.xml` and is defined in the `models` folder in our component's administrative area. We are not editing the core user XML files.

```
<?xml version="1.0" encoding="utf-8"?>
<user>
    <params group="com_mycomponent">
        <param name="myparameter"
               type="text"
               size="20"
               default=""
               label="MY PARAMETER"
               description="MY PARAMETER DESCRIPTION" />
    </params>
</user>
```

To use this file, we must use the `JUser::getParameters()` method. This method allows us to tell Joomla! about our bespoke `users.xml` file.

```
// define path to the XML file
$path = JPATH_COMPONENT_ADMINISTRATOR . DS . 'models';
// load the XML file and get the JParameter object
$params =& $user->getParameters(true, $path);
```

We can now use the `JParameter::render()` method to generate HTML form elements that can be used to enable editing of the bespoke user parameters.

```
// output parameters
echo $params->render('bespokeparams', 'com_mycomponent');
```

Because this is sensitive data, we should also make use of the token in the form.

```
echo JHTML::_('form.token');
```

All of this form data should obviously be used in an *edit user* type page. The next half of this recipe explains how to deal with the form submission. For security reasons, we check the token before continuing.

```
// make sure the token is valid
JRequest::checkToken() or jexit('Invalid Token');
```

The next step is to retrieve the input data and set the parameters in the user object.

```
// load the raw array of params
$rawParams = JRequest::getVar(
    'bespokeparams',
    array(),
    'POST',
    'ARRAY'
);
// build an array from the raw array
$besokeParams['myparameter'] = $rawParams['myparameter'];
// bind with the user's parameters
$params->bind($bespokeParams);
```

Now that we have bound the input data with the user's parameters, we need to save the changes.

```
// save changes to the user
if ($user->save()) {
    JError::raiseNotice("200", JText::_("Saved User"));
}
```

That's it! All done!

How it works...

XML files are used by `JParamater` to define data. When we automatically load XML files for `JUser` parameters, the name of the XML file relates to the `usertype`. The only exception is `user.xml`; this is a default file. For example, if we wanted to have different parameters for the `usertype` publisher, we would need to create a file named `publisher.xml`. For more information, refer to the *Getting the user's group ID and type* recipe earlier in this chapter.

We purposely set the `group` of the `<params>` element to that of the extension name. This ensures that we keep our data separate from other data. A design flaw exists in `JParameter`, which means when we render a `JParameter` object, the data is always taken from the default group. In other words, our data is not logically separated from other data. Therefore, we need to be careful when choosing names for each of our bespoke parameters.

The `JUser::getParameters()` method accepts two parameters. The first defines whether or not we want to load the XML metadata. The second optionally defines an alternative location, in our case this is the `models` folder.

The token is included in the form to help prevent various security attacks. For more information about using the token, refer to the *Using the token* recipe in Chapter 2, *Keeping Extensions Secure*.

When dealing with the input data, we must be very cautious. If we are not, we could easily end up with an injection weakness. The `JParameter::bind()` method is not choosy, it will bind with any data. This is why we process the raw parameters data before binding.

The `JUser::save()` method is self explanatory, it literally saves changes made to the `JUser` object to the database. It is important to deal with any database `params` field carefully, using `JUser` to save the changes rather than directly editing the database ensures that we do not corrupt any other data held in the `params` field. Remember, this field contains compound data.

There's more...

This recipe explains one way to achieve extending the user parameters field. The following two subsections suggest two alternatives:

Set rather than bind

Binding is a good and simple option for dealing with parameters. However, it is also perfectly acceptable to set each parameter individually. For more information, refer to the previous recipe, *Setting the user's parameters*.

```
// bind with the user's parameters
$params->set('myparameter', $rawParams['myparameter']);
```

Forget about XML

The recipe uses an XML file to define data. There is only any need to define data in this way if we want to use `JParameter` to render HTML form elements. It is perfectly possible to skip this step entirely. Instead, we could simply output fields manually. The disadvantage of this approach is that it is less flexible. However, if we are only saving one to two extra user parameters, this may make more sense.

```
<input type="text"
       size="20"
       class="text_area"
       value="<?php echo $params->get('myparameter'); ?>"
       name="myparameter"/>
```

See also

The previous two recipes, *Getting the user's parameters* and *Setting the user's parameters*, explain how to interact with a user's parameter data.

Sending an email to the user

Email is a good mechanism for providing confirmation of actions, for example confirmation that an order has been received in a shopping cart. In Joomla! we can send emails to any email address. This recipe explains how to send an email to the currently logged in user.

Only send emails to users who want email notifications

Depending on the context of the email, it is a good idea to only send emails to users who have explicitly requested email notification. For example, system notifications are only sent to user's who have set their `sendemail` parameter to `true`.

Getting ready

To complete this recipe we need the `JUser` object that represents the current user. For more information, refer to the *Getting the user* recipe.

```
$user =& JFactory::getUser();
```

How to do it...

The quick and easy way to send an email is to use the static `JUtility::sendMail()` method. This method has a very long signature! The following table describes the parameters we can pass to this method, *only the first five of the eleven parameters are required*:

Parameter	Default	Description
`from`		Email address from which the emails will appear to originate
`fromname`		Name of person or organization from which the emails appear to originate
`recipient`		Email address to which we want to send the email (this can be an array of email addresses)
`subject`		Subject of the email
`body`		Content of the email
`mode`	`false`	Content can be plain text or HTML, by default the mode is `false` (plain text)—it is easiest to think of this as an *is HTML* flag
`cc`	`null`	Email address to which we want to send a carbon copy of the email (this can be an array of email addresses)
`bcc`	`null`	Email address to which we want to send a blind carbon copy of the email (this can be an array of email addresses)
`attachment`	`null`	Path to a file we want to attach to the email (this can be an array of file paths)
`replyto`	`null`	Email address to which replies will be sent (this can be an array of email addresses, but if it is, `replytoname` must also be an array of corresponding names—not all email clients are capable of handling multiple `replyto`)
`replytoname`	`null`	Name of person or organization to which replies will be sent

Despite the number of parameters, the method signature is relatively easy to understand. To use this method we first need to get and build the data we are going to pass to the method. We'll begin by getting the *from* details from the Joomla! configuration.

```
// get the Joomla! configuration
$config    =& JFactory::getConfig();

// get the email 'from' details
$from      = $config->getValue('mailfrom');
$fromname  = $config->getValue('fromname');
```

We get the recipient email address from the `$user` object.

```
$recipient = $user->get('email');
```

The body and the subject are very straightforward. If we want to add a personal touch, we can easily include things such as the user's name.

```
// get the users name
$name    = $user->get('name');
$subject = 'My First Joomla! Email';
$body    = "Hi $name \n\nDo you like my email?";
```

All that is left to do is to send the email itself.

```
if (JUtility::sendMail($from, $fromname, $recipient, $subject, $body)
                                                   !== true) {

    JError::raiseNotice(
        '500',
        JText::_('ERROR SENDING EMAIL')
    );
}
```

Notice that we check the mixed return value of `JUtility::sendMail()` to check if the email was sent successfully. The return value will always be `true` on success and a `JException` object on failure.

Common problems

Many of the problems associated with sending email stem from incorrect configuration, and the error messages we receive often fail to point us towards this. If you encounter problems, always start by making sure that the Joomla! Global Configuration—Mail Settings are correct.

How it works...

Behind the scenes Joomla! uses a `JMail` object. The `JMail` objects are very powerful; there is not a great deal that we cannot do with these that we cannot do with a fully fledged email client. The power of the `JMail` object comes from its parent class, `PHPMailer`. This class is a part of the PHPMailer library. For more information about the PHPMailer library, refer to `http://phpmailer.codeworxtech.com/`.

There's more...

The static `JUtility::sendMail()` method is a no nonsense way of quickly sending emails. It does not however provide us with the same power as directly using a `JMail` object. In this section, we look at how to use a `JMail` object to achieve the same result as in the *How to do it section*.

We retrieve the mailer using the static `JFactory::getMailer()` method. The mailer is a JMail object that is preconfigured based on the Joomla! Global Configuration Server settings.

```
// get the JMail object
$mailer =& JFactory::getMailer();
```

To this object we add the recipient.

```
// add recipient
$mailer->addRecipient($recipient);
```

Now we compose the email itself. The composed email consists of a subject line and a plain text body.

```
// compose the email
$mailer->setSubject($subject);
$mailer->setBody($body);
```

Sending HTML emails

To send an HTML email using the mailer, we use the `JMail::isHTML()` method to tell the mailer we want to send the email in HTML format. For best results when sending HTML emails, in addition to setting the body, set the value of the `AltBody` instance variable. This is a plain text alternative for email clients that cannot read HTML emails.

We are now ready for the real magic, sending the email! For this we use the `JMail::Send()` method. This method returns `true` on success and a `JException` object on failure. *Note that if the method does fail, a notice will be raised. For this reason, we may not need to display an error message of our own.*

```
// send email
if ($mailer->Send() !== true) {
    // uh oh, sending of email failed!
}
```

See also

It can be useful to include a user's name and username in an email. For more information, refer to the *Getting the user's name and username* recipe, earlier in this chapter.

For more information about `JMail`, refer to the official API documentation at `http://api.joomla.org`.

5

Multilingual Recipes

This chapter contains the following recipes:

- ▶ Creating a translation
- ▶ Translating some text
- ▶ Determining the character length of a UTF-8 string
- ▶ Removing leading and trailing UTF-8 whitespace
- ▶ Comparing UTF-8 strings
- ▶ Finding a UTF-8 string in a UTF-8 string
- ▶ Executing a regular expression on a UTF-8 string
- ▶ Reversing a UTF-8 string
- ▶ Extracting a substring from a UTF-8 string
- ▶ Replacing occurrences of a UTF-8 string in a UTF-8 string
- ▶ Accessing characters in a UTF-8 string by position
- ▶ Converting a string from one encoding to another
- ▶ Creating a UTF-8 aware database installation script

Introduction

As much as we English-speaking countries would like to believe, talking slower and louder doesn't really constitute the ability to converse with people who don't speak English. It is easy to overlook multilingual requirements when we are not used to having to battle with translations ourselves. In Joomla!, there are several ways to make our extensions multilingual.

Two things we do need to be aware of are character sets and character encodings. A character set defines a set of characters, for example the Latin alphabet. A character encoding defines the numeric representations of characters from one or more character sets. For example, the Latin character A is defined by the ASCII character encoding as 65.

ASCII (American Standard Code for Information Interchange) is probably the most widely known character encoding. ASCII is a 7-bit encoding that uses a single byte to represent a single character (only the last 7 bits are ever utilized, and thus the highest-order bit is always 0). The problem with this is that we are limited to 128 (2^7) characters.

Do not confuse ASCII with ISO-8859-1 or Windows-1252. These character encodings are ASCII compliant, but use 8 bits, allowing a total of 256 (2^8) characters.

On the face of it, 128 sounds like a lot of characters—after all there are only 26 characters in the alphabet. But then there are uppercase, lowercase, numbers, symbols, and non-printing characters. And that's just the Latin alphabet; we haven't even looked at other alphabets such as Cyrillic and Arabic, let alone some of the more complex syllabic alphabets!

Of course, we don't want to become experts in every known alphabet. What we want is an easy way of encoding characters. Joomla! uses Unicode to enable us to do this. Unicode is a character encoding developed in tandem with the **UCS (Universal Character Set)**. The great thing about Unicode is its completeness. It defines over 100,000 characters, which is far in excess of the likes of ASCII! For more information about Unicode, refer to http://www.unicode.org.

Joomla! uses **UTF-8 (Unicode Transformation Format 8)**, an 8-bit multibyte Unicode Transformation Format. UTF-8 has seen widespread adoption by the Internet community. This is extensively due to the fact that the Unicode characters corresponding to the ASCII characters are represented in the same way in UTF-8 as they are in ASCII. This often means that little change is required to make the existing applications Unicode compliant. The following table demonstrates just how much more flexible UTF-8 is compared with ASCII and ISO-8859-1:

Alphabet	Character	ASCII	ISO-8859-1	UTF-8
Latin	G	71 (1 byte)	71 (1 byte)	71 (1 byte)
Latin	z	122 (1 byte)	122 (1 byte)	122 (1 byte)
Latin Supplement	£	Undefined	163* (1 byte)	163* (2 bytes)
Latin Supplement	Ÿ	Undefined	255* (1 byte)	255* (2 bytes)
Cyrillic	Ж	Undefined	Undefined	1046 (2 bytes)
Cyrillic	ҽ	Undefined	Undefined	1213 (2 bytes)
Arabic	ض	Undefined	Undefined	1590 (2 bytes)
Arabic	ت	Undefined	Undefined	1658 (2 bytes)

Alphabet	Character	ASCII	ISO-8859-1	UTF-8
CJK Compatibility†	アパ ート	Undefined	Undefined	13056 (3 bytes)
CJK Compatibility†	ワツ ト	Undefined	Undefined	13143 (3 bytes)
Hangul Syllables	가	Undefined	Undefined	44032 (3 bytes)
Hangul Syllables	흎	Undefined	Undefined	55118 (3 bytes)

* Although these ISO-8859-1 characters have the same numeric value as the UTF-8 equivalent, they are represented differently in memory—notice the number of bytes.

† Chinese, Japanese, and Korean *Han unified* character set:

For a complete Unicode character map, refer to `http://www.unicodemap.org/`.

PHP (prior to PHP 6) does not natively support UTF-8. PHP always assumes that one byte is equivalent to one character. Luckily, Joomla! provides us with ways of combating this. In addition to explaining how to manage extension translation, this chapter explains how to deal specifically with UTF-8 strings.

Use a UTF-8 aware editor

It's not only PHP that has difficulties understanding UTF-8. It is important when creating translations to use a UTF-8 aware editor. For more information, refer to the documentation for your text editor or IDE (most IDEs support UTF-8, but require setup).

HTML entities

When using UTF-8, HTML entities become almost entirely redundant. For example, the copyright symbol © no longer needs to be represented as `&copy` or `&#169` because the symbol is explicitly defined in UTF-8 as the two-byte value `0xC2A9`. Consequently, we should not use the PHP `htmlentities()` function. Instead, we need to only make use of the PHP `htmlspecialchars()` function. When using this function, we should always use it in the following form: `htmlspecialchars($rawString, ENT_QUOTES, 'UTF-8')`.

Creating a translation

Translations are defined in the INI files. There are normally two translation files for every language and every extension. One of these files is for the frontend and the other for the backend. For each language there is a folder. The folder name conforms to RFC 3066 (http://www.ietf.org/rfc/rfc3066.txt). The following table shows some example language tags as defined by RFC 3066:

Language	Tag
Arabic, Morocco	ar-MA
Chinese, China	zh-CN
English, Great Britain	en-GB
English, United States	en-US
French, France	fr-FR
German, Germany	de-DE
Russian, Russia	ru-RU

This recipe explains how to create a language file for an extension in Joomla!. For existing translations, refer to http://extensions.joomla.org/extensions/languages/. There is also an accredited translations project at http://joomlacode.org/gf/project/jtranslation/.

Getting ready

We need an editor that supports UTF-8 encoding. In this recipe, we use the Windows- and Linux-compatible editor **SciTE** or **SCIntilla based Text Editor** (http://www.scintilla.org/SciTE.html).

How to do it...

We start by opening **SciTE**. Before we do anything, we must change the encoding. *Changing the encoding later may result in file corruption.* To change the encoding, navigate to **File | Encoding** and select **UTF-8**.

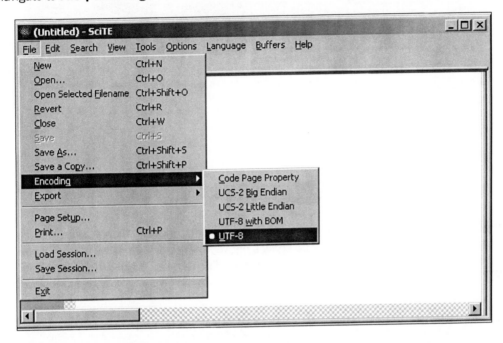

The first thing we do is give the file a header that describes the contents of the file. This normally includes the author, copyright, and license details. It is also a good idea to add a reminder about UTF-8. *In an INI file, a hash indicates a comment.*

```
# Author Packt Publishing
# Copyright (C) 2009
# License http://www.gnu.org/licenses/gpl-2.0.html GNU/GPL
#
# Note: All INI files need to be saved as UTF-8 - No BOM
```

Now we need to save the file. If we are saving a frontend language file, the file must be saved in the `languages/lang-tag/` folder. If we are saving a backend language file, the file must be saved in the `administrator/languages/lang-tag/` folder *where* `lang-tag` *is the language tag, for example,* `en-GB`.

The filename is constructed as `lang-tag.extension.ini` *where* `lang-tag` *is the language tag, for example,* `en-GB` *and* `extension` *is the extension name, for example,* `com_mymultilingualcomponent`.

We can now start defining translations in the file. Translations are defined in the usual KEY=VALUE INI style. The KEY is the name of the translation string and the VALUE is the value that the string translates to. The KEY should always be uppercase and it is generally best to restrict the KEY to ASCII characters.

In the example above, we define three translations— MULTILINGUAL, PACKT, and J15COOKBOOK. Notice that there are no spaces between the KEY and the equals sign, and the VALUE and the equals sign. This example is especially simple because it only includes ASCII characters. So let's try a more complex example. The following is a Chinese translation:

 Translations in Joomla! define translations of phrases. We do not translate each individual word. Remember that language constructs vary extensively and word-to-word translation often results in incoherent gobbledygook. *Note that a phrase can contain one to many words.*

How it works...

Joomla! loads translation INI files if they exist, and the loaded translations are used when we use the static `JText` class. For information about using a translation, refer to the next recipe, *Translating some text*. Joomla! also handles which translation to load, that is to say, Joomla! knows whether or not the site is being viewed in English, or German, or any other language.

There's more...

The first subsection describes how to add additional useful SVN data to the language header. The second subsection explains how to determine what needs translating.

SVN

Something we didn't mention about the headers is that it is common practice when using SVN or similar to include repository details, especially revision numbers and author details. If we are using SVN, this is expressed as the `$Id$` keyword or just for the revision `$Revision$`.

```
# $Revision$
# Author Packt Publishing
# Copyright (C) 2009
# License http://www.gnu.org/licenses/gpl-2.0.html GNU/GPL
#
# Note: All INI files need to be saved as UTF-8 - No BOM
```

It may be necessary to enable keyword substitution in order for this to work correctly. To do this in Tortoise SVN as discussed in Chapter 1, *Development using JoomlaCode.org and SVN*, use the **TortoiseSVN | Properties** context menu.

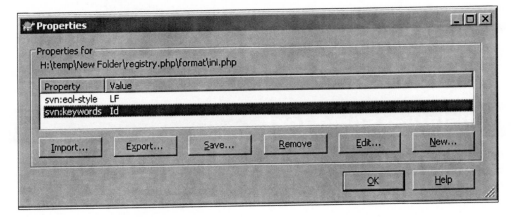

Alternatively, we can use the `svn propset` command. For more information about keywords and properties in SVN, refer to `http://svnbook.red-bean.com/`.

What to translate?

Knowing what to translate is often a bigger problem than the actual translation process. Joomla! has a handy ability that we can use to inform us which translations have failed because no translations are defined. The only downside of this functionality is that we have to browse to every page in our extension in order to find all of the missing translations.

To enable this feature, browse to **Global Configuration | System** and enable **Debug Language**.

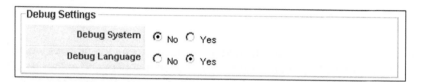

Now when we browse through our site, we should notice that a large amount of text is encapsulated in bullet marks or question marks. Bullet marks indicate that the text was successfully translated, whereas question marks indicate that no translation exists. In instances where no translation exists, the value that we should be using as the KEY will be displayed.

 For a more complete report, we can enable *Debug System* and a summary of the translations will be displayed at the bottom of every page.

See also

For more information about SVN, refer to Chapter 1, *Development using JoomlaCode.org and SVN*. The next recipe, *Translating some text*, explains how to use the defined translations.

Translating some text

Whenever we output any text that will be visible to the user, we should always translate that text. In Joomla!, we do this by using the static `JText` class and the defined translations. This recipe explains how to use `JText` to output a translation of a phrase.

How to do it...

The static `JText::_()` method translates a string and returns the result. The fact that the method returns the result as opposed to outputting the result means that the method is very versatile, for example, we can output the result or assign it to a variable.

```
// output translation
echo JText::_('TRANSLATE ME');

// assign translated text to a variable
$translation = JText::_('TRANSLATE ME');
```

 Many of the methods in the Joomla! framework that accept a user-friendly string/message will automatically translate values. For this reason, it is important to make sure that we only use `JText` where necessary.

How it works...

The `JText::_()` method works by loading the global `JLanguage` object and using this to translate the text into the current locale. Translation will only occur if a translation for the string exists. Translations are defined in special language files, as described in the previous recipe, *Creating a translation*. If a translation does not exist, the original string is returned.

When the original string is used to define a translation, it's converted to uppercase (using the PHP non UTF-8 aware `strtoupper()` function); and if there is a leading underscore, it is stripped. For these reasons, it is generally best to translate strings that are all uppercase and use only the ASCII character set.

It is generally a good idea to use some sort of standard when translating strings. For example, translations for error messages pertaining to form validation might all be prefixed with `FORM_VALIDATION_ERROR`. This does two important things—it provides logical separation of translations and helps provide semantic meaning.

 Although translation keys are defined in uppercase, `JText` takes care of this for us. So, it is perfectly acceptable to use mixed case strings when using `JText`.

There's more...

There are some other useful things we can do with `JText`, including making translations JavaScript safe and using the PHP style `sprintf()` and `printf()` type functionality.

JavaScript safe

If we are inserting translated text into some JavaScript, it is possible when using the `JText::_()` method to tell `JText` that we want the returned value to be JavaScript safe.

```
// some JavaScript alert
alert("<?php echo JText::_('JS ALERT', true); ?>");
```

The second parameter we pass to `JText::_()` tells `JText` to add slashes to the resultant string. By default, `JText::_()` is not JavaScript safe.

This works not just for JavaScript. JavaScript is an implementation of ECMAScript, and thus we are actually making an ECMAScript-safe string. Another well-known implementation of ECMAScript is ActionScript, the Adobe Flash scripting language.

Sprintf and printf

The `JText::sprintf()` method is comparable to the PHP `sprintf()` function. It allows us to insert formatted values into a string. The PHP `sprintf()` function uses the percent sign (%) to indicate an insertion point of a formatted value—"Ah Cripes" I hear you call, a weird character!! Luckily for us, the % sign is in the ASCII character map, which means there are no issues with using the % sign in a translation name.

```
// output translation
echo JText::sprintf('I ATE %d CAKES IN THE %s',
                    $numberOfCakes,
                    $location);
```

The `JText::sprintf()` method does not translate the extra parameters. For example, in the previous code, `$location` is not translated. We can overcome this by manually translating the value.

```
// output translation
echo JText::sprintf('I ATE %d CAKES IN THE %s',
                    $numberOfCakes,
                    JText::_($location));
```

For more information, refer to the PHP `sprintf()` documentation at `http://php.net/sprintf/`.

Also available is the JText::printf() method. This is comparable to the PHP printf() function. It is very similar to JText::sprintf(), except that it outputs the string and returns the length of the outputted string. This method is not generally very useful in Joomla! because the initial string is translated and, therefore, we can't be certain of the original string length. For this reason, it is generally preferable to use the JText::sprintf() method.

```
// output translation
$length = JText::printf('I ATE %d CAKES IN THE %s',
                        $numberOfCakes,
                        JText::_($location));
```

For more information, refer to the PHP printf() documentation at http://php.net/printf/.

 The static JText::printf() method returns the length of the string in bytes, not characters.

See also

To define translations, refer to the previous recipe, *Creating a translation*.

Determining the character length of a UTF-8 string

In the introduction, we explained that UTF-8 is a multibyte character encoding. That is to say, a single character can be represented by one or more bytes. The PHP strlen() function (prior to PHP 6) is not UTF-8 compliant. The strlen() function simply counts the number of bytes. This recipe explains how to determine the number of characters in a multibyte UTF-8 string.

How to do it...

We use the static JString::strlen() method to calculate the number of characters in a given string.

```
// get length of $string in characters
$characters = JString::strlen($string);
```

If we want, we can also use the PHP `strlen()` function to calculate the number of bytes in a string. *This can sometimes be useful for dealing with storage requirements.*

```
// get length of $string in bytes
$bytes = strlen($string);
```

How it works...

To explain the use of `JString::strlen()` in a better way, we can use an example. The CJK Compatibility Ideograph-FA2D 鶴 is represented in UTF-8 as three bytes. The following table describes the character in more detail and includes the UTF-8 representation:

鶴	CJK Compatibility Ideograph-FA2D
Bytes	3
Unicode decimal	64045
Unicode binary	11111010 00101101
UTF-8 representation	11101111 10101000 10101101

As we can see, three bytes are required to represent the character using UTF-8. If we used the PHP `strlen()` function to determine the length of a string that contained only this character, the result would be 3. If we used the PHP `JString::strlen()` method to determine the length of a string that contained only this character, the result would be 1.

```
$bytes       = strlen('鶴');            // results in 3
$characters = JString::strlen('鶴');   // results in 1
```

Removing leading and trailing UTF-8 whitespace

A common task when manipulating strings is to remove whitespace characters from either end of the string. In ASCII, we classify whitespace characters as any of the following:

Character	Description	ASCII Decimal	ASCII Hexadecimal
" "	Ordinary space	32	0x20
"\t"	Tab	9	0x9
"\n"	New line (Line Feed/LF)	10	0xA
"\r"	New line (Carriage Return/CR)	13	0xD
"\0"	NULL	0	0x0
"\x0B"	Vertical tab	11	0xB

This recipe explains how to remove ASCII whitespace characters and other characters from the start and end of a string.

How to do it...

If all we want to do is remove the leading and trailing ASCII whitespaces from a string, we use the normal PHP `trim()` function.

```
// strip leading and trailing ASCII whitespace
$noSpacesString = trim($rawString);
```

If we want to remove any non-ASCII leading or trailing characters, we must use the `JString::trim()` method. Unlike the PHP `trim()` function, this method is UTF-8 safe.

```
// ASCII whitespace and UTF-8 non breaking space 0xA0
$whitespace = " \t\n\r\0\x0B";

// strip leading and trailing $whitespace characters
$noSpacesString = JString::trim($rawString, $whitespace);
```

How it works...

It is not necessary to use `JText::trim()` when we only want to strip ASCII characters. Remember, ASCII uses 7 bits and thus a byte always starts with `0`. In UTF-8, the ASCII map is still available. Any byte in a UTF-8 string that does not represent an ASCII character always starts with `1`. Therefore, removing ASCII characters with PHP `trim()` is perfectly safe.

So what about this non-breaking space? We're almost certainly familiar with —the Unicode character `0xA0` is the Unicode representation of this character. In the example, we define the `$whitespace` variable, which includes the usual ASCII whitespace characters and the UTF-8 encoded Unicode character `0xA0`. To create a non-breaking space in Windows use *Alt+0160*, and in Mac OS use *OPTION+SPACE*. Linux is a bit more complex, so you will need to refer to your distribution and/or editor documentation.

The non-breaking space is a good example of a Unicode character we might want to remove from the start or end of a string. There are many whitespace characters in Unicode. For more information, refer to `http://en.wikipedia.org/wiki/Space_(punctuation)` and `http://en.wikipedia.org/wiki/Newline`.

There's more...

Sometimes it is useful to trim whitespaces from just the left or right of a string. The same rule applies to the PHP `trim()` function. If we are only stripping ASCII characters, we should use the PHP functions `ltrim()` and `rtrim()`. On the other hand, if we are including UTF-8 characters in the whitespace definition, we must use the `JString::ltrim()` and `JString::rtrim()` functions.

See also

For some more sophisticated ways of dealing with character stripping, refer to the *Executing a regular expression on a UTF-8 string* recipe.

Comparing UTF-8 strings

This recipe explains how to compare two UTF-8 strings. Note that when dealing with UTF-8, the concept of upper and lowercase characters does not apply to all alphabets. These alphabets are known as unicameral or unicase.

How to do it...

If we are comparing two case-sensitive strings, we use the PHP `strcmp()` function.

```
if (strcmp($stringOne, $stringTwo) == 0) {
    // $stringOne is equal to $stringTwo
}
```

On the other hand, if we want to perform a case-insensitive comparison, we need to use the `JString::strcasecmp()` method.

```
if (JString::strcasecmp($stringOne, $stringTwo) == 0) {
    // $stringOne is equal to $stringTwo
}
```

How it works...

The case-sensitive PHP `strcmp()` function compares bytes. Therefore, it is safe to use it when comparing binary data. When we perform a case insensitive comparison we rely on the transformation of all characters to the same case. The PHP case insensitive `strcasecmp()` function is not UTF-8 aware, the function will therefore fail to properly transform the string case. The Joomla! `JString::strcasecmp()` method is UTF-8 aware, and so it transforms all characters to lowercase before comparing the strings.

It is important to be aware of the fact that there are some issues with case mapping in Unicode. One such example is detailed in the following quote taken from Unicode Consortium (2006), The Unicode Standard, Version 5.0, Addison-Wesley Professional:

> *Case mappings may produce strings of different lengths than the original. For example, the German character U+00DF β Latin small letter sharp s expands when uppercased to the sequence of two characters "SS".*

See also

For some more sophisticated ways of comparing strings, refer to the next but one recipe, *Executing a regular expression on a UTF-8 string*.

Finding a UTF-8 string in a UTF-8 string

This recipe explores the methods in the static `JString` class that enable us to locate UTF-8 strings within other UTF-8 strings. The following table summarizes the methods. For more information, refer to the PHP function equivalent documentation at `http://php.net/manual/ref.strings.php`.

Method	Description
`JString::strpos()`	Finds the first position of the needle in a haystack
`JString::strcspn()`	Determines the length of segment before the mask is encountered
`JString::strspn()`	Determines the length of segment containing the mask
`JString::strrpos()`	Finds the last position of the needle in the haystack
`JString::stristr()`	Gets the remainder of the haystack from the start of the needle (case insensitive)

> The `JString` class does not emulate UTF-8 safe equivalents of all the PHP string functions. The `JString` class only emulates PHP string functionality that is not UTF-8 safe. For example, `strstr()` is UTF-8 safe and thus there is no equivalent defined within `JString`.

How to do it...

The following examples explain how to use the identified `JString` methods. In each example, we will use the Greek haystack defined as follows (includes some Greek UTF-8 characters).

```
$haystack = "Joomla! είναι ένα CMS";
```

Many of these methods use character positions. Character positions in a string are calculated starting from zero. For example, the character at position zero in the haystack is J. The following table describes the exact position of each character in the haystack:

Haystack																				
0	1	2	3	4	5	6	7	8	9	10	11	12	13	14	15	16	17	18	19	20
J	o	o	m	l	a	!		ε	ί	v	α	l		έ	v	α		C	M	S

The JString::strpos() method finds the starting position of the complete needle in the haystack. Optionally, we can provide this method with the third parameter $offset. This can be used to define the character position from which we want to start searching for the needle. If the needle is not found, this method returns Boolean false.

```
$needle = 'έvα';
$needlePosition = JString::strpos($haystack, $needle);
// $needlePosition = int(14)
```

> The method JString::strpos() can return both zero and Boolean false. Therefore, when testing for the failure of location of the needle, use ($needlePosition === false).

The JString::strcspn() method, determines the number of characters in the haystack before any occurrence of any of the characters in the needle (opposite of JString:: strspn()). We can optionally provide this method with the third and fourth parameters $start and $length. These can be used to define the starting character position and maximum length in which we want to search.

```
$needle = 'vί';
$cleanCharacters = JString::strcspn($haystack, $needle);
// $cleanCharacters = int(9)
```

The JString::strspn() method, determines the number of characters in the haystack before any occurrence of characters that are not in the needle (opposite of JString:: strcspn()). We can optionally provide this method with the third and fourth parameters $start and $length. These can be used to define the starting character position and maximum length in which we want to search.

```
$needle = 'aJlmo';
$cleanCharacters = JString::strspn($haystack, $needle);
// cleanCharacters = int(6)
```

The `JString::strrpos()` method, locates the start position of the last instance in the haystack of the complete needle. Unlike the PHP-equivalent function, this method does not include an optional offset parameter. This is a confirmed bug in the `JString` API, which may be addressed in due course. For more information, please refer to `http://joomlacode.org/gf/project/joomla/tracker/?action=TrackerItemEdit&tracker_item_id=15416`.

```
$needle = 'να';
$lastNeedlePosition = JString::strrpos($haystack, $needle);
// lastNeedlePosition = int(15)
```

The `JString::stristr()` method, gets the remainder of the haystack from the start point of the first occurrence of the needle. This is a UTF-8 aware case-insensitive equivalent of the PHP function `strstr()`. In the following example, the value of `$needle` is the uppercase equivalent of *ένα*.

```
$needle = 'ΕΝΑ';
$remainderOfString = JString::stristr($haystack, $needle);
// $remainderOfString = string(10) "ένα CMS"
```

See also

For some more sophisticated ways of finding UTF-8 strings in UTF-8 strings, refer to the next recipe, *Executing a Regular Expression on a UTF-8 string*.

Executing a regular expression on a UTF-8 string

Regular expressions are powerful tools for inspecting and manipulating strings. Luckily, using UTF-8 does not preclude us from using regular expressions. However, we do have to be a little more vigilant. This recipe explains how to safely execute a UTF-8 aware **PCRE (Perl Compatible Regular Expression)** in PHP.

How to do it...

The first thing we do is define the regular expression. Let's imagine we want to search for the Russian word **Книга** (book) in a string. We define each letter based on its Unicode hexadecimal value. The following table describes the five Unicode characters in the Russian word book:

Character	Description	Unicode hexadecimal
К	CYRILLIC CAPITAL LETTER KA	41A
н	CYRILLIC SMALL LETTER EN	43D
и	CYRILLIC SMALL LETTER I	438
г	CYRILLIC SMALL LETTER GHE	433
а	CYRILLIC SMALL LETTER A	430

Each Unicode character is defined in a regular expression as $\x{HEX}$. In order for the regular expression engine to understand Unicode values, we must include the /u modifier.

```
// define pattern for Russian book
$pattern = '/\x{41A}\x{43D}\x{438}\x{433}\x{430}/u';
```

Now we can use the pattern with any of the normal PHP preg functions.

```
// example haystack
$haystack = "The Russian word Книга means 'book'";

// perform Regular Expression
$numberOfMatches = preg_match($pattern, $haystack, $array);
```

How it works...

To put this all into context, in the example the value of $numberOfMatches will be int(1) and the value of $array will be array(1) { [0]=> string(10) "Книга" }. That is to say, there has been a total of one successful match and that Книга was the complete match for the pattern. *Note that the identified length of Книга is 10 because it is measured in bytes, not characters.*

This recipe uses the PHP PCRE function preg_match(). The syntax of the pattern indicated applies to all PHP PCRE functions. For more information, go to http://php.net/manual/book.pcre.php. The other popular Regular Expression PHP functions—often referred to as ereg, or to give them their proper name **POSIX ERE (Portable Operating System Interface, Extended Regular Expressions)**—are not UTF-8 compliant and are deprecated as of PHP 5.2.0. So they should be avoided in preference of PCRE.

PHP provides us with multibyte string functions. _These functions are UTF-8 compliant; remember that UTF-8 is a multibyte character encoding._ Included among these are the POSIX ERE flavor functions such as `mb_ereg()`. For more information, refer to `http://php.net/manual/function.mb-ereg.php`.

 A good place to look for advice about regular expressions is `http://www.regular-expressions.info/`. For PHP-specific information, refer to `http://www.regular-expressions.info/php.html`.

See also

For some simpler ways of comparing strings and locating strings in strings, refer to the previous two recipes, _Comparing UTF-8 strings_ and _Finding a UTF-8 string in a UTF-8 string_.

For some simpler ways of dealing with substrings, refer to the recipes, _Extracting a substring from a UTF-8 string_ and _Replacing occurrences of a UTF-8 string in a UTF-8 string_.

Reversing a UTF-8 string

This recipe explains how to reverse the characters in a UTF-8 string. For example, by reversing the `Reverse!` string, we would get the value `!esreveR`.

How to do it...

To reverse a UTF-8 string, we must use the static `JString::strrev()` method.

```
// reverse string
$reversedString = JString::strrev($string);
```

How it works...

Unlike the PHP `strrev()` function, the static `JString::strrev()` method is UTF-8 aware. Using the PHP function could potentially corrupt the string if there are any UTF-8 characters in the string that are represented by more than one byte. Consider the CJK Unified Ideograph 字. This character is represented in UTF-8 as:

11100101 10101101 10010111

If we use the PHP `strrev()` function, the bytes will be reversed. This will corrupt the string! On the other hand, if we use the static `JString::strrev()` method, the three bytes will be recognized as a single atomic character. Therefore, they will maintain their order.

See also

The *Accessing characters in a UTF-8 string by position* recipe later in this chapter may also be of interest.

Extracting a substring from a UTF-8 string

This recipe explains how to safely extract a portion of a UTF-8 string based on character positions.

How to do it...

To extract a substring from a UTF-8 string, we must use the static `JString::substr()` method. We supply to this method a starting position (defined as the number of characters from the start of the string), the length of the substring (in characters), and the string from which we want to extract the substring.

```
$subString = JString::substr($subject, $start, $length);
```

How it works...

The substring is defined based on two values, `$start` and `$length`. To help explain, we can use the following diagram:

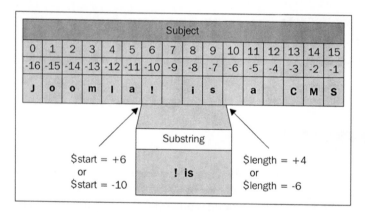

In this example, we can define the substring as `$start = +6` and `$length = +4`. In plain English, this equates to "the substring starts at character position six and is four characters long". There are other ways of defining `$start` and `$length`.

It is possible to define $start based on the offset from the start or the end of the string by changing the sign of $start. For example, a value of +6 indicates an offset of six characters from the start of the string, whereas a value of -10 indicates an offset of ten characters from the end of the string.

Like $start, changing the sign of $length changes the meaning. A positive value such as +4 indicates four characters from the start offset, whereas a negative value such as -6 indicates an offset from the end of the string at which to stop.

 Character positions in a string are calculated starting from zero. In other words, the character at position zero in the previous example is J and the character at position one is o.

 $length is not required, and omitting it will return all of the remaining string.

See also

To replace a substring with an alternative string, refer to the next recipe, *Replacing occurrences of a UTF-8 string in a UTF-8 string*.

To learn about extracting substrings based on patterns instead of character positions, refer to the *Executing a regular expression on a UTF-8 string* recipe earlier in this chapter.

Replacing occurrences of a UTF-8 string in a UTF-8 string

This recipe explains how to replace the occurrences of one string (search) with another string (replacement) in an existing string (subject) where the strings are UTF-8 encoded. For example, we can replace occurrences of Ꝛ with R in the string Ꝛeplace my Ꝛs with Rs to give the value Replace my Rs with Rs. This example can be considered a form of manual transliteration. Refer to the *Converting a string from one encoding to another* recipe later in this chapter for more information about transliteration.

How to do it...

For case-sensitive replacements, we can use the normal PHP str_replace() function.

```
$newString = str_replace($search, $replace, $subject);
```

For case-insensitive replacements, we must use the static
`JString::str_ireplace()` method.

```
$newString = JString::str_ireplace($search,
                                   $replace,
                                   $subject);
```

To replace a substring identified by its character position in a UTF-8 string, we must use
the static `JString::substr_replace()` method. The substring is defined based on the
integer values `$start` and `$length`. Unlike the PHP `substr_replace()` function in which
these values represent byte positions, in the `JString::substr_replace()` method these
integers represent character positions.

```
$newString = JString::substr_replace($subject,
                                     $replace,
                                     $start,
                                     $length);
```

How it works...

The PHP `str_replace()` function is safe when dealing with case-sensitive replacements
because it is binary safe.

When we perform case-insensitive replacements, it is necessary to pair values based on their
case. For example, A is paired with a. We must use the static `JString::str_ireplace()`
method because the equivalent PHP `str_ireplace()` function does not have knowledge of
these case pairings outside of the ASCII character set. For example, the Cyrillic character Dje,
represented as ђ in lowercase and Ђ in uppercase, would not be properly treated using the
normal PHP function.

Any form of position in a string should always be defined based on character position. Using
the static `JString::substr_replace()` method ensures that the `$start` and `$length`
values are treated as character positions and not byte positions. The following diagram
illustrates how this method might be used:

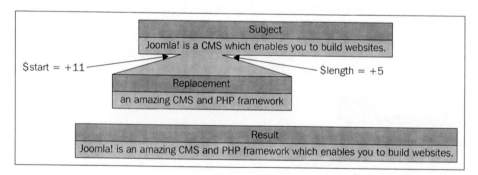

For more information about defining substrings in terms of $start and $length, refer to the previous recipe, _Extracting a substring from a UTF-8 string_.

 To insert a string at a character position, define an empty substring by specifying the $length value of zero.

See also

To learn more about extracting a substring based on a pattern instead of character positions, refer to the _Executing a regular expression on a UTF-8 string_ recipe earlier in this chapter.

Accessing characters in a UTF-8 string by position

It is common to want to access a character at a given position in a string. In PHP, we would normally use the $string[$position] syntax. The problem with this is that prior to PHP 6, $position defined the byte position and not the character position. This recipe explains how to convert a string to an array of characters so that we can access each character individually.

How to do it...

To convert a string into an array, we use the static JString::str_split() method.

```
// split string into an array of characters
$charArray = JString::str_split($string);

// access the second character using the array
$secondChar = $charArray[1];
```

There's more...

It can also be useful to split a string into segments bigger than a single character. We can define the number of characters we want in each element of the array by using the second optional $split_len parameter (which is one, by default).

```
// split string into an array of double characters
$doubleCharArray = JString::str_split($string, 2);
```

If we use the array to modify the string because the array and string are not bound in any way, it will be necessary to rebuild the string. The easy way to do this is to use the PHP `implode()` or `join()` function.

```
$string = implode($charArray);
```

Converting a string from one encoding to another

It is not unusual to encounter systems in which several encodings are present, especially when dealing with legacy systems. In some cases, we won't have any control over this; for example, reading in data from an external web service that encodes data using ISO-8859-1. This recipe explains how to convert a string from one encoding to another.

How to do it...

To covert a string from one encoding to another, we use the static `JString::transcode()` method. This method accepts three parameters—the original encoding, the desired encoding, and the string to convert.

```
// convert ISO-8859-1 string to a UTF-8 string
$utf-8-string = JString::transcode('ISO-8859-1',
                                   'UTF-8',
                                   $iso-8859-1-string);
```

How it works...

The static `JString::transcode()` method maps characters of one encoding to another. For example, if the `$iso-8859-1-string` variable contained the character β represented as the binary value `11011111`, it would be converted to the UTF-8 binary value `11000011 10011111`.

In instances where a direct equivalent does not exist, this method will attempt to perform transliteration. This is the action of representing one alphabet in another. For example, converting a UTF-8 string that contains the Unicode Latin Extended-B character ƒ (LATIN SMALL LETTER F WITH HOOK) into an ISO-8859-1 string will convert the character into an ASCII lowercase f.

 Transliteration is not a complete solution; it will not always be possible to substitute a character with another character. In these instances, the characters will simply be discarded.

Creating a UTF-8 aware database installation script

This recipe explains how to deal with UTF-8 when creating a component installation package. Joomla! components that install new tables to the database generally supply an SQL file that is referenced in the extension XML manifest file.

Joomla! requires MySQL version 3.23 or above (MySQL 6.x is not currently supported). Support for Unicode, and more specifically UTF-8, was introduced in MySQL 4.1. For this reason, multilingual components should supply two SQL files—one for UTF-8 aware databases and one for non-UTF-8 aware databases.

Getting ready

Before we create any SQL files, we need to address that pesky XML manifest file. Joomla! does the hard work for us and all we really need to do is point Joomla! towards two separate SQL files. We do this by providing two `<file>` elements in the `<sql>` element and defining the `charset` attribute for each.

```
<?xml version="1.5" encoding="utf-8"?>
<!DOCTYPE install SYSTEM "http://www.joomla.org/xml/dtd/1.5/component-
install.dtd">
<install>
    ...
    <install>
        <sql>
            <file driver="mysql" charset="utf8">install.sql</file>
            <file driver="mysql"
                        charset="">install.noutf8.sql"</file>
        </sql>
    </install>
    ...
</install>
```

How to do it...

Every field that is defined as the type `varchar` or `char` must be scaled up in a non UTF-8 aware database to accommodate UTF-8 characters. In Joomla!, it is widely accepted that tripling the field size is an adequate increase. For example, a `char(20)` field becomes a `char(60)` field.

Sometimes this isn't possible. For example, we cannot triple the size of a `varchar(255)` field because the `varchar` type is limited to a maximum of 255 bytes. Under these circumstances, we must change the field type to `text`.

The following example shows two SQL scripts side by side, both of which create the `#__mytable` table. One of the scripts is designed for UTF-8 aware databases and the other for non-UTF-8 aware databases.

UTF-8 aware	Non UTF-8 aware

```CREATE TABLE `#__mytable`
(
  `id` int(11) NOT NULL auto_increment,
  `name` char(30),
  `description` varchar(255),
  PRIMARY KEY (`id`)
) CHARSET=utf8;```
	```CREATE TABLE `#__mytable`
	(
	  `id` int(11) NOT NULL auto_increment,
	  `name` char(60),
	  `description` text,
	  PRIMARY KEY (`id`)
	) CHARSET=latin1;```

How it works...

When Joomla! installs a component, it looks for SQL files identified by the manifest file. The SQL file that is executed is identified by the `driver` and `charset` attributes. *Joomla! only officially supports MySQL, so most installers only provide SQL files where the `driver` is `mysql`.* The `charset` attribute is used to identify whether or not the SQL file is designed for a database that does or does not support UTF-8 character encoding. The value of `charset` should always be `utf8` or a null string.

A UTF-8 character is limited to a maximum of six bytes. The current highest Unicode mapping value is `0x10FFFF`, which requires five bytes. The majority of characters that we are likely to use are within the `0x0` through `0xFFFF` range, which requires a maximum of three bytes. This is why we only triple the field sizes. For a complete description, refer to `http://unicode.org/Public/UNIDATA/Blocks.txt`.

We define the character set in the example table creation queries. This is not actually necessary and is often omitted as it is assumed that the database will default to UTF-8 and Latin-1 respectively. However, including the character set in the table creation queries guarantees that we are using the correct character sets.

It is worth taking a moment to explore character sets and collations. For more information, refer to `http://dev.mysql.com/doc/refman/5.1/en/charset-general.html`.

6
Interaction and Styling

This chapter contains the following recipes:

- ▶ Getting page and component parameters
- ▶ Adding CSS to a page
- ▶ Overriding component templates
- ▶ Adding JavaScript to a page
- ▶ Creating a modal window
- ▶ Generating modal content
- ▶ Updating an element using Ajax and MooTools
- ▶ Updating an element based on a form using Ajax and MooTools
- ▶ Providing an Ajax response from a component
- ▶ Enabling pagination in a list of items

Introduction

This chapter contains recipes that explain how to create stylized interactive user interfaces. The best and most versatile extensions are always the most configurable. The first recipe in this chapter looks at how to get page and component parameters.

It is always a good idea to define the parameters that determine the look and feel of the pages. For example, when we create a menu link to an article, we can individually define which icons to display, such as PDF, print, and email. This sort of configuration can be extended to almost anything, for example choosing whether or not to use Ajax in a page.

In this chapter we explain how to harness Ajax. We need to put to rest some common misconceptions about Ajax. Ajax is not an acronym; it doesn't stand for asynchronous JavaScript and XML, and isn't synonymous with **XMLHttpRequest (XHR)**.

So what exactly is Ajax? Ajax can be thought of as a collection of technologies, including JavaScript, CSS, XML, and the DOM. It enables us to create rich user interfaces that don't require a complete reload of the page every time a user completes an action that requires new data. Jesse Garrett is credited with coining the term Ajax. Here's what he has to say (`http://www.adaptivepath.com/ideas/essays/archives/000385.php`):

> *An Ajax application eliminates the start-stop-start-stop nature of interaction on the Web by introducing an intermediary—an Ajax engine—between the user and the server.*

Avoid Ajax for the sake of Ajax

It is easy to get carried away when adding Ajax capabilities to any web application, and Joomla! is no exception. Before adding any Ajax capabilities, it is worth considering the actual benefits it will bring to the users. Ajax applications are notoriously difficult to design. It is essential to make sure that Ajax is considered during the design phase.

Getting page and component parameters

This recipe explains how to retrieve parameters defined by the current menu item. This is something we are likely to use only within a component.

How to do it...

In order to access the page parameters, we need access to the application, sometimes referred to as **mainframe**. To get this, we use the static `JFactory::getApplication()` method.

```
// get the application object
$application =& JFactory::getApplication();
```

The page parameters are represented in a `JParameter` object. To retrieve this object, we use the `getParams()` method.

```
// get the page parameters
$params =& $application->getParams();
```

We can get all of the component parameters and page parameters from this object.

The `getPageParams()` method is an alias of the `getParams()` method.

How it works...

Component parameters are defined per component in the `config.xml` file located in the component's admin folder. Parameters specific to views are defined in the view's `metadata.xml` file. The `parameters` object that is retrieved in this recipe is based on a combination of the parameters defined in these two files. There are also generic system parameters defined for all of the menu items such as `page_title`.

The values of the parameters are based on the component configuration and the current menu item parameters. Remember that the current menu item parameters can include a redefinition of the component parameters. If we take a look at a menu item, we will see a number of parameters presented on the righthand side. In the following screenshot, we can see four distinct parameter sections—**Basic**, **Advanced**, **Component**, and **System**:

The **Basic** and **Advanced** parameters are defined by the view. In this instance, that view is the content component view *section*. The **Component** parameters are the parameters defined by the component. Lastly, the **System** parameters are defined by Joomla! itself in the `administrator/components/com_menus/models/metadata` XML files.

See also

To learn more about parameters, including how to work with them and how to define them, refer to Chapter 9, *Keeping it extensible and modular*.

Adding CSS to a page

This recipe explains how to add **Cascading Style Sheets (CSS)** to an HTML-generated document.

Getting ready

In order to add CSS to the document, we need the document object. Remember to always use the `=&` assignment operator so as not to accidentally create a copy of the document object.

```
$document =& JFactory::getDocument();
```

How to do it...

To add a link to a CSS document to the HTML `<head>` tag in the form of a `<link>` tag, we use the `JDocument::addStyleSheet()` method. This is known as an **external stylesheet**.

```
$document->addStyleSheet('http://example.org/styles.css');
```

Alternatively, we can declare styles in a `<style>` tag in the HTML `<head>` tag. This is known as an **internal stylesheet**. To do this, we use the `JDocument::addStyleDeclaration()` method.

```
// define the internal styles
$style = '#someElement {color: sienna;} ';
// add the styles to the document
$document->addStyleDeclaration($style);
```

Avoid inline CSS

We should try to avoid the use of inline styles in extensions (other than templates) because it reduces the flexibility of our extensions.

There's more...

Both the JDocument::addStyleSheet() and JDocument::addStyleDeclaration() methods accept a second optional parameter. This parameter defines the **MIME (Multipurpose Internet Mail Extensions)** type of the document with which we are linking. The default value is text/css. In fact, it is difficult to think of a scenario where an alternative would be of use. Indeed, there are no instances in the Joomla! Core or Joomla! Core components where this second parameter is put to use.

> **Stylesheets not being applied? MIME type is used as a guide!**
>
> Although we can specify the MIME type for an external stylesheet, browsers treat this only as a guide. It is the MIME type returned by the server that has overriding precedence. If a stylesheet is not being applied correctly, check that the server is providing the correct MIME type.

The JDocument::addStyleSheet() method also provides third and fourth optional parameters. These are used to determine the media type to which the stylesheet applies and to define the additional attributes we want associated with the <link> tag.

```
// define style sheet
$stylesheet = 'http://example.org/printStyles.css';
$type = 'text/css';
$media = 'print';
$attribs = array('charset' => 'US-ASCII');
// add style sheet to the HTML document
$document->addStyleSheet($stylesheet, $type, $media, $attribs);
```

For more information about the various media types, refer to http://www.w3.org/TR/REC-html40/types.html#type-media-descriptors.

A sneaky shortcut

There is a handy shortcut for adding an external stylesheet. The static JHTML::stylesheet() method can be used in instances where the CSS document we are linking to resides in the current Joomla! installation.

```
// define style sheet location
$stylesheet = 'myStyleSheet.css';
$path = 'components/com_mycomponent/assets/';
// add style sheet
JHTML::stylesheet($stylesheet, $path);
```

The JHTML::stylesheet() method accepts the following three parameters:

- The name of the stylesheet.
- The path relative to the root of the Joomla! installation.
- An associative array of additional attributes that we want applied to the <link> tag.

Both the second and third parameters are optional. However, outside the Joomla! Core it is unusual not to supply the second. If we omit the second parameter, it is assumed that the path is media/system/css/.

 As the path is an HTTP path, we use forward slashes as directory separators instead of using the environment-defined DS directory separators.

Overriding component templates

This recipe explains how to override default **model-view-controller (MVC)** component templates within a template extension. For the purpose of this example, we will override the article template from the content component.

How to do it...

The first thing we need to do is identify the template we want to override. The templates are located in the component's views/viewname/tmpl folder. For example, the article templates for the content component are located in components/com_content/views/article/tmpl.

In this instance, there are seven files of which three are PHP and thus are templates. These files are default.php, form.php, and pagebreak.php. We want to override the template that displays an article. This means we want to override default.php. Therefore, we need to make a copy of the file.

But where does it go? Overriding is achieved based on the site template. If we wanted to override the template in our template extension—let's call it **Wasps**—we would copy the file to templates/wasps/html/com_content/article/default.php.

 We should only declare overrides in our own template extensions. That is to say, modifying existing templates such as the Joomla! accessible template **Beez** is essentially the same as hacking the core. It is perfectly acceptable to repackage an existing template and modify it as required.

We are now in a position to modify the copied file. On all pages where the template Wasps is used, the overriding `default.php` template will be used.

How it works...

When Joomla! loads a template in an MVC component, it first looks for an override in the site template. These overrides are always located within the template's `html` folder. If an override is located, it is used in preference to the component's own templates.

There's more...

It isn't just component templates that can be overridden in the site template. The following table describes all of the other files that we can override in the root of the `html` folder:

Filename	Description
`modules.php`	Look and feel of modules
`pagination.php`	Look and feel of the pagination user controls, generated by `JPagination` objects; see the *Enabling pagination in a list of items* recipe at the end of this chapter

The following table describes all of the files we can override in the root of the templates folder:

Filename	Description
`component.php`	Component-only template; see the *Generating modal content* recipe later in this chapter
`error.php`	Fatal error template
`index.php`	General layout of all the HTML pages
`offline.php`	Displayed when the site is down for maintenance

Adding JavaScript to a page

This recipe explains how to add JavaScript to an HTML-generated document.

Getting ready

In order to add JavaScript to the document, we need the document object. Always remember to use the `=&` assignment operator so as to avoid accidentally creating a copy of the document object.

```
$document =& JFactory::getDocument();
```

How to do it...

To add a link to the HTML `<head>` tag in a JavaScript document, in the form of a `<script>` tag, we use the `JDocument::addScript()` method.

```
$document->addScript('http://example.org/script.js');
```

Alternatively, we can declare JavaScript in a `<script>` tag in the HTML `<head>` tag. To do this, we use the `JDocument::addScriptDeclaration()` method.

```
// define the internal styles
$script = "alert ('Some JavaScript Alert')";
// add the styles to the document
$document->addScriptDeclaration($script);
```

There's more...

The `JDocument::addScript()` and `JDocument::addScriptDeclaration()` methods accept a second optional parameter. This parameter defines the MIME type of the script, the default value of which is `text/javascript`. Examples of other scripting languages include Tcl (`text/tcl`) and VBScript (`text/vbscript`).

```
// add some VBScript
$document->addScript('http://example.org/script.vb','text/vbscript');
```

Big scripts

When we declare large scripts, it can be useful to use the **heredoc** string syntax. This syntax allows us to write a string without the need to escape quotation marks.

```
$script = <<<SCRIPT
var Account = new Class({
  options: {
    name: "Packt Publishing's Account",
    number: "0000001",
    \$amount: 10
  },
  initialize: function(options){
    this.setOptions(options);
  }
});
Account.implement(new Options);
SCRIPT;
```

Alternatively, as of PHP 5.3.0, we can use the **nowdoc** string syntax. This is similar to heredoc, except that no parsing occurs. This means that the inner strings such as `$amount` will not be evaluated as the value of the equivalent PHP variable.

```
$script = <<<'SCRIPT'
var Account = new Class({
  options: {
```

```
    name: "Packt Publishing's Account",
    number: "0000001",
    $amount: 10
  },
  initialize: function(options){
    this.setOptions(options);
  }
});
Account.implement(new Options);
SCRIPT;
```

See also

For information about using JavaScript to create an Ajax-enabled application, refer to the *Updating an element using Ajax and MooTools* and *Updating an element based on a form using Ajax and MooTools* recipes later in this chapter.

Creating a modal window

This recipe explains how to create a modal window. A **modal window** is a child window that blocks interaction with the parent window until the modal window is closed.

How to do it...

In order to enable modal windows, we must load the modal behavior. We do this using JHTML.

```
JHTML::_('behavior.modal');
```

To create a modal window, all we need to do is create a normal HTML hyperlink, but apply the CSS class modal as follows:

```
<a href="<?php echo $link; ?>" class="modal">
  My Modal Window
</a>
```

How it works...

When we load the modal behavior, we are telling the document that we want to include the **SqueezeBox** JavaScript, which deals with modal windows. This JavaScript automatically attaches itself to any hyperlinks that are specified as the CSS class modal.

An HTML element can have more than one CSS class

It is possible to apply more than one CSS class to an HTML element. For example, to apply the modal and hyperlink CSS classes, we would do the following class="hyperlink modal".

For more information about SqueezeBox, refer to
`whttp://digitarald.de/project/squeezebox/`.

There's more...

It is possible to define alternative selectors. By default the selector is `a.modal`, that is, `<a>` tags of the `modal` class. We could change this to `a.mymodal`, as shown in the following example:

```
JHTML::_('behavior.modal', 'a.mymodal');
```

There are a number of additional options that we can provide in the form of an associative array. The following table summarizes the options:

Option	Description
ajaxOptions	Options that are specific to the MooTools `Ajax` class
onClose	JavaScript function executed when the modal window is closed
onHide	JavaScript function executed when the modal window is hidden
onMove	JavaScript function executed when the modal window is moved
onOpen	JavaScript function executed when the modal window is opened
onResize	JavaScript function executed when the modal window is resized
onShow	JavaScript function executed when the modal window is shown
onUpdate	JavaScript function executed when the modal window is updated
size	Initial size of the modal window is expressed as an associative array with two values, x and y; for example, `array("x" => 100 "y" => 100)`

All of these options can be defined in the third parameter—an associative array. For example, we could do the following to set the size of a modal window to 300px by 150px and display an alert when a modal window is closed:

```
// define modal options
$modalOptions = array (
   'size' => array('x' => 300, 'y' => 150),
   'onClose' => '\function() {alert("modal window closed");}'
);
// load modal JavaScript
JHTML::_('behavior.modal', 'a.modal', $modalOptions);
```

Backslash for literal values

We use a backslash to indicate that we want a value to be treated literally. In the example, we can see that the `onClose` value starts with a backslash. If it did not, it would be treated as a regular JavaScript string.

Overriding options on a per-window basis

The options described in the table earlier in this recipe are those that can be defined as default values for all modal windows on a page. It is possible to override the default values within each modal window hyperlink. The overriding values are defined in the `rel` attribute.

```
<a href="<?php echo $link; ?>"
  class="modal"
  rel = "{
    size: {x: 400, y: 200},
    onClose: function() {alert('my modal window closed')}
  }">
  My Modal Window
</a>
```

There are additional options that we can specify in the `rel` attribute. The following table summarizes the additional options. *Placing any of these options in the options array when calling* `behavior.modal` *will not work.*

Option	Description
handler	The way in which to handle the modal content; handlers include `adopt`, `iframe`, `image`, `string`, and `url`
sizeLoading	The size of the modal window while the content loads; it's expressed in the form `{x: 200, y: 150}`
marginImage	The margin used when using the `image` handler, which is expressed in the form `{x: 20, y: 20}`
adopt	The ID of an element in the current page to adopt for the modal content
closeWithOverlay	A Boolean option to allow closing of the modal window when the overlay is clicked on; the default value is `true`
zIndex	**Z-index** (layer) on which the modal window is created; the default value is `65555`
overlayOpacity	The opacity of the layer that hides the parent window; it's expressed as a value between `0.0` and `1.0` with the default value being `0.7`
classWindow	The CSS class/classes to apply to the modal window, `sbox-window`
classOverlay	The CSS class/classes to apply to the overlay, `sbox-overlay`

See also

The next recipe explains how to generate content for a modal window using Joomla!.

Generating modal content

This recipe explains how to generate content that is suitable for use within a modal window.

How to do it...

To generate HTML modal content—content that is not cluttered with the usual template and various modules—we can use the special template `component`.

We can define the use of this template in the request by setting the value of `tmpl`, as shown in the following example:

```php
<?php
// build the modal link
$link = JRoute::_('index.php?option=com_mycomponent&tmpl=component');
?>
<a href="<?php echo $link; ?>" class="modal">
  My Modal Window
</a>
```

Note that the actual value of `$link` would likely include a great deal of request parameters such as `task`. Alternatively, we can force the special template `component` on to the response by setting the request value of `tmpl` before the application renders.

```php
JRequest::setVar('tmpl', 'component');
```

How it works...

There are actually four special templates—`component`, `error`, `index`, and `offline`. Each of these templates can be thought of as a root template file. In most instances, the `index` template file is used. When a major error occurs, the `error` template file is used. When the site is down for maintenance, the `offline` template file is used. And finally, the `component` template file is used when all we want to render is the component that has been invoked by the request.

> In the backend, there are special templates; these are `component`, `cpanel`, `error`, `index`, and `login`. The `cpanel` template is used for the main administrative control panel. The `login` template is used for the administrative login page. There is no `offline` template file because the administrative backend is still accessible when the system is down for maintenance.

We can test the use of the `tmpl` request value on any component. For example, if we view an article normally and then add the `&tmpl=component` to the end of the URI, we will see only the component output. In the following example, we can see to the left the normal view of the *Joomla! License Guidelines* article and to the right, we can see the same article using the component template:

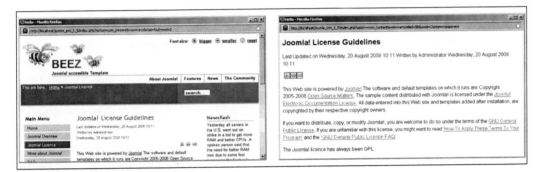

See also

For information about creating a modal window in which to load content, refer to the previous recipe *Creating a modal window*.

Updating an element using Ajax and MooTools

This recipe explains how to update an element in a page using MooTools. To achieve this, we use the MooTools `Ajax` class. The use of the MooTools `Ajax` class eliminates the need for us to get bogged down by browser-specific quirks.

Getting ready

The first thing we need to do is add the MooTools library to the page in which we want to add Ajax capabilities.

```
// add mootools to the page
JHTML::_('behavior.mootools');
```

How to do it...

We need an element on the page to update:

```
<div id="someID">
  <p>Update this element please!</p>
</div>
```

Next we will create a button, which will update the `someID` element when we click on it.

```
<input type="button"
       id="ajaxButton"
       value="<?php echo JText::_('UPDATE'); ?>" />
```

It is generally best to avoid declaring JavaScript in the `onClick` attribute. Instead, we will declare the script in the `document` header and attach it to the button programmatically. It is essential that we attempt to do this only when the **Document Object Model (DOM)** is loaded. Therefore, we create a `domready` event handler.

```
// define the script
$script = <<<SCRIPT
window.addEvent('domready', function() {
  $('ajaxButton').addEvent('click', function () {
    new Ajax(
      'index.php?option=com_mycomponent&id=$id&format=ajax',
        {
          method: 'get',
          update: 'someID'
        }
    ).request();
  });
});
SCRIPT;
// add the script to the document
$document =& JFactory::getDocument();
$document->addScriptDeclaration($script);
```

How it works...

Attaching the `click` event handler is a bit of pain, and it increases the size of the required code. However, it ensures that everything that might be required by the event is loaded before the event can be triggered. In our example, we retrieve the button using the MooTools $ function and simply add an event handler for `domready`. This will add the desired `click` event handler.

MooTools really is our savior here as it does all the hard work for us. All we have to do is plug in the basic options. On closer inspection, we can see that when the button is clicked, a new `Ajax` object is created. This object is passed the URI of the data we want to retrieve, and an object literal that defines some extra options.

In this case, we tell the object that we want to retrieve `index.php?option=com_mycompon ent&id=$id&format=ajax`. The options tell the object that we want to use the `GET` method (by default this is `POST`), and that we want to use the response to update the contents of the element with the `someID` ID.

> For information about Ajax responses, refer to the next recipe, *Providing an Ajax response from a component*. This recipe also explains the purpose of the `format` request value `ajax` that is used in the example URI.

The last thing we do is execute the `request()` function. This is when the magic actually occurs. Forgetting to include this will prevent the request from taking place.

We can think of the object itself as a throwaway object. That is to say, as soon as the `onClick` event has completed, the object is discarded. Should the event occur a second time, a new object will be created and will subsequently be discarded.

There's more...

The following table describes some of the options we can pass when creating a new `Ajax` object:

Option	Description
data	Post data to send with the request; used only when the method is `POST`.
update	The element or ID of the element that we want to update—technically, this is not required. When we don't want to update an element directly from the response, simply ignore this option.
onComplete	The function to execute once the request has been successfully completed.
evalScripts	A Boolean option to execute any JavaScript found embedded in the response.
evalResponse	A Boolean option to evaluate the entire response as JavaScript (there are security issues with this, and usage should be carefully considered).

See also

For information about using a form with Ajax, refer to the next recipe, *Updating an element based on a form using MooTools*.

To discover how to handle Ajax requests, refer to the *Providing an Ajax response from a component* recipe later in this chapter.

To learn more about correctly embedding JavaScript in a page, refer to the *Adding JavaScript to a page* recipe earlier in this chapter.

Updating an element based on a form using Ajax and MooTools

This recipe explains how to update an element in a page based on a form using MooTools. This recipe uses the MooTools `Ajax` class to achieve this. Using the MooTools `Ajax` class eliminates the need for us to get bogged down by browser-specific quirks.

Getting ready

The first thing we need to do is add the MooTools library to the page in which we want to add Ajax capabilities.

```
// add mootools to the page
JHTML::_('behavior.mootools');
```

How to do it...

We need an element on the page to update and a form from which we get values to update the element. We will place the form inside the element we want to update, so as to prevent the form from being submitted more than once.

```
<div id="someID">
  <form id="ajaxForm">
    <textarea name="comment"></textarea>
    <input type="button" id="ajaxButton"
       value="<?php echo JText::_"UPDATE"); ?>" />
    <!-- hidden fields -->
    <input type="hidden" name="option" value="com_mycomponent"/>
    <input type="hidden" name="format" value="ajax"/>
  </form>
</div>
```

For information about Ajax responses, refer to the next recipe, *Providing an Ajax response from a component*. This recipe also explains the purpose of the hidden `format` field.

Included in the form is a button, which will update the `someID` element when we click on it. It is generally best to avoid declaring the JavaScript inline, for example, in an `onClick` attribute. Instead, we declare the script to handle the button `click` event in the document header and attach it to the button programmatically. It is essential that we only attempt to do this once the DOM is loaded. Therefore, we create a `domready` event handler.

```
// define the script
$script = <<<SCRIPT
window.addEvent('domready', function() {
  $('ajaxButton').addEvent('click', function () {
    new Ajax(
      'index.php',
        {
            data: $('ajaxForm'),
            method: 'post',
            update: 'someID'
        }
    ).request();
    });
});
SCRIPT;
// add the script to the document
$document =& JFactory::getDocument();
$document->addScriptDeclaration($script);
```

How it works...

Attaching the `click` event handler is a bit of a pain, and it increases the required code. However, it ensures that everything that might be required by the event is loaded before the event can be triggered. In our example, we retrieve the button using the MooTools $ function and simply add an event handler for `domready` that will later add the desired `click` event handler.

MooTools really is our savior here as it does all the hard work for us. All we have to do is plug in the basic options. On closer inspection, we can see that when the button is clicked, a new `Ajax` object is created. This object is passed the URI of the data we want to retrieve, and an object literal that defines some extra options.

In this case, we tell the object that we want to retrieve `index.php`. The options tell the object that we want to pass the values in `ajaxForm` via the `POST` method, and that we want to use the response to update the contents of the element with the `someID` ID.

The last thing we do is execute the `request()` function. This is when the magic actually occurs. Forgetting to include this will prevent the request from taking place.

We can think of the object itself as a throwaway object. This means that as soon as the `click` event has completed, the object is discarded. Should the event occur a second time, a new object will be created and will subsequently be discarded.

An alternative approach is to use the `Element.send()` function of MooTools. This is used in conjunction with the `Element.send` property. The property defines the parameters for the Ajax request and the method performs the request. For more information, refer to `http://mootools.net/docs/Request/Request`.

See also

For information about using a basic hyperlink with Ajax, refer to the previous recipe, *Updating an element using Ajax and MooTools*.

To discover how to handle Ajax requests refer to the next recipe, *Providing an Ajax response from a component*.

To learn more about correctly embedding JavaScript in a page, refer to the *Adding JavaScript to a page* recipe, earlier in this chapter.

Providing an Ajax response from a component

This recipe explains how to provide an Ajax-friendly response from a component. This recipe is designed to be used in conjunction with the *Updating an element based on a form using Ajax and MooTools* or *Updating an element using Ajax and MooTools* recipe. This recipe assumes we are building an MVC Joomla! component.

How to do it...

An Ajax response needs to be a pure, uncluttered response that only includes the output generated by the component. To achieve this, we must use the RAW document.

We define the use of this document in the request by setting the value of `format`, as shown in the following example. Note that the actual URI would likely include more request parameters.

```
index.php?option=com_mycomponent&format=raw
```

The great thing about the RAW document is that it becomes the default document if the specified format is not known. For example, defining the value of `format` as `ajax` would have the same effect.

When we build a Joomla! MVC component, we must create a new view in order to take advantage of this document type. As we already know, a normal HTML view class is always located in a file named `view.html.php`. When using the RAW document, we create the corresponding view in a file named `view.raw.php`. If we have opted to use a format name such as `ajax`, the name of the file will be `view.ajax.php`. The advantage of using a custom format name is that it is semantically clear and allows us to create many different views using the RAW document.

Using templates with RAW views

When creating a view for a RAW document, it is still possible to use a template from the `tmpl` folder as with the HTML views.

How it works...

Joomla! uses a `JDocument` object to represent and handle the document that is ultimately returned in the response. There are five different `JDocument` types. Out of these, four are of special interest and are described in the following table:

Type	MIME	MVC template	Description
Feed	`application/rss+xml` `application/atom+xml`	`view.feed.php`	RSS or Atom feeds
HTML	`text/html`	`view.html.php`	Normal HTML output
PDF	`application/pdf`	`view.pdf.php`	Adobe PDF
RAW	`text/html`	`view.raw.php`	Any other type of document

When we specify the format of a response, we are telling Joomla! which type of `JDocument` we want to use. For the purpose of Ajax requests, the RAW document is a winner! In fact, for anything other than a feed, PDF or normal HTML response, the RAW document will definitely be the format of choice.

Do not use the component template to achieve this

It might be tempting when dealing with HTML snippets to think that the component template is a suitable solution. However, this template provides a complete HTML document. For more information, refer to the *Generating modal content recipe*, earlier in this chapter.

There's more...

Providing snippets of HTML is not always the best way of responding to an Ajax request. It certainly isn't the most robust as there is no specific error-reporting available. There are many alternative formats we can use, and the most popular are undoubtedly JSON and XML.

JSON (JavaScript Object Notation) uses a subset of the JavaScript literal syntax. JSON is essentially a serialized encoding. Do not confuse JSON with object literals. JSON is a subset of the JavaScript literal syntax and is especially easy to work with from a JavaScript client.

Use MooTools JSON object to unserialize JSON

MooTools provides us with a handy object that can be used for JavaScript serialization. Instead of using the JavaScript eval() function, which poses some inherent security risks, we should use the JSON.decode() method. For more information, refer to http://mootools.net/docs/core/Utilities/JSON.

JavaScript is an implementation of **ECMAScript (ES)**. Technically, JSON uses a subset of the **ES3** literal syntax. In the proposed **ES5** specification, JSON will take on a bigger role. For more information, refer to http://ecmascript.org/.

As of PHP 5.2.0, PHP provides some handy JSON functions among which json_encode() is of particular note. This function can be used to encode PHP data as JSON data. For more information, refer to http://php.net/manual/function.json-encode.php.

JSON and remote procedure calls (RPC)

JSON-RPC provides a comprehensive **JSON**-based transmission protocol. For more information, refer to http://groups.google.com/group/json-rpc/web and the *Using a custom JDocument in a component (PHP 5 only)* recipe in the next chapter.

Extensible Markup Language (XML), unlike JSON, tends to be more suited to larger applications, and applications that that are serving content to disparate systems. Joomla! includes the **phpxmlrpc** library and the `JSimpleXML` class for dealing with XML. It is perfectly acceptable to choose XML for data interchange. However, in comparison with JSON, XML generally requires more development time for both the client and server.

For this reason, it is usually best we save all of that XML goodness for those all important **web services** that require a greater level of interoperability. JSON and JSON-RPC are normally perfectly adequate for systems that are designed specifically with Ajax in mind.

XML-RPC web services should be implemented as plugins

Joomla! has a plugin type specifically for dealing with XML-RPC web services. Should we want to create an XML-RPC web service with which our Ajax will interact, we should create a plugin.

See also

For information about using a basic hyperlink to initiate an Ajax request, refer to the *Updating an element using Ajax and MooTools* recipe.

For information about using a form to initiate an Ajax request, refer to the *Updating an element based on a form using Ajax and MooTools* recipe.

Enabling pagination in a list of items

This recipe explains how to enable **pagination** when viewing lists of items.

How to do it...

To use Joomla! pagination, we need three integer values. They are as follows:

- `$limit` specifies the maximum number of items to display on a page
- `$limitstart` specifies which item is the first to be displayed on the current page
- `$total` is the total number of items

The value of `$limit` is persistent. That is to say, the number of items that a user chooses to display on a page is retained during their session. To retrieve the value of `$limit`, we use the `getUserStateFromRequest()` application method.

```
// get the application object
$app =& JFactory::getApplication();
// define the state context
```

```
$context = 'com_mycomponent.list.';
// get the limit
$limit = $app->getUserStateFromRequest($context.'limit', 'limit', 0,
                                                               'int');
```

The `$limitstart` value is retrieved in the same way as `$limit` in the backend.

```
// get the limitstart (backend)
$limitstart = $app->getUserStateFromRequest($context.'limitstart',
                                       'limitstart', 0, 'int');
```

The `$limitstart` value is retrieved differently in the frontend.

```
// get the limitstart (frontend)
$limitstart = JRequest::getInt('limitstart', 0);
```

The `$limitstart` value can cause problems if the value of `$limit` has been adjusted. We can combat this by correcting the value as necessary.

```
$limitstart = ($limit != 0 ? (floor($limitstart / $limit)
                                   * $limit) : 0);
```

There are several ways to get the value of `$total`. In an MVC component, we typically create a `getTotal()` method in the model. The usual ways of calculating this value include using the protected `JModel::_getListCount()` method, the `JDatabase::getNumRows()` method, and directly querying the database using the MySQL aggregate `COUNT()` function. For example:

```
SELECT COUNT(*) AS `total`
FROM `#__items_table`
WHERE `published` = 1;
```

Once we have the pagination parameters, we need to get the data we want to display in the paginated list. We use the MySQL `LIMIT` clause to extract only the data we want. If we are getting the data in a `JModel` and are using the `JModel::getList()` method, we simply pass the values of `$limitstart` and `$limit`.

```
// get page data restricted by limitstart and limit
$pageData = $this->getList($sql, $limitstart, $limit);
```

Alternatively, if we are directly using the `JDatabase` object, we pass the values of `$limitstart` and `$limit` when we set the query.

```
// get the database object
$db =& JFactory::getDBO();
// get page data restricted by limitstart and limit
$db->setQuery($sql, $limitstart, $limit);
$pageData = $db->loadObjectList();
```

Pagination in Joomla! allows for the display of all items. When all items are selected for display, the value of $limit will be 0. In these instances, we don't need to limit the data using $limitstart and $limit.

The last thing we do after we have outputted the page data is provide the user with the user controls necessary to navigate the paginated data. To achieve this, we use a JPagination object.

```
// import JPagination class
jimport('joomla.html.pagination');
// create JPagination object
$pagination = new JPagination($total, $limitstart, $limit);
```

To generate the controls, we use the JPagination::getListFooter() method.

```
echo $pagination->getListFooter();
```

This should give us something similar to the following screenshot:

 When outputting the pagination user controls in the backend, it is normal to place them inside the <tfoot> of the adminList table.

How it works...

To help better understand what is going on, we'll use the following example:

	Betty	Andy	John	Lisa	Elizabeth	Vicky	Roger	Douglas	Robert	Marry	Amy	Ryan	Anna	Hannah	Kevin	Paul	Chloe	Alice
	0	1	2	3	4	5	6	7	8	9	10	11	12	13	14	15	16	17
$limit = 5	Page 1					Page 2					Page 3					Page 4		
$limit = 10	Page 1										Page 2							
$limit = 20	Page 1																	

In this example, the paginated data is a list of names. Beneath this is each item's indexed position in the list. A definition of each page based on the value of $limit is displayed beneath this.

If we wanted to see page two with a maximum of 10 items per page, we would define the page as $limit = 10 and $limitstart = 10. On the other hand, if we wanted to see page four with a maximum of five items per page, we would define the page as $limit = 5 and $limitstart = 15.

When we retrieve the value of $limit and $limitstart using the getUserStateFromRequest() application method, we are requesting persistent values that can be updated based on the request. We pass this method four parameters—the name of the state data, the name of the request data, the default value, and the type of value.

Notice how we use $context to define the name of the state data. This ensures that the persistent value of $limit is specific to lists in com_mycomponent. It is possible to use other values for $context. For example, to make the state data specific to *names*, we might use com_mycomponent.names.list.

Unlike $limit, the value of $limitstart is persistent only when viewing paginated lists in the backend. We can prove this by navigating away from and back to the paginated data in the frontend and backend. We will notice that the page we return to is remembered in the backend, while it is reset to page one in the frontend. This is why we simply retrieve the value of $limitstart from the request in the frontend.

There's more...

The JPagination class doesn't just provide the getListFooter() method to create pagination user controls. The class provides more fine-grained options such as getLimitBox() and getPagesCounter(). For more information, refer to the official Joomla! API site at http://api.joomla.org/.

7
Customizing the Document

This chapter contains the following recipes:

- ▶ Setting the document title
- ▶ Setting the document generator
- ▶ Setting the document description
- ▶ Adding metadata to the document
- ▶ Changing the document character set
- ▶ Changing the document MIME type
- ▶ Controlling client caching of responses
- ▶ Creating a PDF in a component
- ▶ Creating an RSS or Atom feed in a component
- ▶ Outputting a RAW document from a component
- ▶ Using a custom JDocument in a component (PHP 5 only)

Introduction

This chapter discusses the ways in which we can modify the response by working with the Joomla! document object. Joomla! uses a JDocument object to handle response data. Because JDocument is abstract, the Joomla! document object will always be a subtype of JDocument. The classes that extend JDocument are intended for different response formats. The following table describes the classes and their purposes:

Class	Format	Default MIME type	Purpose
JDocumentError	error	text/html	Display a fatal error
JDocumentFeed	feed	application/rss+xml or application/atom+xml	Syndication feed, RSS, or Atom
JDocumentHTML	html	text/html	Default document used for all typical Joomla! responses
JDocumentPDF	pdf	application/pdf	Adobe PDF representation
JDocumentRAW	raw*	text/html	All other circumstances

 * JDocumentRAW is unique as it handles all *unknown* formats. For example, if a requested format is XML, the document will be a JDocumentRAW object.

So what exactly does the format column represent? When a request is made, Joomla! uses the value of the request variable format to determine which document type to use. We really see this only when we retrieve something other than an HTML document, because this always defaults to html. For example, when we request an article as a PDF, we use a URI similar to this:

```
http://example.org/index.php?option=com_content&view=article&id=5&
format=pdf
```

The JDocumentError class is slightly different from the others. We should never really need to interact directly with this. We can, of course, invoke this document indirectly by raising a fatal error. For more information, refer to Chapter 11, *Error handling and reporting*.

The Joomla! document object and views in Joomla! MVC components are closely related. For each format that we provide a view, we create a new JView subclass. For example, when we examine the content component, we can see that the article view supports HTML and PDF simply by the presence of the view.html.php and view.pdf.php files.

This chapter also deals with the static JResponse class. This class is used to define the HTTP response, *including the HTTP headers*.

The separation between JResponse and the JDocument object is not always as clear as one would hope. However, this is somewhat inevitable because the two are inextricably linked—the response describes and includes the document output. For example, outputting an HTML response will require the response Content-Type header field to be set accordingly, that is, as text/html.

Setting the document title

This recipe explains how to set the title of the current document. The exact meaning of *title* will depend on the type of document. For example, in an HTML document, this is the value encapsulated in the <head> tag.

Getting ready

Before we do anything, we need the global document object.

```
$document =& JFactory::getDocument();
```

How to do it...

To set the title of the document, we use the JDocument::setTitle() method.

```
$document->setTitle('My Unique Title');
```

If we are outputting an HTML document, this should generate something like this:

```
<title>My Unique Title</title>
```

There's more...

Menu items can also define page titles. Thus, the actual title we use should not necessarily be the title of whatever we are viewing. To deal with this, we should use something along these lines:

```
// get the component and page parameters
$application =& JFactory::getApplication();
$params      =& $application->getParams();

// get the page title
$pageTitle = $params->get('page_title', $defaultTitle);

// set the document title
$document->setTitle($pageTitle);
```

See also

For more information about parameters, refer to the *Getting page and component parameters* recipe in the previous chapter.

Setting the document generator

This recipe explains how to set the name of the piece of software that generated the page. The exact meaning of *generator* will depend on the type of document. For example, in an HTML document, this value is used in a `<meta>` tag.

Getting ready

Before we do anything, we need the global document object.

```
$document =& JFactory::getDocument();
```

How to do it...

To set the generator, we use the `JDocument::setGenerator()` method. Remember that in HTML the value of generator is designed to identify the piece of software used to generate the page, not the author. For more information, refer to `http://www.w3.org/html/wg/markup-spec/#meta.name`.

```
// set the generator
$document->setGenerator('My Component');
```

If we are outputting an HTML document, this should generate something like this:

```
<meta name="generator" content="My Component" />
```

See also

To learn more about adding metadata to the document, see the next but one recipe, *Adding metadata to the document*.

Setting the document description

This recipe explains how to set the document description. The exact meaning of *description* will depend on the type of document. For example, in an HTML document, this value is used in a `<meta>` tag.

Getting ready

Before we do anything, we need the global document object.

```
$document =& JFactory::getDocument();
```

How to do it...

To set the description, we use the `JDocument::setDescription()` method. The description value is used by applications such as search engines to help determine the content of a page.

```
// set the description
$document->setDescription("A Joomla! 1.5 recipe");
```

If we are outputting an HTML document, this will generate something like this:

```
<meta name="description" content="A Joomla! 1.5 recipe" />
```

See also

To learn more about adding metadata to the document, refer to the next recipe, *Adding metadata to the document*.

Adding metadata to the document

This recipe explains how to add metadata to the document. The exact meaning of *metadata* will depend on the type of document. For example, in an HTML document, this is used to generate `<meta>` tags.

Getting ready

Before we do anything, we need the global document object.

```
$document =& JFactory::getDocument();
```

How to do it...

To add metadata to the document, we use the `JDocument::setMetaData()` method. For example, to set the value of the keywords metadata, we would do the following:

```
// set the keywords metadata
$document->setMetaData('keywords', 'Joomla! Cookbook');
```

If we are outputting an HTML document, this will generate something like this:

```
<meta name="keywords" content="Joomla! Cookbook" />
```

If we want to add an `http-equiv` `<meta>` tag, we must provide the third parameter with the `$http_equiv` Boolean value. For example, to add the `http-equiv` metadata `Expires`, we would do the following:

```
// set the expiry date
$expiresDate = 'Mon, 23 Mar 2009 15:48:00 GMT';
$document->setMetaData('Expires', $expiresDate, true);
```

If we are outputting an HTML document, this will generate something like this:

```
<meta http-equiv="Expires"
      content="Mon, 23 Mar 2009 15:48:00 GMT" />
```

 `http-equiv` metadata is intended to override the HTTP header fields. The `Expires` header is used to specify when a cache should be considered stale. For information about HTTP header fields, refer to `http://www.w3.org/Protocols/rfc2616/rfc2616-sec14.html#sec14`.

See also

To set description and generator metadata, we do not use the `JDocument::setMetaData()` method. For more information, refer to the previous two recipes, *Setting the document description* and *Setting the document generator*.

Changing the document character set

This recipe explains how to change the document character set. *By default, the character set is UTF-8, a multibyte Unicode character encoding.* For a complete description of character encoding, refer to Chapter 5, *Multilingual Recipes*.

Getting ready

Before we do anything, we need the global document object.

```
$document =& JFactory::getDocument();
```

How to do it...

To change the document character set, we use the `JDocument::setCharset()` method. For example, this will set the character set to US-ASCII:

```
// set the character set
$document->setCharset('us-ascii');
```

How it works...

The character set defines the way in which the characters are encoded in the response data. For most document types, for example HTML, the document can only have one encoding. Composite document types, such as `multipart/alternative`, may use several encodings. In these instances—relatively rare, at least for Joomla!— it is necessary to micromanage the character encoding of each part.

The character encoding is passed as part of the HTTP response headers. The following example shows a set of HTTP headers where the character set has been changed to US-ASCII:

Field	Value
Date	Mon, 23 Mar 2009 10:26:26 GMT
Server	Apache/2.2.8 (Win32) PHP/5.2.6
Expires	Mon, 1 Jan 2001 00:00:00 GMT
Last-Modified	Mon, 23 Mar 2009 10:26:26 GMT
Content-Type	text/html; charset=us-ascii

Setting the character set in a document doesn't necessarily guarantee that the defined character set is used by the client. For example, in an HTML document it is possible to override the encoding defined in the response headers using an `http-equiv <meta>` tag.

```
<meta http-equiv="content-type" content="text/html; charset=utf-8" />
```

Modern browsers often attempt to automatically detect character encoding even if the encoding has been explicitly defined. We can never guarantee that a client will heed the response specified character set.

See also

For more information about character encodings, refer to Chapter 5, *Multilingual Recipes*.

The next recipe, *Changing the document MIME type*, explains how to modify the HTTP header `Content-Type`. Or put simply, it shows how to change what the document represents; for example, a JPEG image.

Changing the document MIME type

This recipe explains how to change the **MIME (Multipurpose Internet Mail Extensions)** type of the document. Changing this enables us to inform the client what the data we are sending represents. In Joomla!, we generally only use this when we have invoked the RAW document.

Getting ready

Before we do anything, we need the global document object.

```
$document =& JFactory::getDocument();
```

How to do it...

To modify the document MIME type, we use the `JDocument::setMimeEncoding()` method.

```
$document->setMimeEncoding('text/plain');
```

Note that the MIME type we provide is just the MIME type and nothing else. For example, `"text/html; charset=utf-8"` is not valid because it also includes the `Content-Type` parameter `charset`.

XHTML MIME type

Even modern browsers have difficulty understanding the XHTML MIME type `application/xhtml+xml`. Unless the client explicitly tells us that it does accept this MIME type, we should use `text/html`. For more information, refer to `http://www.w3.org/TR/xhtml-media-types/#media-types`.

How it works...

The MIME type is used to define the way in which the data being transferred has been encoded, for example `image/jpeg`. This, in turn, tells the client how to handle the response. For example, the headers of an HTTP response might look like this:

Field	Value
Date	Mon, 23 Mar 2009 10:26:26 GMT
Server	Apache/2.2.8 (Win32) PHP/5.2.6
Expires	Mon, 1 Jan 2001 00:00:00 GMT
Last-Modified	Mon, 23 Mar 2009 10:26:26 GMT
Content-Type	image/jpeg; charset=utf-8

So when would we want to change the MIME type? A good example is when we have used the database to store binary data. For example, it is not uncommon to use a database to store thumbnails. To serve a thumbnail, we would need to output the raw binary data and change the MIME type to suit the image format. For more information, refer to the *Outputting a RAW document from a component* recipe later in this chapter.

 We would not normally include the `charset` parameter when specifying a MIME type of `image/xxx`. However, we cannot prevent this because it is built into the Joomla! framework. For more information, refer to the implementation of `JDocument::render()`.

See also

For information about changing the value of the Content-Type parameter `charset`, refer to the previous recipe, *Changing the document character set*.

Controlling client caching of responses

This recipe explains how to control client caching of responses. By default, Joomla! always assumes that caching by clients should not be allowed. However, in instances where we are dealing specifically with data we know will not change, or will only change occasionally, allowing a client to cache a response can be beneficial, as it could significantly reduce the load on the server. *Note that client caching is completely separate from Joomla!'s own cache.*

How to do it...

To allow clients to cache responses, we use the static `JResponse::allowCache()` method.

```
// allow clients to cache the response
JResponse::allowCache(true);
```

How it works...

The HTTP 1.1 protocol (`http://www.ietf.org/rfc/rfc2616.txt`) defines caching as:

> *A program's local store of response messages and the subsystem that controls its message storage, retrieval, and deletion. A cache stores cacheable responses in order to reduce the response time and network bandwidth consumption on future, equivalent requests. Any client or server may include a cache, though a cache cannot be used by a server that is acting as a tunnel.*

When we allow client caching in Joomla!, it explicitly defines an expiration time using the HTTP `Expires` header field. This is always calculated based on the current time plus 900 seconds (15 minutes).

Unfortunately, it is not generally possible to change the expiry time. For a potential work-around, refer to the last recipe in this chapter, *Using a custom JDocument in a component (PHP 5 only)*, and consider overriding the `JDocument::render()` method.

However, there is a way in which we can define an overriding expiry time. The `Cache-Control` header field was added in HTTP 1.1 and is recognized by the majority of clients. We can provide a maximum age that a cache should allow a cached entity to reach. And what's good about this is that it overrides the `Expires` header field.

To add this to the response, we use the `JResponse::setHeader()` method. The following example sets the maximum age to 1800 seconds (30 minutes).

```
// set the maximum age in seconds
JResponse::setHeader('Cache-Control', 'max-age=1800');
```

> To force a client browser to reload a cached page in Windows and *NIX environments, use *Ctrl + F5*, and in Mac OS environments use *Cmd + F5*. Note that this may differ depending on your browser.

There's more...

It is a good practice to inform the document when the response was last updated. This is achieved using the `JDocument::setModifiedDate()` method. This method accepts one parameter, the modified date.

```
// get the document object
$document =& JFactory::getDocument();

// set the modified date
$document->setModifiedDate('Mon, 23 Mar 2009 12:07:31 GMT');
```

The date must be provided as a string in the `HTTP-date` format, as defined in *RFC 2616 section 3.3.1*. This method does not accept `JDate` objects. However, we can use the `JDate::toRFC822()` method to generate a suitable date string.

```
// get JDate object that represents the current date and time
$jdateObject =& JFactory::getDate();

// set the modified date using the JDate object
$document->setModifiedDate($jdateObject->toRFC822());
```

The modified date is used directly to set the `Last-Modified` header field. This field is used primarily for caching purposes. To quote RFC 2616:

> The **Last-Modified** entity-header field value is often used as a cache validator. In simple terms, a cache entry is considered to be valid if the entity has not been modified since the **Last-Modified** value.

 Setting the modified date when caching is disabled will not work.

Creating a PDF in a component

This recipe explains how to create a PDF view in a Joomla! MVC component. Adding PDF views is a relatively quick process, and it significantly improves the functionality of a component.

Getting ready

Like any other view format, we must create a new `JView` subclass to create a PDF view. This should be located in the corresponding view's folder and the file should be named `view.pdf.php`. For example, for the `myview` view in the `mycomponent` component, we create the `components/com_mycomponent/views/myview/view.pdf.php` file, in which we place the `MycomponentViewMyview` class, which extends `JView`.

How to do it...

The first thing we do is override the `display()` method in order to change the PDF document. We modify the document using the mutator methods. The first method changes the document title, this is the title normally shown in the title bar of the PDF viewer.

```
$document->setTitle($title);
```

The next method changes the filename. This is especially useful if the user is likely to save the file, as this will be the default name the user is prompted to save the file as.

```
$document->setName($filename);
```

The next method sets the document description, sometimes referred to as the subject. This should only be a very brief description of the document.

```
$document->setDescription($description);
```

The next method sets the document metadata. Currently, only keywords are supported. *It is possible to set other metadata, but it will not be used in the document.*

```
$document->setMetaData('keywords', $keywords);
```

So far, all of the methods do not print anything to the body of the PDF itself. The next method adds a common header to every page. Note that the header text itself is not formatted.

```
$document->setHeader("My PDF Document Title\nMy Subtitle");
```

Lastly, we can add content to the main body of the PDF document. We achieve this in the normal way by simply outputting the content.

```
echo 'This is my PDF! ';
```

The outputted data can be formatted using some basic HTML tags. The following tags are supported:

Type	Tags
Format	`<b>, <u>, <i>, <strong>, <em>, <sup>, <sub>, <small>, <font>`
Heading	`<h1>, <h2>, <h3>, <h4>, <h5>, <h6>`
Indentation	`<blockquote>`
Linked	`<a>, <img>`
List	`<ol>, <ul>, <li>`
Spacing	`<p>,  , <hr>`
Table	`<table>, <tr>, <td>, <th>`

See also

For information about working with other document types, refer to the remaining recipes in this chapter—*Creating an RSS or Atom feed in a component*, *Outputting a RAW document from a component*, and *Using a custom JDocument in a component (PHP 5 only)*.

Creating an RSS or Atom feed in a component

This recipe describes how to create an **RSS (Really Simple Syndication)** or **Atom** (RFC 4287) feed.

 Joomla! 1.5 does not always generate valid Atom feeds. However, this does not prevent the Atom feeds from working correctly. For more information, refer to `http://validator.w3.org/feed/`.

Getting ready

Like any other view format, we must create a new `JView` subclass to create a feed view. This should be located in the corresponding view's folder and the file should be named `view.feed.php`. For example, for the `myview` view in the `mycomponent` component, we create the `components/com_mycomponent/views/myview/view.feed.php` file. Here, we place the `MycomponentViewMyview` class, which extends `JView`.

Itemized with regular updates

There are only any grounds to create a feed when dealing with itemized data that is updated on a regular basis. For example, the latest news about Joomla! can be found at `http://www.joomla.org/announcements.feed?type=atom`.

How to do it...

Unlike the other document formats, the feed document does not handle direct output. To modify the feed, we must tell the document object everything we want to do. We start by modifying the document itself. At the very least, we need to set the title of the document.

```
// get the document
$document =& JFactory::getDocument();

// set the feed title
$document->setTitle('My Feed');
```

There are other things we might want to set in the feed using the `JDocumentFeed::set()` method. For example, we can set the copyright notice.

```
// set the feed title
$document->set('copyright', '(c) 2009 Packt Publishing');
```

Next, we add the items to the document we want to appear in the feed. To do this, we need to iterate over the data we are adding. In each iteration, we create a new `JFeedItem` object and add it to the document. The following example assumes that `$currentRecord` is the current object we are using to create a feed item:

```
// create new item
$item = new JFeedItem();

// set the required feed item data
$item->set('title',       $currentRecord->name);
$item->set('link',        $currentRecord->url);
$item->set('description', $currentRecord->description);
```

Once we have created a new `JFeedItem` object, we must add it to the document.

```
// add the feed item
$document->addItem($item);
```

How it works...

The values we can set in the document using the `JDocumentFeed::set()` method are detailed in the following table. The RSS and Atom columns show how these values are used by Joomla! to create the RSS and Atom feeds respectively. *Note that these do not necessarily correspond to the RSS and Atom requirements.* For more information, refer to `http://www.rssboard.org/rss-specification` and `http://www.ietf.org/rfc/rfc5023.txt`.

Name	Description	RSS	Atom
category	Category to which the channel belongs	OPTIONAL	NO
copyright	Copyright notice	OPTIONAL	NO
docs	URI to documentation describing the format(1)	OPTIONAL	NO
editor	Name of the managing editor	OPTIONAL (2)	OPTIONAL
editorEmail	Email address of the managing editor	NO	OPTIONAL
image	Object of the `JFeedImage` type that defines an image associated with the feed	OPTIONAL	NO
lastBuildDate	Date when the feed was last built	IGNORED (3)	NO
pubDate	Date when the channel was last published	OPTIONAL	NO
rating	PICS rating; refer to `http://www.w3.org/PICS/`	OPTIONAL	NO
skipDays (4)	Days of the week when an aggregating client—client that combines several feeds—should not bother updating the feed	OPTIONAL	NO
skipHours (5)	Hours when an aggregating client—client that combines several feeds—should not bother updating the feed	OPTIONAL	NO
syndicationURL	Automatically generated URI to Atom feed	IGNORED	IGNORED
ttl	Maximum number of minutes to cache feed	OPTIONAL	NO (6)
webmaster	Email address of the webmaster	OPTIONAL	NO

(1) For RSS this should be `http://www.rssboard.org/rss-specification`

(2) For RSS this should be the email address of the managing editor

(3) Last build date is always now (unless cached)

(4) In the string form `<day>Saturday</day><day>Sunday</day>`

(5) In the string form `<hour>n</hour><hour>n+1</hour>`

(6) Atom uses HTTP caching, for more information refer to the *Controlling client caching of responses* recipe earlier in this chapter

Items in the feed are represented as `JFeedItem` objects. The following table describes values in these objects that we can set. The RSS and Atom columns show how these values are used by Joomla! to create the RSS and Atom feed items respectively. *Note that again these do not necessarily correspond to the RSS and Atom requirements.* For more information, refer to `http://www.rssboard.org/rss-specification` and `http://www.ietf.org/rfc/rfc5023.txt`.

Name	Description	RSS	Atom
author	Name or email of the user who created the item (1)	OPTIONAL	OPTIONAL
authorEmail	Email address of the user who created the item	NO	NO
category	Name of category in which the item resides	OPTIONAL	NO
comments	URI of the page where comments about the item are available	OPTIONAL	NO
description	Description of the item, for example introduction text to a content item	REQUIRED	OPTIONAL
date (2)	Date when the item was published	OPTIONAL	OPTIONAL
enclosure	Object of the `JFeedEnclosure` type that defines a related media object, for example an MPEG	OPTIONAL	OPTIONAL
guid	Globally Unique Identifier (3)	OPTIONAL	NO
link	URI to the full story	REQUIRED	REQUIRED
pubDate	see date instead	NO	NO
source	RSS channel to which the item belongs	NO (4)	NO
title	Name or title of the feed item	REQUIRED	REQUIRED

(1) For Atom this should be an email address, for RSS this should be a username
(2) This is not technically part of `JFeedItem`, but the document renderers use this instead of `pubDate`
(3) Usually easiest to use the URI for the item
(4) Not yet implemented

There's more...

Creating feeds is all well and good, but there is little point in creating them unless the users know how to access them. The following RSS icon was created by Mozilla and has since been accepted as the standardized feed icon for RSS 1.0, RSS 2.0, and Atom 1.0 feeds. For more information, refer to `http://www.mozilla.org/foundation/feed-icon-guidelines/`.

The first place we tend to add links to feeds is in the content of a web page. When we do this, we need only create a normal hyperlink with a few extra attributes. Those attributes are `rel` and `type`, and they should be used as shown in the following code snippet:

```
<a rel="alternate"
   type="application/rss+xml"
   href="<?php echo $rssLink; ?>">Feed</a>
```

Getting rel right

The `rel` attribute is used to identify the relationship between the current document and the link. We use `alternate` when the link specifies an alternative way of viewing the current page. For more information, refer to `http://www.w3.org/TR/html4/struct/links.html#h-12.2`.

Most modern browsers are capable of displaying a feed icon in one of their toolbars if the web site informs the browser that there is an alternative way of viewing the current content as a feed. For example, if we browse to the Joomla! announcements page in Firefox, a feed icon appears in the address bar.

To tell a browser about feeds, we must add a `<link>` tag to the document header. To do this, we use the `JDocumentHTML::addHeadLink()` method. *Note that this only works for HTML documents.*

```
// get the document
$document =& JFactory::getDocument();

// add the link tag
$attribs = array("type" => "application/rss+xml",
                 "title" => "My RSS Feed");
$document->addHeadLink($rssLink, "alternate", "rel", $attribs);
```

The previous example deals explicitly with RSS. Ideally, we should also add an Atom link. This will allow the user to choose his or her preferred format. This will output something like this:

```
<link href="rss.xml"
      rel="alternate"
      type="application/rss+xml"
      title="My RSS Feed" />
```

See also

For information about working with other document types, refer to the previous recipe *Creating a PDF in a component* and the remaining recipes in this chapter, *Outputting a RAW document from a component* and *Using a custom JDocument in a component (PHP 5 only)*.

Outputting a RAW document from a component

This recipe explains how to output a document other than an HTML, PDF, or Feed document. For the purposes of this recipe, we will output a text file.

How to do it...

To output a raw document, we must specify the format in the request. For example:

```
http://example.org/index.php?option=com_mycomponent&format=text
```

The next stage is to create a `JView` subclass capable of handing the format `text`. The view name must be `view.text.php`. This should be located in the relevant view folder. For example, for the `myview` view in the `mycomponent` component, the file will be located in `components/com_mycomponent/views/myview/`. The file must contain the `MycomponentViewMyview` class, which extends `JView`.

```
/**
 * Text view class
 */
class MycomponentViewMyview extends JView {
}
```

In this class, we override the `JView::display()` method. In this method, we change the MIME type of the response and we output the response.

```
/**
 * Text view class
 */
class MycomponentViewMyview extends JView {
    /**
     * Display the view
     *
     * @param string $tpl template file (not used)
     */
    function display($tpl = null) {
```

```
// get the document
$document =& JFactory::getDocument();

// set the MIME type
$document->setMimeEncoding('text/plain');

// get the item we want to display
$item =& $this->get('Data');

// output the text file
echo $item->title . "\n\n" . $item->text;
    }
}
```

How it works...

Selecting the `format` in the request determines the type of document. The table in the chapter introduction describes each of the document types. In this instance, we are invoking `JDocumentRaw` by using a `format` value that none of the other `JDocument` classes can handle.

By default, the `JDocumentRaw` class uses a MIME type of `text/html`. It is perfectly safe to change this to suit the data we are returning to the browser. In the example, we set the MIME type as `text/plain`.

Outputting data in a RAW document is no different from any other view. We simply throw out the data exactly as we want it to be sent in the response.

There's more...

It can be useful to instruct the browser to *download* the response as opposed to displaying it inline. We can achieve this by changing the disposition of the response body.

```
// change disposition of this MIME part
JResponse::setHeader('Content-Disposition', 'attachment');
```

We can use the static `JResponse::setHeader()` method to replace or add any MIME headers to the response. For more information, refer to the official Joomla! API site at `http://api.joomla.org`.

It is possible to use templates in the same way as we do for HTML views. Remember that templates are handled by the `JView::render()` and `JView::loadTemplate()` methods. Thus, there is nothing we need to do differently from an HTML view to use templates in a raw view.

See also

For information about working with other document types, refer to the previous two recipes *Creating a PDF in a component* and *Creating an RSS or Atom feed in a component*, and refer to the next recipe *Using a custom JDocument in a component (PHP 5 only)*.

Using a custom JDocument in a component (PHP 5 only)

This recipe explains how to create and use a custom JDocument in a component. For the purposes of this recipe, we will create a JDocument class to handle **JSON-RPC**.

 This recipe will work only if the server is running PHP 5 or newer because of the way in which objects are handled prior to PHP 5.

 This example uses the PHP JavaScript Object Notation extension. This extension is available only as of PHP 5.2.0 or PECL json 1.2.0. For more information, refer to `http://php.net/manual/book.json.php`.

How to do it...

We start by creating a new JDocument class. We will create a class named JDocumentJSONRPC. Although the location of this class is unimportant, if we are following the normal Joomla! way of doing things, the best place to put this is probably in the `classes` folder in the root of the component's administrative folder. We begin by defining the class. The class extends the abstract JDocument class.

```
/**
 * JDocumentJSONRPC class, provides an easy interface to
 * display a JSON RPC response.
 */
class JDocumentJSONRPC extends JDocument {
    /**
     * Class constructor
     *
     * @param array $options Associative array of options
     */
```

```
function __construct($options = array()) {
    // let the parent class do its bit
    parent::__construct($options);

    // set the MIME type
    $this->setMimeEncoding("application/json");
}
}
```

A JSON-RPC response is always an object, and it always contains jsonrpc, id, and result or error. The value of jsonrpc is static, so we will ignore that for now and add the rest to our class.

```
var $_id     = 0;
var $_result = null;
var $_error  = null;
```

For each of these we supply a mutator that will allow us to set the values.

```
/**
 * Sets the repsonse ID. This value should always be equal
 * to the incoming request ID.
 *
 * @param  int    $id Response ID
 * @access public
 */
function setId($id) {
    $this->_id = intval($id);
}


/**
 * Sets the result of the procedure call.
 *
 * @param  mixed  $result Procedure call result
 * @access public
 */
function setResult($result) {
    // flush the error, we don't need it any more
    $this->_error  = null;

    // define the result
    $this->_result = $result;
}

/**
 * Sets the error
```

```
 *
 * @param   int      $code       Error code
 * @param   string  $message  Error message
 * @access  public
 */
function setError($code, $message) {
    // flush the result, we don't need it any more
    $this->_result = null;

    // define the error object
    $this->_error = new stdClass();
    $this->_error->code = intval($code);
    $this->_error->message = (string)$message;
}
```

The last method we add is where the magic occurs. The `JDocument::render()` method is used to generate the output from the request, and the method returns that output as a string. We need to override this method in order to create our JSON-RPC response.

```
function render($cache = false, $params = array()) {
    // create the response object
    $response            = new stdClass();
    $response->jsonrpc = "2.0";
    $response->id        = $this->_id;

    // set the error or result
    // these are always mutually exclusive
    if (is_object($this->_error)) {
        $response->error = $this->_error;
    } else {
        $response->result = $this->_result;
    }

    // let the parent deal with the headers
    parent::render($cache, $params);

    // return the JSON-RPC response
    return json_encode($response);
}
```

We're nearly there! Only one thing is left to do. Joomla! is built such that the document object is always created from one of the core `JDocument` classes. What we need to do is replace the current Joomla! document object with an instance of our `JDocumentJSONRPC` class.

```
$document =& JFactory::getDocument();
$document = new JDocumentJSONRPC();
```

We are now ready to start using our custom JDocument! For example, we could set an error.

```
$document->setError(-32601, 'Procedure not found.');
```

This will produce the following:

```
{"jsonrpc":"2.0","id":0,"error":{"code":-32601,"message":"Procedure
not found."}}
```

Or on a more positive note, we might have something like this:

```
$result = "Joomla! 1.5 Cookbook";
$document->setResult($result);
```

This will produce the following:

```
{"jsonrpc":"2.0","id":0,"result":"Joomla! 1.5 Cookbook"}
```

How it works...

Jumping in and replacing the Joomla! document object is obviously something that we won't find in the normal Joomla! documentation, especially because it requires PHP 5. But that doesn't make it unadvisable. The much anticipated translation tool **Nooku**, from Joomlatools, uses exactly the same approach to deal with the DBO.

Of course, we must replace the document object as early as possible. Failure to do so could result in unexpected behavior. In fact, the best time and place to do this is at the start of the component's root file. Here's an example:

```
// use the format request value to check for document type
if (JRequest::getCmd("format") == "jsonrpc") {
    // get the class
    require_once($pathToJDocumentJSONRPC_Class);

    // replace the document
    $document =& JFactory::getDocument();
    $document =  new JDocumentJSONRPC();
}
```

Notice how we use the format request value. This is the same value that is used to normally determine the JDocument class we want to use. It also happens to mean that the document we are replacing will be of the type JDocumentRAW.

There's more...

Our example explicitly uses JSON-RPC. So, is there a way we can use the example class in the real world? Indeed there is. But one thing is missing—there is no parsing of the JSON-RPC request.

 All examples in this recipe are based on the proposed JSON-RPC 2.0 specification. For more information, refer to `http://groups.google.com/group/json-rpc/web/json-rpc-1-2-proposal`.

JSON-RPC can accept POST and GET requests. However, POST is the preferred format. The following example function `getJSON_RPC_Request()` deals with the POST request data by reading it from `php://input` and decoding it. The example also checks to make sure the request data is valid.

 We use `php://input` as opposed to `$HTTP_RAW_POST_DATA` because `$HTTP_RAW_POST_DATA` is environment specific.

```php
/**
 * Decodes JSON-RPC POST request data
 *
 * @return mixed request object or false on fail
 */
function getJSON_RPC_Request() {
    // only deals with POST requests
    if (JRequest::getVar('REQUEST_METHOD', null, 'SERVER') != 'POST')
    {
        $document->setError(-32600, 'Invalid Request.');
        return false;
    }

    // get raw POST data and decode
    $rawRequest = file_get_contents('php://input');
    $request    = json_decode($rawRequest);
    // check request was successfully decoded
    if ($request == null) {
        $document->setError(-32700, 'Parse Error.');
        return false;
    }
    // check request is an object
    if (!is_object($request)) {
        $document->setError(-32600, 'Invalid Request.');
```

```
        return false;
    }
    // check the request object is valid
    $vars = get_object_vars($request);
    if (!array_key_exists('method', $vars) ||
        !array_key_exists('jsonrpc', $vars)) {
        $document->setError(-32600, 'Invalid Request.');
        return false;
    }
    // set the response ID if an ID was provided
    if (array_key_exists('id', $vars)) {
        $document->setId($request->id);
    }
    // all done!
    return $request;
}
```

This ultimately results in a `$request` object that defines what we should be doing. If an error has been set in the document, we know that we should not attempt to continue because the request is illegal.

See also

For information about working with other document types, refer to the previous three recipes—*Creating a PDF in a component, Creating an RSS or Atom feed in a component,* and *Outputting a RAW document from a component.*

8
Customizing the Backend

This chapter contains the following recipes:

- ▶ Disabling the menu bar
- ▶ Setting the toolbar title and icon
- ▶ Adding common item manipulation buttons to the toolbar
- ▶ Adding common itemized manipulation buttons to the toolbar
- ▶ Adding custom buttons to the toolbar
- ▶ Adding spacers and dividers to the toolbar
- ▶ Adding a help system to a component
- ▶ Creating a filter header for tabular data in an MVC component
- ▶ Filtering tabular data in an MVC component
- ▶ Creating toggle-enabled order column headers for tabular data in an MVC component
- ▶ Ordering tabular data in an MVC component

Introduction

This chapter looks at the common parts of the backend that are manipulated by components. Some of the recipes also apply to the frontend. For example, the filtering and ordering recipes apply to both the backend and the frontend.

To help put this into context, we will use an example. The **Contact Manager** is described by Joomla! as "*allowing you to add contact information to your Joomla! site*". The following screenshot depicts the **Contact Manager** displaying all of the current contacts:

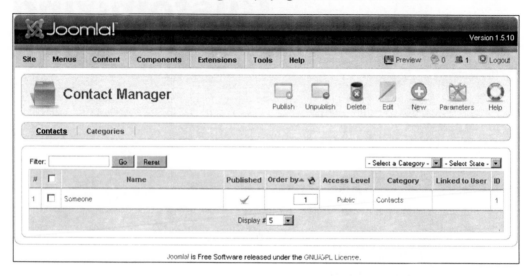

Starting from the top left corner, we see the header (which includes the menu bar and the header modules), the toolbar (which includes an icon, title, and a selection of buttons), the submenu, and the component output. In this instance, the component output consists of three filter options and a table that is currently ordered by the **Order by** column.

Disabling the menu bar

This recipe explains how to disable the menu bar. This is usually a good idea when users are editing something which is checked out, or are halfway through a step-by-step process.

How to do it...

To disable the menu bar, we set the request value of `hidemainmenu` to 1. It is generally best to do this programmatically as and when it is required.

```
// disable the menu bar
JRequest::setVar('hidemainmenu', 1);
```

Alternatively, we can specify this in the request. However, this is less desirable because it leaves us with less control over the status of the menu bar.

```
index.php?option=com_mycomponent&task=sometask&hidemainmenu=1
```

How it works...

Disabling the menu bar prevents users from navigating away from the current page, or at least, navigating away from the current page using the menu bar. The following screenshot is an example in which the menu bar is enabled:

And here is the same menu bar, but this time disabled. Notice that the menus are now grayed out and the links in the modules have been removed. However, the **Preview** button remains active. This is because it opens a new window and, therefore, will not interfere with the current course of events.

See also

Customizing the toolbar is the next logical step. The next recipe, *Setting the toolbar title and icon*, begins by changing the toolbar title and icon.

Setting the toolbar title and icon

This recipe explains how to set the toolbar title and how to change the icon that appears next to the title.

How to do it...

To change the title, we use the static `JToolBarHelper::title()` method.

```
JToolBarHelper::title('My Title');
```

This changes the title and sets the icon to the generic package, as shown in the following screenshot:

 My Title

We can change the icon by additionally specifying a CSS class suffix.

```
// set the toolbar title and icon suffix
JToolBarHelper::title('My Title', 'myicon');
```

Doing this means that we will also need to add some CSS.

```
// create the CSS
$iconStyle = '.icon-48-myicon { background-image: url(components/
                      com_mycomponent/assets/icon-48-myicon.png) }';

// add the CSS to the document
$document =& JFactory::getDocument();
$document->addStyleDeclaration($iconStyle);
```

Now we get a custom title and a custom icon, as shown in the following screenshot:

 My Title

How it works...

Setting the title is easy enough, but what about all the CSS? The second parameter we pass to `JToolBarHelper::title()` is appended to the class name `icon-48-`. In our example, we define the second parameter as `myicon`. Therefore, the name of the class is `icon-48-myicon`.

The sole purpose of this CSS class is to define the icon. This is achieved by using the `background-image` style property. The image should be 48px squared. In our example, we have used a custom image located in our component's `assets` folder.

Once we have defined our CSS, we add it to the global document object. In our example, we added our custom CSS by using the `addStyleDeclaration()` method. If we prefer, we can define the CSS in a separate CSS file and add this to the document using the `addStyleSheet()` method. For more information about adding CSS to a page, refer to Chapter 6, *Interaction and Styling*.

The next four recipes explain how to add buttons and spacers/dividers to the toolbar.

Adding common item manipulation buttons to the toolbar

This recipe explains how to add buttons to the toolbar that are commonly used to manipulate an item of data, that is, a record in a database. *Toolbar buttons should nearly always be used in preference to form buttons.*

Getting ready

The common buttons require the existence of a form named `adminForm`. The buttons described in this recipe require the hidden input field `task` to be present in the form.

How to do it...

To add a button to the toolbar, we use the `JToolBarHelper` helper class. Exactly how we add a button depends on the type of button we want to add. The following example adds a new `addNew` button.

```
// add a new button to the toolbar
JToolBarHelper::addNew();
```

Easy as pie! This gives us the following toolbar:

Now for some more! These three buttons often occur together on pages where we are editing or creating items. The buttons are **Save**, **Apply**, and **Cancel**.

```
// add save, apply, and cancel buttons to the toolbar
JToolBarHelper::save();
JToolBarHelper::apply();
JToolBarHelper::cancel();
```

This gives us the following toolbar:

The next two buttons also often occur together:

```
// add publish and unpublish buttons to the toolbar
JToolBarHelper::publish();
JToolBarHelper::unpublish();
```

This gives us the following toolbar:

How it works...

All of these methods accept two optional parameters. These are the following:

1. The task we want to execute.
2. The name that is displayed beneath the button.

When a user clicks on a button, the task is transferred to the `task` field in the HTML form `adminForm`. This form is then submitted.

There's more...

The fact that we can override the task when we add the buttons to the toolbar means that the buttons are not restrictive. For example, by default, the `addNew` button has a default task of `add`. We could easily change this to something like `new`.

```
// add a new button to the toolbar
JToolBarHelper::addNew('new');
```

This can be useful when, for example, we want several `addNew` buttons, each designed to add something different. In this instance, we will also want to change the text of each button:

```
// 3 add new buttons
JToolBarHelper::addNew('newPaper',    'New Paper');
JToolBarHelper::addNew('newScissors', 'New Scissors');
JToolBarHelper::addNew('newStone',    'New Stone');
```

This gives us the following toolbar:

> We do not need to use JText to translate the button labels, as this is done automatically.

See also

The next recipe describes how to add buttons designed specifically for working with itemized data. To add buttons that fall out of the scope of those provided for us, refer to the *Adding custom buttons to the toolbar* recipe.

Adding common itemized manipulation buttons to the toolbar

This recipe explains how to add buttons to the toolbar that are commonly used to manipulate itemized data, that is, several records in a database. *Toolbar buttons should nearly always be used in preference to form buttons.*

Getting ready

The common buttons require the existence of a form named `adminForm`. The buttons described in this recipe require that the hidden input fields, `task` and `boxchecked`, are present in the form. The `boxchecked` field is a counter that defines the number of selected items, this should be 0 by default. This will be automatically maintained if we use the JHTML types, `grid.checkedOut` or `grid.id`, to create the item checkboxes.

How to do it...

To add a button to the toolbar, we use the `JToolBarHelper` helper class. Exactly how we add a button depends on the type of button we want to add. The following example adds **Publish** and **Unpublish** buttons to the toolbar:

```
// add publishing buttons to the toolbar
JToolBarHelper::publishList();
JToolBarHelper::unpublishList();
```

Easy as pie! This gives us the following toolbar:

This next example adds an **Edit** button to the toolbar.

```
// add edit button to the toolbar
JToolBarHelper::editList();
```

This gives us the following toolbar:

This last example adds a **Delete** button to the toolbar.

```
// add edit button to the toolbar
JToolBarHelper::deleteList();
```

This gives us the following toolbar:

How it works...

When a user presses a button, the task is transferred to the `task` field in the HTML form `adminForm`. This form is then submitted. The buttons that deal exclusively with itemized data (list buttons) work in a slightly different manner to normal buttons. These buttons require items to be selected in the itemized data before they work. The previously mentioned `boxchecked` field is used to determine this. In instances where this field indicates that no items are selected, we will receive a JavaScript alert if we press a list button.

There's more...

Except for the `deleteList()` method, all of these methods accept two optional parameters. These parameters are:

1. The task that we want to execute.
2. The name that is displayed beneath the button.

For an example of how to use this in practice, refer to the previous recipe.

So what about the `deleteList()` method? It has three optional parameters:

1. An optional confirmation message.
2. The task that we want to execute.
3. The name that is displayed beneath the button.

This is very similar to the others!

The extra parameter—the confirmation message—is a message that is used in a JavaScript *are you sure* style confirmation. If we do not provide this, no confirmation message will be displayed.

See also

To learn about adding non-itemized, data-orientated buttons to the toolbar, refer to the previous recipe, *Adding common item manipulation buttons to the toolbar*. To add buttons that fall out of the scope of those provided for us, refer to the *Adding custom buttons to the toolbar* recipe that follows.

Adding custom buttons to the toolbar

This recipe explains how to add a custom button to the toolbar. Adding custom buttons is only necessary when none of the predefined buttons are suitable. For more information about the predefined buttons, refer to the official Joomla! API web site at `http://api.joomla.org`.

Getting ready

The common buttons require the existence of a form named `adminForm`. The buttons described in this recipe require the hidden input field `task` to be present in the form. When creating custom buttons that deal with itemized data, the hidden input field `boxchecked` is also required. The `boxchecked` field is a counter that defines the number of selected items, this should be 0 by default. This will be automatically maintained if we use the JHTML types, `grid.checkedOut` or `grid.id`, to create the item checkboxes.

How to do it...

We will start with a basic button. This includes $task (the value of task to use in the request), $icon (the CSS suffix for the icon class), and $label (the text displayed underneath the button).

```
// define button
$task  = 'doit';
$icon  = 'myicon';
$label = 'My Button';
// add custom button
JToolBarHelper::custom($task, $icon, '', $label);
```

Notice how the third parameter we pass is an empty string. This is because the third parameter, which is used to determine the *on mouse over* icon, is not actually used. The resultant toolbar is shown in the following screenshot:

 My Title

My Button

We're not quite there yet. Next, we need to consider the context of the button. By default, the button is designed to be used with a list of items in which at least one of the items must be selected for the button to work. If we don't want this, we must provide the fifth parameter $listSelect as false.

```
// add custom button for non lists
JToolBarHelper::custom($task, $icon, '', $label, false);
```

We can choose whether or not the menu bar on the next page should be enabled. This requires a hidden hidemainmenu form field. By default, the menu will be enabled. However, the use of this parameter is not advisable. A more manageable solution is described in the *Disabling the menu bar* recipe at the start of this chapter.

```
// add custom button for non lists that disables the menu bar
JToolBarHelper::custom($task, $icon, '', $label, false, true);
```

Now we can finish off the button! To add an icon, we use the CSS class. This is in the form icon-32-suffix. For example, using the previous code, the class will be icon-32-myicon. The following example adds an icon to the document:

```
// define style for button icon-32-myicon
$style = '.icon-32-myicon { background-image: url(components/
                            com_mycomponent/assets/icon-32-myicon.png); }';
// add style to the document
$document =& JFactory::getDocument();
$document->addStyleDeclaration($style);
```

For example, the following uses a clock icon:

There's more...

For even more power over your button, check out the JToolbar class. A global instance of this class is used to handle the toolbar. We can access this object using the static getInstance() method.

```
// get the toolbar
$toolbar =& JToolBar::getInstance('toolbar');
```

This class includes the appendButton() and prependButton() methods. These methods enable us to add buttons to the start and end of the toolbar. This is an example:

```
$toolbar->appendButton($buttonType, $icon, $label, $task, $isList,
                                                     $hideMenu);
```

Perhaps the most impressive trick this class has up its sleeve is the ability to define folders in which custom JButton handlers reside. The JButton classes are used to render buttons. The following table describes the built-in types, all of which are located in the libraries/joomla/html/toolbar/button folder:

Button	Description	Helper methods
Confirm	Standard button with a JavaScript confirmation dialog	
Custom	Entirely custom button, accepts raw HTML	JToolbarHelper::custom()
		JToolbarHelper::customX()
Help	Link to help files—third-party component help systems are normally locally stored files—for more information, refer to the *Adding a help system to a component* recipe	JToolbarHelper::help()
Link	Simple URL	
Popup	Modal window (uses an iframe)	
Separator	Visual separator	JToolbarHelper::spacer()
		JToolbarHelper::divider()
Standard	Most common type of button, accepts name, text, task, list, and hideMenu	

See also

For information about adding predefined buttons to the toolbar, refer to the two previous recipes, *Adding common item manipulation buttons to the toolbar* and *Adding common itemized manipulation buttons to the toolbar.*

Adding spacers and dividers to the toolbar

This recipe explains how to add spacers and dividers to the toolbar. This can be useful because it provides logical separation of buttons.

How to do it...

To add a spacer to the toolbar, we use the `JToolBarHelper::spacer()` method.

```
// add a spacer
JToolBarHelper::spacer();
```

For example, we might want to add a spacer between the button groups, **Save**, **Apply**, and **Cancel**, and **Publish** and **Unpublish**:

Or, we can add a divider by using the `JToolBarHelper::divider()` method.

```
// add a divider
JToolBarHelper::divider();
```

This is shown in the following screenshot:

See also

For information about adding the buttons to the toolbar in the first instance, refer to the previous three recipes.

Adding a help system to a component

This recipe explains how to add a help system to the backend of a component. This type of help system is intended for administrators.

How to do it...

Unlike the core Joomla! component help, third-party component help systems are stored locally as part of the component. We start by creating a folder named `help` in the component's administrative folder. For example, for the `com_mycomponent` component, this would be `administrator/components/com_mycomponent/help`.

In this folder, we must create a folder named `en-GB`. This is where all of the help files will reside. Help files are basic HTML files...nothing fancy! It is normal to name these using a dot notation to separate areas of interest.

The following example contains four help files. The name of each file corresponds to its **reference**. For instance, the reference for the `some.subject.html` file is `some.subject`. The `index.html` file should always be created even if we do not want a help reference named `index`. Creating this file prevents users from snooping (getting file lists) through the help files.

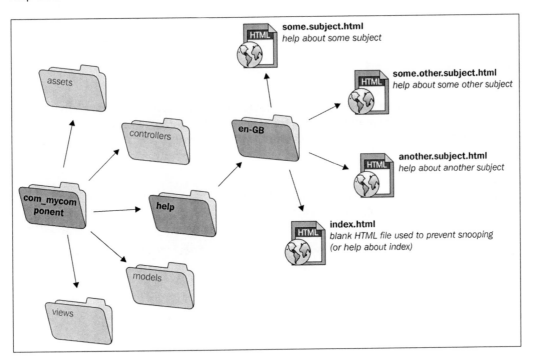

some.subject.html
help about some subject

some.other.subject.html
help about some other subject

another.subject.html
help about another subject

index.html
blank HTML file used to prevent snooping (or help about index)

To use the help files, we add a help button to the toolbar using the static `JToolbarHelper::help()` method. This method accepts two parameters, the file reference and `true`.

```
// add help button for some subject
JToolbarHelper::help('some.subject', true);
```

This gives us the following toolbar:

When we click on the button, we get a pop-up window in which the relevant help file is loaded. *Note that if the file does not exist, we will receive a standard 404 error.*

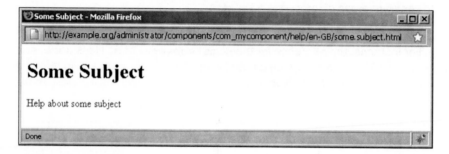

How it works...

In the previous section, we created the `en-GB` folder within the `help` folder. We do this because help files can be created for different languages, the default language being British English or rather `en-GB`. To create help for other languages, simply add the language folder and the translated files.

 Joomla! automatically checks if a folder for the current language exists. If it does not, `en-GB` is assumed.

It is best to keep the structure of the help files very simple. That is to say, we should stick to the basic HTML tags such as `<h1>`, `<hr/>`, and `<p>`. This will make the files easier to manage.

Plain HTML files are not very attractive. Adding some basic styling can increase the readability of the files tenfold. A good place to begin is with the CSS file located in the default Joomla! administrative template `khepri`. In fact, if we aren't doing anything fancy, simply linking to this file should be enough!

```
<link href="../../../../templates/khepri/css/template.css"
      rel="stylesheet"
      type="text/css" />
```

Use the assets folder to store media files

If we require any media files, for example a screenshot in our help files, it is best to place these in the component's `assets` folder. This gives us central control of media files and prevents duplication for the various languages.

Creating a filter header for tabular data in an MVC component

This recipe explains how to create a filter header for tabular data in a Joomla! MVC component. For example, when we look at the core **Contact Manager** component, above the list of contacts, we can see three filters—a plain-text search filter, a category filter, and a state filter.

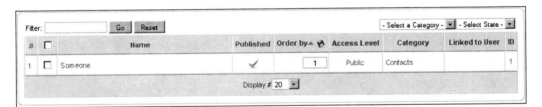

How to do it...

The drop-down selection filters are referred to as **lists**. We create these in the `JView` class and assign them to the view in an array named lists.

The first thing we need to do is create the lists. It is common to use JHTML to achieve this. We'll start with an easy one. We will name the first list as **state**. This list determines the publishing state of the filter, that is, published or unpublished. For this, we need the current state of the list.

```
// get the application
$app =& JFactory::getApplication();

// get the current value for filter_state
$filterState = $app->getUserStateFromRequest('com_mycomponent.
                        filterState', 'filter_state', '', 'word');
```

Step two is to create the lists array and add the state list.

```
// create lists array
$lists = array();

// add state filter
$lists['state'] = JHTML::_('grid.state', $filterState);
```

Now let's move on to a more complex filter, or rather a bespoke filter. Here we create a list using select.genericlist. We start in the same way, that is, by determining the current value for this filter:

```
// get the current value for filter_bespoke
$filterBespoke = $app->getUserStateFromRequest
        ('com_mycomponent.filterBespoke', 'filter_bespoke', '', 'word');
```

Now we need some values represented as objects to add to the drop down. We can create these objects ourselves, or we can use the JHTML type select.option. For the purpose of this example, we will hardcode these objects.

```
// no selection (default)
$optionNone = JHTML::_('select.option', '', JText::_('SELECT CHEESE
                                                OR CHALK'));

// some option for cheese
$optionOne = JHTML::_('select.option', 'cheese', JText::_('CHEESE'));

// some option for chalk
$optionTwo = JHTML::_('select.option', 'chalk', JText::_('CHALK'));

// put it all together!
$options= array($optionNone, $optionOne, $optionTwo);
```

We often filter based on dynamic data. Another way of generating this array would have been to execute a database query using the `JDatabase::loadObjectList()` method.

Now we generate the drop-down list and add it to `$lists`.

```
$lists['bespoke'] = JHTML::_('select.genericlist',
                             $options,
                             'filter_bespoke',
                             'class="inputbox"
                             onchange="submitform();"',
                             'value',
                             'text',
                             $filterBespoke);
```

If we want to include a free text filter, we also add this to `$lists`.

```
// get the search string
$search = $app->getUserStateFromRequest('com_mycomponent.search',
                                        'search', '', 'string');

$search = JString::strtolower($search);

// add to the lists
$lists['search'] = $search;
```

Once we have added all of the necessary lists to the `$lists` variable, we assign the array to the view.

```
$this->assignRef('lists', $lists);
```

Now we can move on to the layout! The corresponding layout should reside in the tmpl folder. *In most instances, this will be* `default.php`. Here we output the lists above the tabular data, but still within the form.

```
<table>
    <tr>
        <td width="100%">
            <?php echo JText::_('Filter'); ?>:
            <input type="text"
                   name="search"
                   id="search"
                   value="<?php echo $this->lists['search'];?>"
                   class="text_area"
                   onchange="document.adminForm.submit();" />
            <button onclick="this.form.submit();">
                <?php echo JText::_("GO"); ?>
            </button>
```

```
        <button
         onclick="document.getElementById('search').value='';
         this.form.getElementById('filter_state').value='';
         this.form.getElementById('filter_bespoke').value='';
         this.form.submit();">
            <?php echo JText::_('RESET'); ?>
        </button>
    </td>
    <td nowrap="nowrap">
        <?php echo $this->lists['bespoke'];?>
        <?php echo $this->lists['state'];?>
    </td>
  </tr>
</table>
```

This should give us a header that looks something like this:

How it works...

The `getUserStateFromRequest()` application method gets a value from the request. If the value is not defined in the request, it gets the last known value from the state data. If there is no previous state data for this value, a default value defined in the method call is used. Thus, filtering options are **stateful**, that is to say, they are remembered between requests.

In our example, we extract three values using this method. `$filterState` is defined by the state value `com_mycomponent.filterState`, this can be overridden by the request value `filter_state`. If neither are known the default value, a null string, is assumed. The value is cast as a `word`.

`$filterBespoke` is similar. `$filterBespoke` is defined by the state value `com_mycomponent.filterBespoke`, this can be overridden by the request value `filter_bespoke`. If neither are known the default value, a null string, is assumed. The value is cast as a `word`.

`$search` is also similar. `$search` is defined by the state value `com_mycomponent.search`, this can be overridden by the request value `search`. If neither are known the default value, a null string, is assumed. The value is cast as a `string`, and converted to lowercase, *this is because free text searches are normally case insensitive*.

The `JHTML` type `grid.state` provides a handy shortcut for generating a publishing state filter. The actual filter is named `filter_state`, hence this is also the name of the request value we use when retrieving this value using the application method `getUserStateFromRequest()`.

The bespoke filter that we generated using the JHTML type list.genericlist required more work. We had to generate the options as objects, define the name of the user control as filter_bespoke, set the CSS class and add some JavaScript, tell list.genericlist the names of the value and text object attributes to create the options, and finally, specify the currently selected option.

The JavaScript is especially important. The submitform() method causes the current form, document.adminForm, to be submitted when a different option is selected. This means that the displayed filter is always the current filter.

That leaves us with the free text search box. Adjacent to this box are two buttons—**Go** and **Reset**. The **Go** button applies the entered filter text. The **Reset** button resets the entire filter. *It is easy to forget that this should reset everything in the filter, and not just the search box.*

The search box is a straightforward textbox named search and displays the lists value search. The **Go** button submits the form using the JavaScript this.form.submit() function. The **Reset** button uses JavaScript to reset each filter user control. In our example, this is search, filter_state, and filter_bespoke.

See also

For information about how to implement the filter, refer to the next recipe, *Filtering tabular data in an MVC component.*

Filtering tabular data in an MVC component

This recipe explains how to filter tabular data in a Joomla! MVC component. This recipe uses the filter header described in the previous recipe to define what is to be filtered.

How to do it...

We filter data in the concrete JModel. The default method used to get the tabular data from a model is getData(). It is a good idea to use a cache for this method response. This will prevent duplicate queries being made to the server. To do this, we need to add a class instance variable.

```
/**
 * Cached getData response
 *
 * @var array
 */
var $_data = null;
```

Now we can build the `getData()` method.

```
/**
 * Get the data from the model
 *
 * @access public
 * @return array
 */
function getData() {
    // only load data if it is not cached
    if (empty($this->_data)) {
        // prepare the SQL and load the data into the cache
        $query       = $this->_buildQuery();
        $limitstart  = $this->getState('limitstart');
        $limit       = $this->getState('limit');
        $this->_data = $this->_getList($query,
                                       $limistart,
                                       $limit);
    }

    return $this->_data;
}
```

Notice how we use the `limitstart` and `limit` model state values to restrict the result set. This is for pagination. For more information, refer to Chapter 6, *Interaction and Styling*.

The query that is executed is built using the protected `_buildQuery()` method. In the following example, we build a `SELECT` query that will get data from the `#__mycomponent_table` table.

```
/**
 * Generates the SQL required to the get the data
 *
 * @access protected
 * @return string
 */
function _buildQuery() {
    $db =& JFactory::getDBO();
    $table = $db->nameQuote('#__mycomponent_table');
    $query = 'SELECT * ' .
            "FROM $table " .
            $this->_buildQueryWhere() . ' ' .
            $this->_buildQueryOrderBy();

    return $query;
}
```

This method is actually quite simple. The only important thing to remember is to use the database object to quote the table name for security reasons.

This method calls two other protected methods, _buildQueryWhere() and _buildQueryOrderBy(). The first of these methods is used to build a WHERE clause where the filtering takes place. The second is used to build an ORDER BY clause. For information about this method, refer to the next recipe, *Ordering tabular data in an MVC component*.

Let's start with an outline for the _buildQueryWhere() method.

```
/**
 * Gets the WHERE clause for the getData query.
 *
 * @access protected
 * @return string
 */
function _buildQueryWhere() {
    // get the application
    $app =& JFactory::getApplication();

    // get the state filter (publishing)
    $state = $app->getUserStateFromRequest(
            'com_mycomponent.filterState', 'filter_state', '', 'word');

    // get the bespoke filter value
    $bespoke = $app->getUserStateFromRequest(
        'com_mycomponent.filterBespoke', 'filter_bespoke', '', 'word');

    // get the free text search filter
    $search = $app->getUserStateFromRequest('com_mycomponent.search',
                                            'search', '', 'string');

    $search = JString::strtolower($search);

    // prepare to build WHERE clause as an array
    $where = array();
    $db    =& JFactory::getDBO();

    // @todo build the WHERE clause

}
```

This initial outline retrieves the values we will use in the WHERE clause. At the end of this method, we must add the code that will build the WHERE clause based on the retrieved values. We'll start with the free text search:

```
// check if we are performing a free text search
if (strlen($search)) {
    // make string safe for searching
    $search = '%' . $db->getEscaped($search, true) . '%';
    $search = $db->Quote($search, false);
    $field  = $db->nameQuote('name');

    // add search to $where array
    $where[] = "LOWER($field) LIKE $search";
}
```

Building secure software is a fundamental part of code engineering. Notice how we pay special attention to the value of $search. This example assumes that we are searching the #__mycomponent_table.name field.

The next filter we will deal with is $bespoke. Note that the value of this must be chalk or cheese.

```
// check if we are filtering based on bespoke
if ($bespoke == 'chalk') {
    // items must be chalk
    $where[] = $db->nameQuote('bespoke') . ' = ' .
                $db->Quote('chalk');
} elseif ($bespoke == 'cheese') {
    // items must be cheese
    $where[] = $db->nameQuote('bespoke') . ' = ' .
                $db->Quote('cheese');
}
```

Next, we'll look at the published state filter. Here we assume that we are using the standard publishing field published.

```
// check if we are filtering based on published state
if ($state == 'P') {
    // items must be published
    $where[] = $db->nameQuote('published') . ' = 1';
} elseif ($state == 'U') {
    // items must not be published
    $where[] = $db->nameQuote('published') . ' = 0';
}
```

Okay, almost there! We now have an array full of little WHERE condition goodies. All we have to do is pull these conditions together to create the final WHERE clause.

```
if (count($where)) {
    // building from array
    $where = ' WHERE '. implode(' AND ', $where);
} else {
    // array is empty... nothing to do!
    $where = '';
}

// all done, send the result back
return $where;
```

How it works...

All of the real legwork is performed in the protected _buildQueryWhere() method. So precisely how does this method work?

Initially, this method retrieves the values we want to use to filter the data. We use the getUserStateFromRequest() application method rather than JRequest to get these values because the filter is stateful, that is, it retains its state between requests. The application getUserStateFromRequest() method is provided with four parameters—the name of the state data, the name of the request value, the default value, and the type of value. The value of $search is converted to lowercase. This is because we want the search to be case insensitive.

We build a $where array in which we store the WHERE conditions. *Using an array makes it easier to deal with the AND operators.*

We take extra care when building the free text search condition. This is necessary for security reasons. For more information about securely using LIKE in a query, refer to Chapter 2. In our example, we have made the search case insensitive by forcing all of the comparison strings to lowercase. In MySQL, case sensitivity depends on string format, character encoding, and the string comparison functions we opt to use. For more information, refer to http://dev.mysql.com/doc/refman/5.0/en/case-sensitivity.html.

When we deal with $bespoke, we make sure that we only use the value of this filter if it is one of the expected values, chalk or cheese. Using the raw value of this filter could potentially lead to code injection.

Similarly, when we deal with the published state, we check for the expected values. However, it is true that we also need to do this because the values supplied by the JHTML type grid.state do not correlate directly to the values used in the database.

The method is wrapped up at the end by combining all of the WHERE conditions!

Use a deeper hierarchy to store filter state data if your component contains several different views of tabular data that can be filtered, for example `com_mycomponent.myentity.filterState` and `com_mycomponent.myotherentity.filterState`.

See also

For information about creating a filter header for tabular data, refer to the previous recipe, *Creating a filter header for tabular data in an MVC component*.

To see how to implement the `_buildQueryOrderBy()` method, refer to the last recipe in this chapter, *Ordering tabular data in an MVC component*.

Creating toggle-enabled order column headers for tabular data in an MVC component

This recipe explains how to order tabular data using column headers to toggle between different orders. For example, we can see in the following screenshot that the tabular data is ordered by the **Term** column and it is **ascending**:

How to do it...

We must assign the current ordering options to the view. We do this in the view's `display()` method. Like normal filters, the ordering options are also added to lists, as described in the *Creating a filter header for tabular data in an MVC component* recipe earlier in this chapter.

We append `order` and `orderDirection` to the lists. These are determined using the application `getUserStateFromRequest()` method. *Note that* `$defaultOrderField`, *used in the following example, should be the name of the field on which we want to order the data by default:*

```
// get the application
$app =& JFactory::getApplication();

// get the current field with which to order the results
$lists['order'] = $app->getUserStateFromRequest('com_mycomponent.
            filterOrder', 'filter_order', $defaultOrderField, 'word');

// get the direction in which to order the results
$lists['orderDirection'] = $app->getUserStateFromRequest(
            'com_mycomponent.filterOrderDirection', 'filter_order_Dir',
                                            'DESC', 'cmd');

if (strtoupper($lists['orderDirection']) == 'ASC') {
    $lists['orderDirection'] = 'ASC';
} else {
    $lists['orderDirection'] = 'DESC';
}
```

If we have not already done so, once we have added all of the necessary lists to the `$lists` variable, we assign the array to the view.

```
$this->assignRef('lists', $lists);
```

Now we can move on to the layout. The corresponding layout should reside in the `tmpl` folder. *In most instances, this will be* `default.php`. The HTML table in which the tabular data is displayed contains headings for each column. To make these toggles for ordering, we use the JHTML type `grid.sort`. In the following example, we use the JHTML type `grid.sort` to create the column header for the **Term** column.

```
<th class="title">
    <?php echo JHTML::_('grid.sort',
                    'Term',
                    'term',
                    $this->lists['orderDirection'],
                    $this->lists['order']); ?>
</th>
```

When we call the JHTML type `grid.sort`, we provide four parameters. They are as follows:

1. The name of the column we want to display in the column (we do not need to use JText to translate this value).
2. The name of the field this column uses to order the data.
3. The current direction in which the data is ordered.
4. The name of the field that is currently being used to order the data.

The toggles that are created within the table column headers require two hidden input fields to be present in the form. These are `filter_order` and `filter_order_Dir`.

```
<input type="hidden"
       name="filter_order"
       value="<?php echo $this->lists['order']; ?>" />
<input type="hidden"
       name="filter_order_Dir"
       value="<?php echo $this->lists['orderDirection']; ?>" />
```

See also

The next recipe, *Ordering tabular data in an MVC component*, explains how to apply the ordering options to a concrete `JModel`.

Ordering tabular data in an MVC component

This recipe explains how to order tabular data. For information about creating tabular order user controls, refer to the previous recipe.

Getting ready

This recipe uses the concrete `JModel` method `buildQuery()` described in the *Filtering tabular data in an MVC component* recipe. It is necessary to implement this method first. Note that although ordering and filtering are not the same, they tend to occur in unison.

How to do it...

The `buildQuery()` method calls the protected `_buildQueryOrderBy()` method. This method determines the `ORDER BY` clause. There are two aspects to ordering—what to order by and the direction in which to order. We start by creating the method.

```
/**
 * Builds an ORDER BY clause for the getData query
 *
 * @return string
 */
function _buildQueryOrderBy() {
    // @todo build method
}
```

Now for the inner working of the method! To create the ORDER BY clause, we will need the application object and the database object.

```
// get the application and DBO
$app =& JFactory::getApplication();
$db  =& JFactory::getDBO();
```

The field on which to order is determined by the stateful input value `filter_order`. As this is stateful, we use the `getUserStateFromRequest()` application method.

```
// determine what to order by
$defaultOrderField = 'field_name';
$order = $app->getUserStateFromRequest('com_mycomponent.
        filterOrder', 'filter_order', $defaultOrderField, 'word');
```

 For extra security, check that the value of order is equal to the name of a field on which we want to allow ordering.

The direction of the ordering is also stateful. It is defined by the input value `filter_order_Dir`.

```
// get the direction in which to order the results
$orderDirection = $app->getUserStateFromRequest('com_mycomponent.
        filterOrderDirection', 'filter_order_Dir', 'ASC', 'cmd');
// make sure direction is ASC or DESC is
if (strtoupper($lists['orderDirection']) == 'ASC') {
    $orderDirection = 'ASC';
} else {
    $orderDirection = 'DESC';
}
```

We ensure that the value of $orderDirection is always ASC or DESC (ascending or descending). The value defaults to ascending (that is, increases in value). For example, the lists 1, 2, 3 and A, B, C are in an ascending order.

Almost done! All we need to do is put the pieces together.

```
// return the ORDER BY clause
return ' ORDER BY ' . $db->nameQuote($order) .
                        " $orderDirection ";
```

It is important to use the JDatabase::nameQuote() method for security reasons. For more information, refer to Chapter 2, *Keeping Extensions Secure*.

> Use a deeper hierarchy to store the order state data if your component contains several different views of tabular data that can be ordered, for example `com_mycomponent.myentity.filterOrder` and `com_mycomponent.myotherentity.filterOrderDirection`.

See also

For information about creating toggle-enabled column headings, refer to the previous recipe, *Creating toggle-enabled order column headers for tabular data in an MVC component*.

To see how the `_buildQueryOrderBy()` method slots into the bigger picture, refer to the *Filtering tabular data in an MVC component* recipe earlier in this chapter.

9
Keeping it Extensible and Modular

This chapter contains the following recipes:

- ▶ Loading plugins
- ▶ Invoking a plugin
- ▶ Creating a Joomla! search plugin
- ▶ Creating your own library and import function
- ▶ Installing a plugin programmatically during a component installation
- ▶ Managing categories the easy way
- ▶ Defining JParameters using XML
- ▶ Creating a `JParameter` object
- ▶ Rendering a `JParameter` object
- ▶ Saving `JParameter` data
- ▶ Getting and setting values in a `JParameter` object
- ▶ Defining your own `JParameter` type

Introduction

CBD (Component Based Development) is a popular approach used in modern software systems to create flexible and reusable code. Even if you're not familiar with the term, you will be familiar with the approach, as Joomla! relies on it!

When we talk about extensions in Joomla!, we are actually referring to software components; and I don't mean Joomla! components. Joomla! components, plugins, and modules are all considered to be of the stereotype «component». The following diagram loosely depicts a handful of Joomla! extensions in terms of their component-based relationship with Joomla!:

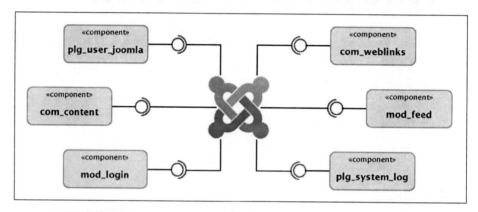

The so-called *lollipops* identify interfaces that the components realize (implement). The *sockets* identify the interfaces that are used by Joomla!. In this diagram, we have not identified the exact interfaces. This is in part due to the nature of PHP and the way in which Joomla! invokes the various extensions.

PHP is a **weak typed** language that implements **type juggling**, although this is somewhat blurred by the introduction of **type hinting** in PHP 5. For a good introduction to UML component diagrams, refer to http://www.ibm.com/developerworks/rational/library/dec04/bell/.

So what's so great about **CBD**? Well again, we already know this! When we go looking for Joomla! extensions, we want to find extensions that do something specific. We want this because it is quicker and cheaper than creating bespoke software.

It's not just when we come to administer Joomla! that the usefulness of CBD can kick in. As extensions can call other extensions—in particular plugins—as a developer, we can reduce our development time and effort while simultaneously creating a more flexible extension.

Consider the core Joomla! **Content** component. This component includes several hooks that allow plugins to react to events raised in the component. For example, the `onAfterDisplayContent` event is used to allow plugins to insert content directly after the main content body of an article is displayed. *This is often used to add comments in forms.*

 Do not confuse CBD and Event Driven Programming. Although the two may occur together, they are fundamentally different.

This chapter looks at ways in which we can use CBD to ease the development of our extensions and make our extensions more flexible.

Loading plugins

This recipe explains how to load plugins. It is necessary to import plugins prior to triggering plugin events.

How to do it...

To import a group of plugins, we use the static `JPluginHelper::importPlugin()` method.

```
JPluginHelper::importPlugin('myplugins');
```

Sometimes it can be useful to load a single plugin. In these instances, we simply provide the second parameter with the name of the plugin in the group we want to load.

```
JPluginHelper::importPlugin('myplugins', 'aplugin');
```

How it works

Plugins are grouped based on their type. There are eight core plugin types, for example **authentication**, **content**, and **editors**. We can define our own types. In the previous section, the type of plugins we imported was `myplugins`, all of which are located in the `plugins/myplugins` folder.

There's more...

If we need additional control over the import, we can use the third and fourth optional parameters, `$autocreate` and `$dispatcher`. These control how the plugins participate in the **Observer** pattern.

When `$autocreate` is `true`—as is the default—instances of class-based plugins are instantiated and become observers of the **subject**. By default, `$dispatcher` is the Joomla! `JDispatcher` object that fulfills the subject role (sometimes referred to as **observable**). We can visualize this relationship as shown in the following diagram:

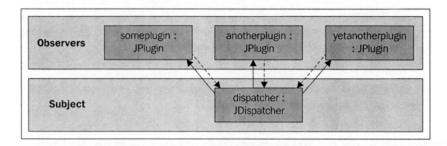

The solid arrows indicate updates. These occur when an event is triggered by the dispatcher. The dashed arrows indicate requests made by the observers to the dispatcher. In the Joomla! event model, this occurs very rarely because all of the data that is required is usually passed in the event notification.

So why would we want to use a different dispatcher? Because the Joomla! `JDispatcher` object is accessible from any scope, we have little control over its observers. Using a different subject gives us complete control over what is or what isn't observing.

And for that matter, why would we not want to use `$autocreate`? Plugins do not have to be utilized using the *Joomla! way*. For example, we might want to create a plugin that acts as a library. For more information, refer to the *Creating your own library and import function* recipe later in this chapter.

See also

To learn how to use a plugin once it is loaded, refer to the next recipe, *Invoking a plugin*.

Invoking a plugin

This recipe explains how to invoke imported plugins. Plugins can be defined as classes or functions. This recipe focuses on class implementations because this is the norm.

Getting ready

In order to invoke a plugin, we need the Joomla! `JDispatcher` object. *Remember to use the `=&` operator so as not to inadvertently create a copy of the object.*

```
$dispatcher =& JDispatcher::getInstance();
```

How to do it...

To invoke a plugin, we use the `JDispatcher::trigger()` method. In its most basic form, we pass the name of the event we want to trigger, for example `onSomethingJustHappened`:

```
$dispatcher->trigger('onSomethingJustHappened');
```

Most events send additional data to the plugins letting them know more about what just happened. To pass additional data, we pass an array as the second parameter.

```
$data = array('Look', 'Some', 'Data');
$dispatcher->trigger('onSomethingJustHappened', $data);
```

> When the data being passed includes objects, remember to explicitly pass by reference (for example, `$data = array(&$myobject)`) unless coding specifically for PHP 5, in which case objects are always passed by reference.

Plugins can return values. The `JDispatcher::trigger()` method returns an array which contains all of the return values. It is common for plugins to return Boolean values, for example:

```
// trigger event onSomethingJustHappened
$data = array('Look', 'Some', 'Data');
$result = $dispatcher->trigger('onSomethingJustHappened', $data);

// check for failure
if(in_array(false, $result)) {
    // uh oh at least one of the plugins returned false!
}
```

How it works

Plugins define methods that handle specific events. When we trigger an event using the dispatcher, it updates all observing objects. These objects, all of the type `JPlugin`, call their respective methods and pass to them the data array as a list of arguments. For example, consider this scenario:

```
$data = array('Look', 'Some', 'Data');
$dispatcher->trigger('onSomethingJustHappened', $data);
```

Where a plugin has the method:

```
function onSomethingJustHappened($arg1, $arg2, $arg3)
```

We can assert that the `onSomethingJustHappened()` method will be called with the parameters `'Look'`, `'Some'`, and `'Data'`.

See also

Plugins can react to invocation only if they are loaded! For information about loading plugins, refer to the previous recipe, *Loading plugins*.

Creating a Joomla! search plugin

This recipe explains how to create a Joomla! search plugin. Joomla! search plugins enable users to search multiple resources through the standard Joomla! **Search** component. In this recipe, we will create a search plugin that searches *Foobars*. We will name this plugin `plg_foobar`.

How to do it...

We start by creating the `foobar.php` file, which is named after the plugin. Because we are creating an installable Joomla! plugin package, we will create this file outside of Joomla! to start with; we will be able to tweak it later. The plugin class that is defined in this file must be named in the form `plgSearchPluginname`. So, if we are searching *Foobars* and our plugin is called *foobar*, the class must be named `plgSearchFoobar`.

```
jimport('joomla.plugin.plugin');
/**
 * Plugin that searches Foobars
 */
class plgSearchFoobar extends JPlugin {
    // @todo implement methods
}
```

There are two events that can be fired on search plugins, `onSearch` and `onSearchAreas`. The `onSearch` event performs the actual search, whereas the `onSearchAreas` event retrieves an array of areas in which the plugin is capable of searching. We will start by implementing `onSearchAreas`.

```
/**
 * Gets an associative array of areas in which we can search
 *
 * @return array
 */
function &onSearchAreas() {
    static $areas = array('foobar' => 'Foobars');
    return $areas;
}
```

Next, we need to implement `onSearch`. This method is inherently more complex as the method declaration clearly shows.

```
/**
 * Foobar Search method. Gets an array of objects, each
 * of which contains the instance variables title, text,
 * href, section, created, and browsernav
 *
 * @param string $text Search string
 * @param string $phrase Matching option, exact|any|all
 * @param string $ordering What to order by,
 *                              newest|oldest|popular|alpha|category
 * @param array  $areas Areas in which to search, null if search all
 * @return array Objects representing foobars
 */
function onSearch($text, $phrase='', $ordering='', $areas=null) {
      // @todo
}
```

Okay, that's the method declaration addressed. Now let's move on to the actual search implementation. We start by checking if the user has opted to search our area, that is, `foobar`.

```
// check we can handle the requested search
if (is_array($areas) && !in_array('foobar', $areas)) {
  // not one of our areas... leave it alone!
  return array();
}
```

Assuming we don't exit the method at this point, we will need the database object. So let's get that now:

```
// get the things we will need
$db =& JFactory::getDBO();
```

The rest of the method is all about building a database query that will handle the search. The first thing we will build is the WHERE clause. To build this, we use `$text` and `$phrase` where `$text` is the string we are searching for and `$phrase` is the type of search—_exact match_, _match all_, or _match any_. For the purposes of this example, we will assume that we are searching on the `#__foobars.foobar` field. _In most cases, searches will occur across several fields._

```
// build SQL conditions WHERE clause
$conditions = '';
switch ($phrase) {
  case 'exact':
    // build an exact match LIKE condition
    $text = $db->Quote('%'.$db->getEscaped($text, true).'%', false);
    $conditions = $db->nameQuote('foobar')." LIKE $text";
```

```
      break;
    case 'all':
    case 'any':
    default:
      // prepare the words individually
      $wordConditions = array();
      foreach (preg_split("~\s+~", $text) as $word) {
        $word = $db->Quote('%'.$db->getEscaped($word, true).'%', false);
        $wordConditions[] = $db->nameQuote('foobar')." LIKE $word";
      }
      // determine the glue and put it all together!
      $glue = ($phrase == 'all') ? ') AND (' : ') OR (';
      $conditions = '('.implode($glue, $wordConditions).')';
      break;
  }
```

Next, we will determine the order of the results. This can be one of the five values, popular, alpha, category, oldest, or newest. By default, we assume the ordering to be newest.

```
  // determine ordering
  switch ($ordering) {
    case 'popular':
      $order = $db->nameQuote('hits') . ' DESC';
      break;
    case 'alpha':
    case 'category':
      $order = $db->nameQuote('foobar') . ' ASC';
      break;
    case "oldest":
      $order = $db->nameQuote('created') . ' ASC';
      break;
    case "newest":
    default:
      $order = $db->nameQuote('created') . ' DESC';
      break;
  }
```

We are almost there! Now it's time to complete the query and return the results. In the following example, we extract the bare minimum as expressed in the DocTags at the start of this recipe.

```
  // complete the query
  $query = 'SELECT foobar AS title, text, created, '
  . $db->Quote('Foobars') . ' AS section, '
  . $db->Quote('2') . ' AS browsernav, '
  . ' CONCAT("index.php?option=com_foobar&id=", id) AS href'
```

```
.  ' FROM '  . $db->nameQuote('#__foobar')
.  " WHERE ($conditions) "
.  " ORDER BY $order";
$db->setQuery($query);
$rows = $db->loadObjectList();
return $rows;
```

That's the leg work done. All that is left to do now is packaging the plugin. For this, we must create an XML manifest file and archive the two files. A quick and easy way to do this is to copy and amend an existing manifest file from another search plugin (search plugins are located in the `plugins/search` folder). Our XML manifest file should look like this:

```xml
<?xml version="1.0" encoding="utf-8"?>
<!DOCTYPE install SYSTEM "http://www.joomla.org/xml/dtd/1.5/plugin-
install.dtd">
<install version="1.5" type="plugin" group="search">
  <name>Search - Foobar</name>
  <author>Packt Publishing</author>
  <creationDate>April 2009</creationDate>
  <copyright>
    Copyright (C) 2009 Packt Publishing. All rights reserved.
  </copyright>
  <license>http://www.gnu.org/licenses/gpl-2.0.html GNU/GPL</license>
  <authorEmail>author@example.org</authorEmail>
  <authorUrl>http://www.example.org</authorUrl>
  <version>1.0</version>
  <description>ENABLES SEARCHING OF FOOBARS</description>
  <files>
    <filename plugin="foobar">foobar.php</filename>
  </files>
  <params></params>
</install>
```

Notice that the `<install>` attribute `group` is `search`. This determines what type of plugin we have created. Also notice that the PHP file we created, described in the `<files>` tag, includes the plugin attribute set to `foobar`. This identifies the file as the file which will be invoked for the Search – Foobar plugin. Once we have done this, all we need do is zip the XML and PHP files together and install them as we would any other plugin.

For a copy of the plugin created in this recipe, download the code bundle for this book from `http://www.packtpub.com/files/code/8143_Code.zip`.

How it works

The array that is returned by the `onSearchAreas()` method is associative. The keys are unique identifiers for each area the plugin is capable of searching. The value is the text the user will see that describes the area. This is an array, which means that one plugin can have the ability to search several areas! To put areas into context, consider the search user interface:

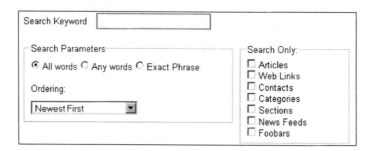

The **Search Only** field set is populated with areas. Included here are **Foobars** as defined in the example plugin.

In the example, we search the database. Search plugins are not limited to searching the database. Provided that `onSearch` returns an array of objects containing the instance variables described in the following table, we can search any resource!

Name	Description
`title`	Name of the item.
`text`	Descriptive text.
`href`	URI to the item. This will be pushed through `JRoute`, so there is no need for us to do this manually.
`section`	Where the item is located. This is generally a static piece of text unless the resource we are searching uses a suitable form of categorization.
`created`	Date and time when the item was created.
`browsernav`	1 == Navigate away from browser
	2 == Same window

If we are searching the database, it is worth noting that most plugins will search across several fields. For example, the core content plugin searches the `title`, `introtext`, `fulltext`, `metakey`, and `metadesc` fields.

To perform the actual search, we rely on the `LIKE` string comparison function. Whenever we use this function, we must pay extra attention to security. Used correctly, the DBO will prevent SQL injection. For more information, refer to Chapter 2, *Keeping Extensions Secure*.

There's more...

If any of the output created by the plugin needs to be translated to the current locale, we can manually load the language file for the plugin like this:

```
JPlugin::loadLanguage('plg_search_foobar');
```

As with all plugins, it is possible to define plugin parameters in the plugin manifest file. To retrieve these settings in the plugin, we can use the static `JPluginHelper::getPlugin()` method and create a new `JParameter` object.

```
$plugin =& JPluginHelper::getPlugin('search', 'foobar');
$pluginParams = new JParameter($plugin->params);
```

If we are searching data that may contain HTML, we can use the static `SearchHelper` class to make sure we do not accidentally search the HTML tags themselves. First, we must load the class as follows:

```
require_once(JPATH_SITE.DS.'administrator'.DS.'components'.DS
              .'com_search'.DS.'helpers'.DS.'search.php');
```

We must then iterate over the objects which we believe match the search criteria. We pass each object to the `SearchHelper::checkNoHTML()` method. This determines if the object's instance variables (identified by their names in the passed array) contain the value of `$searchText` and that that value is not hidden within any HTML markup.

```
$hasSearchTerm = SearchHelper::checkNoHTML($object, $searchText,
                                           array('text'));
```

See also

Search plugins often come as a part of a bigger product, usually headed up by a component. To learn how to package a plugin within a component installer, refer to the *Installing a plugin programmatically during a component installation* recipe.

Creating your own library and import function

This recipe explains how to create a library. Joomla! 1.5 does not explicitly support library extensions and, therefore, we must improvise. In this recipe, we look specifically at using a plugin in lieu of library extensions.

 Library extensions will be implemented in Joomla! 1.6. For more information, visit `http://joomlacode.org/gf/project/joomla/tracker/?action=TrackerItemEdit&tracker_item_id=10778`.

How to do it...

First, we need to create the plugin PHP file. We will call our plugin `mylibrary` and hence name the file `mylibrary.php`. This file contains a function similar to `jimport()` that will import parts of `mylibrary`. Before we define the function, we need to decide where our library files will be placed. It is a good practice to create a folder with the same name as the plugin (this should prevent conflicts between plugins):

```
/**
 * Path to My Library
 */
define('MYLIBRARY_PATH', dirname(__FILE__) . DS . 'mylibrary');
```

Now let's look at the function. We will call this `myimport()`. This function is incredibly simple because it delegates the work to the static `JLoader::import()` method.

```
/**
 * My file importer. Uses dot separators to define namespaces.
 *
 * @param string $path Path to file to import
 * @return boolean
 */
function myimport($path) {
  return JLoader::import($path, MYLIBRARY_PATH, 'mylibrary');
}
```

Next, we create a folder named `mylibrary` in which we place all of our library files and folders.

To use the plugin, we need to create the XML manifest file and package the plugin. The following example is an XML manifest file that defines the library as `mylibrary` and also as a part of the plugin group `library`. Notice that the `mylibrary` folder in which we placed the library files and folders is included in the `<files>` element.

```
<?xml version="1.0" encoding="utf-8"?>
<install version="1.5" type="plugin" group="library">
  <name>Library - My Library</name>
  ...
  <files>
    <filename plugin="mylibrary">mylibrary.php</filename>
    <folder>mylibrary</folder>
  </files>
  ...
</install>
```

Once we have created the plugin (packaged the files in a ZIP file), we can install it and start using it. *Remember to enable the plugin after installation*. The following example shows how we import the plugin—thus declaring the `myimport()` function—and import the `myclass.php` library file.

```
// import My Library
JPluginHelper::importPlugin("library", "mylibrary", false);
// import MyClass from My Library
myimport("myclass");
```

For a copy of the plugin created in this recipe, download the code bundle for this book from `http://www.packtpub.com/files/code/8143_Code.zip`.

How it works

The `myimport()` function uses the static `JLoader::import()` method to which it passes three parameters. The first is the path to the file we want to import, expressed as a namespace; for example, `something.someclass`. The second parameter is the physical path to the `mylibrary` folder. In this instance, we have defined this as the `MYLIBRARY_PATH` constant. The third parameter is the **key**.

The key is essentially a prefix used by `JLoader` to determine a key path, which in turn is used to determine whether or not something has been loaded. In other words, because we can call the static `JLoader::import()` method several times, it is necessary for `JLoader` to prevent repeat actions that could potentially re-declare the existing code. The key must be unique to the library. If it is not, conflicts could occur that could prevent libraries from loading correctly.

When we import the plugin, notice that we provide a third parameter to the static `JPluginHelper::importPlugin()` method. This parameter, set to `false`, determines whether or not we want to **autocreate** the plugin. This is not necessary for our library plugin because unlike a normal plugin, it does not define a class or set of functions that act as observers.

There's more...

A useful trick that we can perform is **autoloading**. This is a feature of PHP 5 that allows us to load classes on the fly. The static `JLoader::register()` method enables us to register class names to files. When an unknown class is used, but has been registered to `JLoader`, PHP will autoload the file.

```
JLoader::register('MyClass', $pathToMyClass);
```

For more information about autoloading, refer to `http://php.net/autoload`.

See also

See also

For more information about autocreate and `JPluginHelper::importPlugin()`, refer to the earlier recipe, *Loading plugins*.

Installing a plugin programmatically during a component installation

This recipe explains how to programmatically install an extension during a component installation. This is useful when distributing a component that requires/supports additional plugins and modules.

Getting ready

All of the programming expressed in this recipe occurs in the `com_install()` function declared in the component installation file. This file is identified by component XML manifest file's `<installfile>` element. Before starting, ensure that the `com_install()` function is declared in this file:

```
/**
 * Installation function for My Component
 */
function com_install() {
  // @todo
}
```

As we know, extensions are normally packaged as archives. For this recipe, we will need to include a plugin package within a component package. Create a folder in the component package named after the plugin we want to install, for example `plg_mylibrary`. Extract the plugin package into this folder.

How to do it...

As we are going to be outputting text in this function, we need to load the language file:

```
// load language file for install output
$lang = & JFactory::getLanguage();
$lang->load('com_mycomponent');
```

The next step is to get a `JInstaller` object and the DBO.

```
// Get installers, DBO, and path to plugin installation files
$componentInstaller =& JInstaller::getInstance();
$installer = new JInstaller();
$db =& JFactory::getDBO();
$pathToPlgMylibrary = $componentInstaller->getPath('source')
                                    . DS . 'plg_mylibrary';
```

Before attempting to install a plugin, we need to ensure that the plugin is not already installed:

```
// get My Library if it is already installed
$query = 'SELECT COUNT(*)'
          . ' FROM ' . $db->nameQuote('#__plugins')
          . ' WHERE ' . $db->nameQuote('element') . ' = '
                    . $db->Quote('mylibrary')
          . ' AND ' .  $db->nameQuote('folder')  . ' = '
                    . $db->Quote('library');
$db->setQuery($query);
$myLibraryInstalled = (bool)$db->loadResult();
```

We can now determine the action that needs to be taken:

```
// work out what to do now
if ($myLibraryInstalled) {
  // already installed
  echo '<p>'.JText::_( 'REQUIRED PLUGIN MY LIBRARY ALREADY
                                    INSTALLED').'</p>';
} else {
  // @todo
}
```

If `$myLibraryInstalled` equates to `true`, we know the plugin is already installed. Therefore, all we do is output some text to that effect. Otherwise, we need to complete the `else` clause by installing the plugin.

```
// Install the plugin My Library
if (!$installer->install($pathToPlgMylibrary)) {
  echo '<p>'.JText::_('FAILED TO INSTALL REQUIRED PLUGIN MY
                                    LIBRARY').'</p>';
} else {
  echo '<p>'.JText::_('INSTALLED REQUIRED PLUGIN MY LIBRARY').'</p>";
}
```

As we already know, whenever we install a new plugin, it is always disabled by default. For that reason, we must now enable the plugin.

```
// publish My Library
$query = 'UPDATE ' . $db->nameQuote('#__plugins')
       . ' SET ' . $db->nameQuote('published') . ' = 1'
       . ' WHERE ' . $db->nameQuote('element') . ' = '
                   . $db->Quote('mylibrary')
       . ' AND ' . $db->nameQuote('folder') . ' = '
                   . $db->Quote('library');
$db->setQuery($query);
if (!$db->query()) {
   echo '<p>'.JText::_('FAILED TO ENABLE REQUIRED PLUGIN MY
                                        LIBRARY').'</p>';
} else {
   echo '<p>'.JText::_('ENABLED REQUIRED PLUGIN MY LIBRARY').'</p>';
}
```

Of course, there is one little detail left to address—the return value.

```
// all done!
return true;
```

For a copy of the component created in this recipe, download the code bundle for this book from `http://www.packtpub.com/files/code/8143_Code.zip`.

How it works

The following flowchart summarizes the process. *For simplification, output is not included in this diagram.*

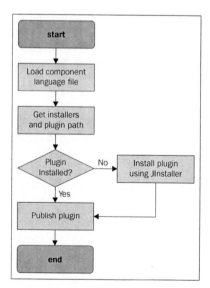

The *Load component language file* step requires that the component includes a language file. As the **Installer** component is accessible only through the backend, the language file is the component's backend language file.

The *Get installers and plugin path* step retrieves two `JInstaller` objects. One is a globally accessible instance of `JInstaller`. We use this to determine the path to the plugin installation files, which are located in the temporary component installation directory. The other is a new instance of `JInstaller`, which we use to process the plugin. We must use a new instance of `JInstaller` because the globally accessible instance is halfway through the installation of the component when `com_install()` is invoked, and `JInstaller` relies on state data.

The *Install plugin using JInstaller* step is undoubtedly the most daunting of all the steps. But in reality, it is quite simple! The `JInstaller` class defines the `install()` method. All we need pass to this method is the path to the unpacked installation files. In our case, this is `$pathToPlgMylibrary`. This method takes care of all the hard work and returns a Boolean value describing the success/failure of the installation.

The *Publish plugin* step is optional. In some cases, it will make sense to publish the plugin only when it was not previously installed. In the example, we assume that the plugin is required by the component and is, therefore, enabled immediately.

See also

For information about the plugin used in this example, refer to the *Creating your own library and import function* recipe earlier in this chapter. Another useful type of plugin to install during a component installation is a search plugin. For more information, refer to the *Creating a Joomla! search plugin* recipe earlier in this chapter.

Managing categories the easy way

This recipe explains how to take advantage of the **Categories** component to manage categories. We often think of categories as being fundamentally linked to content; however, we can use section values (not to be confused with content sections) to separate categories.

How to do it...

When we invoke the Categories component, we can pass a section value. If we want to manage categories for the `com_mycomponent` component, that section value should be `com_mycomponent`.

```
<a href="index.php?option=com_categories&section=com_mycomponent">
  Categories
</a>
```

In most instances, this type of link should be in the Joomla! menus. To achieve this, we must provide the attribute `link` when we define the submenu items in the component manifest file like this:

```
<submenu>
  ...
  <menu link="option=com_categories&amp;
                     section=com_mycomponent">Categories</menu>
  ...
</submenu>
```

 In XML, special characters must be encoded. For example, `&` becomes `&amp;`. For more information, refer to `http://www.w3.org/TR/REC-xml/#syntax`.

When we navigate using the new menu item or the hyperlink, we should see something similar to this:

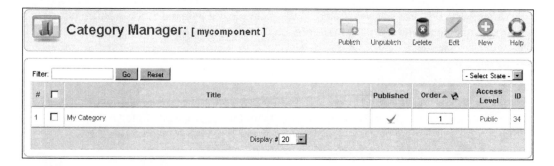

How it works

If we take a peek at the `#__categories` table, we can see precisely how this works in practice. This table includes the `section` field. Looking at this, we can see a handful of other component names. In fact, there are four core components that use the Categories component in this way. They are:

- Banners
- Contact
- Newsfeeds
- Weblinks

This quick and easy approach does have some drawbacks. Most notably, we lose control of the data. We should use this only in instances where our categories are relatively simple and comply with the normal Joomla! Categories data definition.

Defining JParameters using XML

This recipe explains the basic structure of an XML file in which data is defined for use with the JParameter class and JElement subclasses. In most instances, we will find ourselves defining parameters within common XML files, for example, an extension manifest file.

How to do it...

Parameters are defined within the `<params>` element, which must be a direct descendent of the `<root>` element (the name of the `<root>` element is unimportant). Individual parameters are defined in the `<param>` elements. The following example provides a rough outline:

```xml
<?xml version="1.0" encoding="utf-8"?>
<root>
  <params>
    <!-- @todo -->
  </params>
</root>
```

The next step is to define some `<param>` elements. Like most data definitions, parameters have types. The type determines what attributes and subelements are required. We'll start with a simple example, a `text` parameter.

```xml
<param name="aTextParameter"
       type="text"
       default=""
       label="A TEXT PARAMETER"
       description="A TEXT PARAMETER DESCRIPTION" />
```

This defines a text parameter named aTextParameter of the type `text` with a null string default value. The attribute's `label` and `description` form visual aids, where `label` is the name the user will see and `description` is the mouseover hint. The attributes in this example are applicable to nearly all of the parameter types.

Parameters of the type `text` can also define the two optional attributes, `size` and `class`. The `size` attribute is the physical width of the input field (this does not limit the parameter to a specified length). The `class` attribute is the CSS class of the input field. By default, this is `text_area`.

```xml
<param name="aTextParameter"
       type="text"
       default=""
       size="50"
       label="A TEXT PARAMETER"
       description="A TEXT PARAMETER DESCRIPTION"
       class="my_text_area" />
```

Now let's try a more complex parameter, `list`. This parameter type requires the `<option>` subelements. These are very similar to their HTML `<option>` element counterparts.

```
<param name="aListParameter"
       type="list"
       default="one"
       label="A LIST PARAMETER"
       description="A LIST PARAMETER DESCRIPTION">
  <option value="one">ONE</option>
  <option value="two">TWO</option>
</param>
```

Let's try one last example—this time, a calendar. The calendar type allows users to easily select date values.

```
<param name="aCalendar"
       type="calendar"
       default="1867-07-14"
       label="A CALENDAR PARAMETER"
       description="A CALENDAR PARAMETER DESCRIPTION" />
```

How it works

Parameter types relate directly to concrete `JElement` classes. The core concrete `JElement` classes are located in `joomla.html.parameter.element`. For a complete list of `JElement` types, refer to `http://api.joomla.org/Joomla-Framework/Parameter/JElement.html`.

There's more...

As `JParameter` defines data in terms of its relationship to its presentation to the user, it should come as no surprise that there exists a type specifically for separating parameters. The following example creates a blank line, providing a visual queue to the separation of parameter intent:

```
<param name="@spacer"
       type="spacer" />
```

There is a more substantial way of providing separation. `JParameter` supports groups. We can group parameters together to create a logical separation of parameter intent. For example, we can have two values with the name `total` in two separate groups such as `apples` and `bananas`. The grouping relives any ambiguity of the name, for example, `apples.total` and `bananas.total`. By default, all groups are added to an aptly named default group, `_default`. To override this, we must add a `group` attribute to the `<params>` element.

```
<params group="advanced">
```

It's important to understand that we can add several `<params>` elements to the root element.

```xml
<?xml version="1.0" encoding="utf-8"?>
<root>
  <params>
    <param name="aTextParameter"
           type="text"
           default=""
           size="50"
           label="A TEXT PARAMETER"
           description="A TEXT PARAMETER DESCRIPTION" />
  </params>
  <params group="advanced">
    <param name="anotherTextParameter"
           type="text"
           default=""
           size="50"
           label="ANOTHER TEXT PARAMETER"
           description="ANOTHER TEXT PARAMETER DESCRIPTION" />
  </params>
</root>
```

There are some issues with using groups. For more information, refer to the *Rendering a JParameter object* recipe later in this chapter.

See also

The remaining recipes in this chapter deal exclusively with the `JParameter` objects.

Creating a JParameter object

This recipe explains how to instantiate a new `JParameter` object. `JParameter` objects are often used to quickly and easily extend a database. For more information about the database, refer to Chapter 3, *Working with the Database*.

How to do it...

A basic `JParameter` object requires one parameter—the data itself. The data is represented as an INI string. For example:

```php
// define parameters and create a new JParameter object
$myParams = "someParameter=Some Value\n";
$params = new JParameter($myParams);
```

In most instances, we will find that the data in question originates from a database.

```
$params = new JParameter($aRecord->params);
```

The previous recipe, *Defining JParameters using XML*, explained how to create an XML file that describes the `JParameter` data. If we have such a file, we can provide `JParameter` with the path to this file. This is the most common way in which `JParameter` is used.

```
$params = new JParameter($myParams, $pathToXML_File);
```

How it works

The data that is passed to the `JParameter` constructor is a raw INI string. This is parsed by `JParameter` using a `JRegistryFormatINI` object. Groups are denoted in an INI string using INI section identifiers, for example `[somegroup]`. The XML file, if provided, is also parsed in the constructor.

 There are issues with the way in which `JParameter` deals with groups. For more information, refer to the next recipe, *Rendering a JParameter object*.

There's more...

It is possible to load additional data and XML files after instantiation. The `loadINI()` and `loadSetupFile()` methods allow us to do this. Importantly, `JParameter` does not only support INI data. We can use `loadXML()` to load data encoded in an XML format. We can use `bind()` to bind with data defined in a PHP object or array.

See also

For information about creating an XML file, refer to the previous recipe, *Defining JParameters using XML*.

For information about accessing a `JParameter` once it has been created, refer to the *Getting and setting values in a JParameter object* recipe later in this chapter.

Rendering a JParameter object

What sets `JParameter` apart from its parent class `JRegistry` is the ability to define data in an XML metadata file and output that data in a user-friendly format for editing. This recipe explains how we can create a user-friendly form using a `JParameter` object.

Getting ready

In order to generate the form, we need a `JParameter` object. For information about creating a `JParameter` object, refer to the previous recipe. In this recipe, we assume that we already have a `JParameter` object assigned to the `$params` variable.

How to do it...

We start by using the `JParameter::render()` method. This method returns an HTML string that contains a table with embedded form elements based on the XML file that defined the parameters.

```
echo $params->render();
```

Now we should end up with something that looks similar to this:

If more than one group exists in our `JParameter` object, we must render each group separately. The `JParameter::render()` method accepts two optional parameters. The first is the name of the form array, by default this is `params`. The second is the name of the group, by default this is `_default`.

```
// render the default parameters
echo $params->render();

// render the advanced parameters
echo $params->render('advanced', 'advanced');
```

Caveat of rendering groups

When we render any group, the data is always pulled from the `_default` group, irrespective of the group being rendered. This is a known bug, and it should be fixed in Joomla! 1.6 (in development at the time of writing). For more information, refer to `http://joomlacode.org/gf/project/joomla/tracker/?action=TrackerItemEdit&tracker_item_id=15366`

> **Use JavaScript sliders to separate groups**
>
> It is common practice to use JavaScript sliders that are generated using JPane to visually separate groups of parameters. For more information, refer to `http://api.joomla.org/Joomla-Framework/HTML/JPane.html`.

How it works

When we render a JParameter object, JParameter iterates over the parameters defined by the XML file. For each of these, JParameter invokes the corresponding concrete JElement class. The JElement objects are then used to render the data based on the definition.

A feature of rendering a JParameter object is the translation of labels and descriptions. This means that we can define the XML without worrying about multilingual compatibility.

There's more...

A less common, but still useful, way of rendering a JParameter object is to use the JParameter::renderToArray() method. Rendering a JParameter object in the usual way results in a table-based HTML design. The JParameter::renderToArray() method, on the other hand, provides us with greater control. It returns an array of arrays. Each inner array represents a parameter and contains six elements. The following table describes these elements:

0. Name including tooltip
1. HTML form element
2. Description
3. Label
4. Value
5. Name

The following example uses the JParameter::renderToArray() method to output a JParameter object as a list of form elements, each in a separate paragraph.

```
$elements = $params->renderToArray();

foreach($elements AS $element) {
    echo '<p><strong>' . $element[0] . ': </strong><br/>'
                                    . $element[1] . '</p>';
}
```

See also

The previous recipe, *Creating a JParameter object*, explains how to create a `JParameter` object.

The next recipe, *Saving JParameter data*, explains how to handle forms that include a rendered `JParameter` object.

Saving JParameter data

This recipe explains how to save `JParameter` data based on a rendered HTML form as described in the previous recipe, *Rendering a JParameter object*.

How to do it...

When we render a group of parameters, they are submitted as an array in the form. By default this array is called `params`. In the previous recipe, we saw an instance where a group was outputted with an alternative name, `advanced`.

Unfortunately, `JParameter` cannot process the form-submitted data on its own, so we have to improvise. We begin by retrieving the array from the request.

```
// get input array
$params = JRequest::getVar('params', array(), 'POST', 'array');
```

The next stage is to build an INI string based on this array. An easy way to do this is to iterate over the array and build an INI string based exclusively on the array keys and values.

```
// Build parameter INI string
$ini = array();
foreach ($params as $key => $value) {
    // create ini key value pair
    $ini[] = $key . '=' . $value;
}

// convert array to an INI string
$params = implode("\n", $ini);
```

There's more...

There is an obvious issue with this approach—no form of validation is performed on the data. For example, if a value is expected to be an integer, this is not checked. For this level of validation, we must manually implement individual checks.

A less obvious shortcoming is overwriting of the existing data. As the generated form fields are based exclusively on the XML-defined parameters, these fields will not be in the form data if we are storing additional data that is not defined in the XML. To preserve undefined key-value pairs, we could write the returned values back to a `JParameter` object with the old data preloaded and then convert the object to a string using the `JParameter::toString()` method. For more information, refer to the next recipe, *Getting and setting values in a JParameter object*.

See also

For information about rendering a `JParameter` object in a form, refer to the previous recipe, *Rendering a JParameter object*.

Getting and setting values in a JParameter object

This recipe explains how to inspect values stored in a `JParameter` object, and how to store new values and update values in a `JParameter` object.

How to do it...

To get values from a `JParameter` object, we use the `JParameter::get()` method. The following example shows how to get the value of `aRadioParameter`. If the value is not defined, the optional default value is returned. In this case, `$defaultValue`.

```
// get value of aRadioParameter
$value = $params->get('aRadioParameter', $defaultValue);
```

`JParameter` supports grouping. In instances where we want to retrieve a value from a group other than the default group, we provide `JParameter::get()` with a third parameter.

```
// get value of anotherTextParameter from someGroup
$value = $params->get('anotherTextParameter', $defaultValue,
                                              'someGroup'`);
```

The other side of the coin is setting values. The following example sets the value of `aTextParameter` to `$someValue`:

```
// set value of aTextParameter
$params->set('aTextParameter', $someValue);
```

Like the `JParameter::get()` method, `JParameter::set()` accepts a third parameter. This parameter defines the group we want to set the value in. If this parameter is not provided, the default group is assumed.

```
// set value of anotherTextParameter in someGroup
$params->set('anotherTextParameter', $someValue, 'someGroup');
```

How it works

The values defined in a `JParameter` object are initially set when the object is created, usually based on an INI string. For more information, refer to the *Creating a JParameter object* recipe earlier in this chapter.

The `JParameter` class is an extension of the `JRegistry` class. Consequently, much of the interaction is very similar. However, when working with a `JParameter` object, it is essential we use the `get()` and `set()` methods instead of the `JRegistry` methods `getValue()` and `setValue()`.

The default values are used in instances where the data is not defined, or is considered to be not set. In the following raw data example, `aKey` and `yetAnotherKey` are both considered to have data. On the other hand, `anotherKey` is considered to be not set.

```
aKey=someValue
anotherKey=
yetAnotherKey=0
```

The lines in a raw INI string are trimmed during the parsing process. If `anotherKey` were to have a string value of one or more whitespace characters, it would be parsed as a null string.

XML files can define default values for parameters. However, they are not used in any way when retrieving values from a `JParameter` object. They are used solely to provide default values in `JParameter`-rendered forms.

Store extra data in a JParameter object

Although `JParameter` uses XML files to define parameters, we can get and set values for parameters that are not defined in the XML file.

See also

For information about defining parameters, refer to the *Defining JParameters using XML* recipe earlier in the chapter.

Defining your own JParameter type

Joomla! provides us with a number of predefined `JElement` subclasses. We can also think of them as `JParameter` types. The following list identifies these types:

- calendar
- editors
- folderlist
- filelist
- category
- helpsites
- hidden
- imagelist
- languages
- list
- menu
- menuitem
- password
- radio
- section
- spacer
- sql
- text
- textarea
- timezones
- usergroup

Always consider the SQL type

This type can be used to create an options list based on an SQL query. It is often overlooked, but it is a good simple solution.

Not just for form elements

A `JElement` must not necessarily define an HTML form input element. For example, the built-in `spacer` type is for presentation purposes only. Informative `JElements` can also be useful, for example, stating whether or not an optional `PEAR` library is installed.

Getting ready

It is a good idea to keep all concrete implementations of `JElement` in their own folder. When adding concrete implementations of `JElement` to a component, it is conventional to define these classes within a new folder called `elements` in the administrative root of the component. *There is no convention for other extension types.*

In this recipe, we will create a `JElement` that provides a range of integer values. We will call this type `integer`. To create the class, we must first create the PHP file `integer.php`.

How to do it...

In the `integer.php` file, we create a class called `JElementInteger`. In the subclass, we set the value of the `_name` class instance variable and override the `JElement::fetchElement()` method.

```
/**
 * Renders an integer element
 */
class JElementInteger extends JElement {

    /** @var string */
    var $_name = 'Integer';

    /**
     * Gets an HTML form element
     *
     * @param string $name Name of the element
     * @param string $value Current value
     * @param JSimpleXMLElement $node XML metadata
     * @param string $ctrlName Name of array
     * @return string
     */
    function fetchElement($name, $value, &$node, $ctrlName) {
        // @todo
    }
}
```

Once we have done this, it is time to implement the `fetchElement()` method. This method returns an HTML form element that represents a parameter.

```
// get values from node attributes
$maximum   = intval($node->attributes('maximum'));
$minimum   = intval($node->attributes('minimum'));
$increment = intval($node->attributes('increment'));
$value     = intval($value);

// check increment is greater than 0
if ($increment < 1) {
    $increment = 1;
}

// swap maximum and minimum if in wrong order
if ($maximum < $minimum) {
    $oldMaximum = $maximum;
    $maximum = $minimum;
    $minimum = $oldMaximum;
}

// return list of integers using JHTML
return JHTML::_('select.integerlist',
                $minimum,
                $maximum,
                $increment,
                $ctrlName . '[' . $name . ']',
                null,
                $value);
```

To use our new `JElementInteger` class in an XML file, we must tell `JParameter` where our bespoke `JElement` subclass resides. We do this in the `<params>` element using the `addpath` attribute.

```
<params addpath="/administrator/components/com_foobar/elements">
```

To use our new `integer` type, we define a `<param>` element of the `integer` type and provide the `maximum`, `minimum`, and—optionally—`increment` attributes. The following example will create a list of these values: 100, 200, 300, 400, 500, 600, 700, 800, 900, and 1000.

```
<param name="myInteger"
       type="integer"
       default="500"
       label="MY INTEGER"
       description="MY INTEGER DESCRIPTION"
       maximum="100"
       minimum="1000"
       increment="100"/>
```

How it works

Naming conventions are especially important when defining a concrete JElement class. The name of the file and the suffix of the class name relate directly to the <param> element's type attribute. Failure to adhere to the convention will prevent JParameter from loading the JElement subclass.

The fetchElement() method is passed these four parameters:

- $name: This is the actual name of the parameter, for example *myInteger*
- $value: This is the current value of the parameter
- $node: This is a JSimpleXMLElement object, derived directly from the XML file.
- $ctrlName: This is the name of the array to which the parameter is associated, for example params or advanced

The most interesting of all four parameters is $node. In our example, we used the attributes() method to gain access to the attributes defined in the XML <param> element. In this case, they are maximum, minimum, and increment. Similarly, children() and data() are useful methods. The children() method returns an array of child elements, represented as JSimpleXMLElement objects. The data() method gets the data contents of the element. For more information, refer to http://api.joomla.org/Joomla-Framework/Utilities/JSimpleXMLElement.html.

Note that in our JElementInteger class, we used JHTML to generate the actual form field. Using this significantly reduces development time and allows us to concentrate on the fancy bits of the method, such as swapping the maximum and minimum values should they be the wrong way around.

See also

For information about defining parameters, refer to the *Defining JParameters using XML* recipe earlier in the chapter.

10

JObjects and Arrays

This chapter contains the following recipes:

Introduction

In this chapter, we'll discuss how to work with the base `JObject` class and how to work with arrays using the static helper class `JArrayHelper`. The majority of classes in Joomla! inherit from `JObject`. Thus, knowing how to work with `JObject` gives us a basic understanding of how to work with most Joomla! classes.

The JArrayHelper class has a number of handy methods for dealing with arrays and, to some extent, objects. This class is a part of the Joomla! library joomla.utilities. arrayhelper. However, it is not necessary to import the class because it is imported by Joomla! as a matter of course.

As a quick reminder, when we extract arrays from the request data, we should specify the ARRAY type when calling JRequest::getVar(). For example, if we were retrieving the cid array (often used when passing selected itemized data), we would do the following:

```
$cid = JRequest::getVar('cid', array(), 'POST', 'ARRAY');
```

This equates to: From the request, get the cid value with a default value of array() directly from the POST data, and make sure that the value is of the type ARRAY. For more information about working safely with request data, refer to Chapter 2, *Keeping Extensions Secure*.

As of PHP 5, it is possible to define **class member** (a property or method) access. This is achieved using one of the three **access modifiers**: private, protected, or public. These dictate what can interact with the class members. The private members can only be used by the class that defines them. The protected members can only be used by the class that defines them and all subclasses. The public members can be used by anything. Comparatively, in PHP 4, all class members are public. The following example shows how we declare class members using access modifiers:

```
class MyClass {
    public    $somePublicInstanceVariable;
    protected $someProtectedInstanceVariable;
    private   $somePrivateInstanceVariable;

    public    function somePublicMethod() {}
    protected function someProtectedMethod() {}
    private   function somePrivateMethod () {}
}
```

Joomla! 1.5 is, of course, written for PHP 4. If we want to create extensions that are PHP 4 compatible, we cannot use access modifiers. Instead, we can use the Joomla! 1.5 de-facto naming convention of marking members as private and protected using an underscore prefix. The next example is the PHP 4 equivalent of the previous example. We can see that the private and protected instance variable names are prefixed with underscores.

```
class MyClass {
    /**
     * @access public
     */
    var $somePublicInstanceVariable;

    /**
```

```
   * @access protected
   */
  var $_someProtectedInstanceVariable;

  /**
   * @access private
   */
  var $_somePrivateInstanceVariable;

  /**
   * @access public
   */
  function somePublicMethod() {}

  /**
   * @access protected
   */
  function _someProtectedMethod() {}

  /**
   * @access private
   */
  function _somePrivateMethod() {}
}
```

The difficulties with this approach are clear. There is no noticeable difference in the naming convention between the `private` and `protected` members. Also, there is no enforcement of access.

> The example uses DocBlocks in which it defines the access more concisely for documentation purposes. The PHP 5 example does not include the `@access` tags in DocBlocks because PHPDocumentor is capable of parsing PHP 5 access modifiers.

In this chapter, we make a distinction between these two approaches to class member access. We refer to the PHP 5 way of doing things as **access modifiers**, and we refer to the underscore naming convention as **access indicators**. Note that it is possible (and preferable when creating extensions specifically for PHP 5) to use both approaches in tandem:

```
class MyClass {
    public    $somePublicInstanceVariable;
    protected $_someProtectedInstanceVariable;
    private   $_somePrivateInstanceVariable;

    public    function somePublicMethod() {}
    protected function _someProtectedMethod() {}
    private   function _somePrivateMethod () {}
}
```

Magic accessor and mutator methods for PHP 5

As of PHP 5, it is possible to use the __get() and __set() magic methods as a generic way of accessing and modifying class instance variables that are outside of the current scope. For more information, refer to http://php.net/manual/language.oop5.overloading.php.

Getting a JObject property

This recipe explains how to get a value from a JObject. The process described here should always be used in preference of accessing class instance variables directly (unless developing explicitly for PHP 5 environments).

How to do it...

To access a JObject instance variable, we use the get() method. This method accepts two parameters—the name of the instance variable and the default to return if the property is not already set.

```
$value = $myJObject->get('someProperty', 'default value');
```

The default value is optional. If we do not provide this, the default value will be assumed to be null.

There's more...

The JObject::get() method does not take any notice of instance variable access indicators or access modifiers. That is to say, when we use the JObject::get() method, it does not prevent us from getting a property with a name that starts with an underscore, nor does it prevent us from retrieving values that are declared private or protected.

When creating a class that extends a JObject, it is a good idea to override the JObject::get() method to prevent the method from getting data that we want to remain hidden.

See also

We can determine the names of the instance variables of a JObject, as shown in the next recipe, *Getting all of the public JObject properties*.

To set the value of a JObject property, refer to the next but one recipe, *Setting a JObject property*.

Getting all of the public JObject properties

This recipe explains how to retrieve the names of instance variables in a `JObject`. This includes instance variables that are not defined by the class, but have been added on-the-fly.

How to do it...

We can get the names of all the instance variables defined in a `JObject` using the `JObject::getProperties()` method. This method returns an associative array in which the array keys are the object property names and the array values are the object property values.

```
$publicPropertyNames = $myJObject->getProperties();
```

It is also possible to get the names of all the properties, be they `public`, `private`, or `protected`.

```
$allPropertyNames = $myJObject->getProperties(false);
```

How it works

The `JObject::getProperties()` method is only capable of distinguishing between instance variable access using access indicators, that is, the underscore naming convention described in the chapter introduction. This means that if an object contains instance variables that are defined as `private` or `protected` solely using the PHP 5 style access modifiers, the `JObject::getProperties()` method will incorrectly evaluate these as `public`.

See also

To retrieve the value of a `JObject` property, refer to the previous recipe, *Getting a JObject property*.

To set the value of a `JObject` property, refer to the next recipe, *Setting a JObject property*.

Setting a JObject property

This recipe explains how to set a `JObject` property the Joomla! way.

How to do it...

To set a value in a `JObject`, we can use the `JObject::set()` method. This method accepts two parameters—the name of the property we want to set and the value to which we want to set the property.

```
$myJObject->set('someProperty', 'Some Value');
```

This method also returns the old value:

```
$oldValue = $myJObject->set('someProperty', 'Some Value');
```

The second parameter is not required. Omitting this will set the value to `null`. *We can think of this as a way of resetting the value.*

```
$myJObject->set('someProperty');
```

There's more...

The `JObject::set()` method does not take any notice of the instance variable access indicators or access modifiers. That is to say, the method neither prevents us from setting a property with a name that starts with an underscore, nor does it prevent us from setting values that are declared `private` or `protected`.

When creating a class that extends a `JObject`, it is a good idea to override the `JObject::set()` method to prevent the method from setting data that we want to remain `private` or `protected`.

 This method will create new instance variables if they do not already exist. That is to say, if a class does not define a property with the name we provide, this method will create a new property on-the-fly.

See also

To retrieve the value of a `JObject` property, refer to the first recipe in this chapter, *Getting a JObject property*.

It is possible to set more than one property at once. For more information, refer to the next recipe, *Setting a batch of JObject Properties*.

Setting a batch of JObject properties

This recipe explains how to set more than one property of a `JObject` in one simple step.

How to do it...

To set several values in a `JObject`, we need some data. This data must be in the form of an associative array in which the keys relate to the names of the properties.

```
$data = array('x' => 3, 'y' => '5');
```

To set the values of x and y in a `JObject`, we use the `JObject::setProperties()` method.

```
$myJObject->setProperties($data);
```

Like the `JObject::set()` method, this method does not pay attention to access indicators or access modifiers. This method will set all values from the array in the object even if no equivalent class instance variable has been declared.

See also

To set a single property, refer to the previous recipe, *Setting a JObject property*.

Reporting an error in a JObject

In this recipe, we explore how to maintain a history of errors that occur during the life of a `JObject`. The `JObject` class has a number of useful methods we can use to maintain a history of errors. For the most part, errors are expressed as strings. However, it is perfectly acceptable to express errors as `JException` objects and, in PHP 5, as `Exception` objects.

How to do it...

The `JObject::setError()` method is used to report errors. Although this method is technically `public`, generally speaking, we should avoid invoking the method outside of the object itself. *Remember that the error history is supposed to maintain a history of errors that relate specifically to the object, and not to the objects that interact with it.*

At a basic level, we can report an error as a string:

```
$this->setError(JText::_('AN ERROR OCCURED'));
```

If we want the error to be translated, we must do so ourselves, as shown in the above example. (Note the use of `JText`.)

Whenever we raise a Joomla! error, warning, or notice, the `JException` objects are created using the `JError` class. These objects are returned by the various raise methods declared in `JError`. Thus, we can use the `JObject::setError()` method directly after calling a `JError` raise method:

```
// raise a warning
$errorMessage = JText::_('AN ERROR OCCURED');
$error = JError::raiseWarning(500, $errorMessage);

// add the JException object to the object history
$this->setError($error);
```

There's more...

Due to the simplistic nature of the error recording, it can be beneficial to override the `setError()` method with a more comprehensive solution. For example, we could optionally include an error code.

```
/**
 * Add an error message
 *
 * @param   string|object $error Error message
 * @param   int           $code  Error code
 * @access public
 */
function setError($error, $code=0) {
    // if error is not recognized by JError
    // create a JException object
    if (!JError::isError($error)) {
        $error = new JException($error, $code);
    }

    // let JObject take the reins
    parent::setError($error);
}
```

See also

To learn about retrieving errors from a `JObject`, refer to the next two recipes, *Getting an error from a JObject* and *Getting all errors from a JObject*.

Getting an error from a JObject

This recipe explains how to retrieve individual errors from a `JObject` error history.

How to do it...

To retrieve details of the last error that occurred in a `JObject`, we use the `getError()` method. By default, this method always returns the last error as a string.

```
$lastErrorMessage = $object->getError();
```

Error messages are indexed from `0` to the latest error message. We can extract an error based on this index. For example, to extract the third error message, we would use this:

```
$thirdErrorMessage = $object->getError(2);
```

 Extracting an error message may not always be successful. If no errors have occurred or we supply an index value that is out of bounds, the `JObject::getError()` method will return Boolean `false`.

There's more...

As described in the previous recipe, *Reporting an error in a JObject*, an error can be represented as a string, or a `JException` object, or an `Exception` object. The `JObject::getError()` method automatically converts error objects to strings. We can prevent this using the second optional parameter.

```
$error = $object->getError(null, false);
```

This does not guarantee that `$error` will be a `JException` or `Exception` object. It means that if the error was reported as a `JException` or `Exception` object, that object will be returned.

In the example, the last error that occurred is returned. We must supply the first optional parameter in order to supply the second, but we do not know the index position of the last error message. Therefore, we supply a value of `null`. This tells the method to get the last known error.

 Displaying and recording errors can result in **Error Message Information Leaks** (`CWE-209`). Whenever we output error messages, we should not give away too much information—unless we are working in a secure environment. For example, outputting a *file not found* message in which the full path to the file is disclosed can be considered a security weakness.

See also

To add errors to a `JObject`, refer to the previous recipe, *Reporting an error in a JObject*.

To discover how to retrieve all errors from a `JObject`, refer to the next recipe, *Getting all errors from a JObject*.

Getting all errors from a JObject

This recipe retrieves an array that contains a history of all the errors that have occurred during the life of a `JObject`. An example of when this might be useful is retrieving a list of validation errors from a `JModel`.

How to do it...

To extract all errors from a `JObject`, we use the `JObject::getErrors()` method. The array that is returned by this method may include basic error messages described in strings, and `JException` and `Exception` objects. Consequently, we must be careful when processing an array returned by this method; we must not assume that all elements are of a particular type.

```
$errors = $object->getErrors();
```

To cope with the mixed-type elements, we could do something like this:

```
// iterate over mixed errors array
$errorMessages = array();
for ($i = 0, $c = count($errors); $i < $c; $i++) {
  if (JError::isError($errors[$i])) {
    // element is an error object, convert to string
    $errorMessages[] = $errors[$i]->toString();
  } else {
    $errorMessages[] = $errors[$i];
  }
}
```

Displaying and recording errors can result in **Error Message Information Leaks** (`CWE-209`). Whenever we output error messages, we should not give away too much information—unless we are working in a secure environment. For example, outputting a *file not found* message in which the full path to the file is disclosed can be considered a security weakness.

See also

To add errors to a JObject, refer to the *Reporting an error in a JObject* recipe.

To discover how to retrieve a single error from a JObject, refer to the previous recipe, *Getting an error from a JObject*.

Converting an object to an array

It can be useful to convert an object to an array. For example, were we to build a method that expected an array parameter but received an object, if all we are doing with the parameter is interrogating its elements, converting the object to an array will allow us to continue without issue.

How to do it...

We'll use the following class and object to demonstrate. The object has three instance variables: y is private, x is public, and z is public but not defined in the class itself.

```
class MyClass {
   private $y = 0;
   public  $x = 0;
}

$object = new MyClass();
$object->x = 34;
$object->z = 3;
```

We use the JArrayHelper utility class to convert the object.

```
$array = JArrayHelper::fromObject($object);
```

How it works

For each public instance variable within the object, an element with the same key is created in the generated array. When we refer to the public instance variables in this context, we are talking about instance variables defined as public by their access modifiers. The JArrayHelper::fromObject() method does not take any notice of access indicators, that is, class members with names that start with an underscore. So for our example, y is not included because it is declared as private:

```
Array
(
   [x] => 34
   [z] => 3
)
```

Notice that the instance variable z, which is not defined in the class, is transposed irrespective of this.

There's more...

In instances where the originating object contains objects, we can opt to convert them to arrays. We do this by enabling recursion. This will have the effect of converting each instance variable that is an object to an array, and then transposing the result to the final array.

```
$array = JArrayHelper::fromObject($object, true);
```

 Use recursion with caution, as this can potentially lead to a never-ending loop. Consider two objects: the first references the second as a child, while the second references the first as a parent.

It is possible to restrict the instance variables that are transposed using a **Regular Expression (RE)**. Only instance variables whose names match the RE will be transposed. For example, we can prevent instance variables with names that start with an underscore from being transposed:

```
$pattern = '~^[^_]~';
$array = JArrayHelper::fromObject($object, true, $pattern);
```

See also

The next recipe, *Converting an array to an object*, performs the reverse of the operation described in this recipe.

Converting an array to an object

It can be useful to convert an array to an object. For example, if we were to build a method that expected an object parameter but received an array, and if all we are doing with the parameter is interrogating its members, converting the array to an object will allow us to continue without any issue.

How to do it...

We will use the following array as an example. It has three elements, two of which are named (x and y), and one that is not named.

```
$array = array('x' => 34, 'y' => 28, 3);
```

We use the `JArrayHelper` utility class to convert the array.

```
$object = JArrayHelper::toObject($array);
```

How it works

The `JArrayHelper::toObject()` method creates a new `stdClass` object. To this it adds new instance variables based on the array keys. So `$object` will look like this:

```
stdClass Object
(
    [x] => 34
    [y] => 28
    [0] => 3
)
```

There's more...

The resultant object is a `stdClass` object. We can opt to use a different class by supplying the name of the class to the `JArrayHelper::toObject()` method. For example, we could create a `JObject` as follows:

```
$object = JArrayHelper::toObject($array, 'JObject');
```

Note that because `JArrayHelper::toObject()` does not have knowledge of the class in question, it assumes a zero parameter constructor. In other words, the class of object we want to create must provide a constructor that accepts no parameters, or all optional parameters because PHP does not implement overloading in the traditional sense of the word.

The `JArrayHelper::toObject()` method sets object instance variables directly. Therefore, if we are using PHP 5 and the class we specify is using `private` or `protected` access modifiers to declare instance variables and the `JArrayHelper::toObject()` method attempts to set one of those instance variables, a fatal error will be thrown. For example:

```
Fatal error: Cannot access protected property MyClass::$x
```

See also

The previous recipe, *Converting an object to an array*, performs the reverse of the operation described in this recipe.

Getting a column from a multidimensional array

As we already know, a two-dimensional array can be thought of much like a table. The outer array contains all the rows, while the inner arrays represent individual rows. Accessing a column can sometimes seem a bit clumsy. In Joomla!, we can extract the values from any column.

Consider a database query that retrieves a number of rows but only one column in which we are interested. We can simplify the resultant data structure by extracting the column we want as a single array.

 This recipe also applies to an array of objects. This can be useful when using the `JDatabase::loadObjectList()` method.

How to do it...

We will use the following two-dimensional array as an example:

```
$array = array(
    array('aColumn' => 13, 'anotherColumn' => 7),
    array('aColumn' => 21, 'anotherColumn' => 22),
    array('aColumn' => 37, 'anotherColumn' => 19),
);
```

To extract `aColumn` or `anotherColumn`, we use the `JArrayHelper::getColumn()` static method. To this we supply two parameters—the source array and the name of the column (or to be more precise, the name of the index in the inner arrays that contain the values we want to extract).

```
$aColumn = JArrayHelper::getValue($array, 'aColumn');
```

The resultant array in the example will look like this:

```
Array
(
    [0] => 13
    [1] => 21
    [2] => 37
)
```

There is nothing to prevent us from using this method when more complex values are employed. For example, had we used this on a three-dimensional array, the values of elements in the resulting array would have been the arrays in the third dimension.

See also

To safely and securely get an individual value from an array, refer to the next recipe, *Getting a value from an array*.

Getting a value from an array

This is the most insignificant sounding of all the recipes in this chapter! We all know how to get a value from an array. It's simple. We just drop in the index of the element we want and hey presto! We've got our value. The problem is that there's no security involved in this process, so we end up with a raw value.

So why would we need additional security when accessing a value in an array? One good example is processing of form-based multiple-select boxes. In these instances, `JRequest` cannot help us to any great extent. Instead, we need to add in our security after we have retrieved the array using `JRequest`.

How to do it...

The method we use to extract a value from an array is `JArrayHelper::getValue()`. So let's start at the most basic level, grabbing a raw value from an array.

```
$value = JArrayHelper::getValue($myArray, $index);
```

Nothing to get too excited about here! However, this is already different from `$myArray[$index]`. If we were to get the value using `$myArray[$index]` and there was no key equal to `$index`, we would receive a warning. We immediately overcome this using `JArrayHelper::getValue()`. So `JArrayHelper::getValue()` can be useful even for basic array handling.

Next, we can add a default value. The default value is used in instances where the specified index does not exist.

```
$value = JArrayHelper::getValue($myArray, $index, $default);
```

Easy enough!

The real value of `JArrayHelper::getValue()` is in the final parameter we can provide. The last parameter is used to constrain the type of the returned value.

```
$value = JArrayHelper::getValue($myArray, $index, $default,
                                          'INTEGER');
```

The above example ensures that the returned value is an integer. There are other types we can use, as shown in the following table:

Type	Description
INT or INTEGER	Whole number
FLOAT or DOUBLE	Floating point number
BOOL or BOOLEAN	True or false value
ARRAY	Array
STRING	String
WORD	String that only contains the characters a - z, A - Z, underscores, and 0 - 9
NONE	No constraints

See also

For a more complete view of securely dealing with data, refer to Chapter 2, *Keeping Extensions Secure*.

Casting all elements of an array to integers

This method explains how to cast all of the values in an array to integers. An example of when this can be useful is dealing with itemized data. As we know, itemized data often includes checkboxes for each row that allow us to select items. These checkboxes are defined as an array, usually called `cid[]`.

How to do it...

The `JArrayHelper::toInteger()` static method casts all of the values in a given array to integers.

```
JArrayHelper::toInteger($myArray);
```

Notice that this method does not return anything. This is because the array argument is passed by reference. Therefore, we need to be careful if we need to maintain an original copy of the data.

If, for any reason, the array parameter that we pass into the method turns out not to be an array, we can specify a default value to return.

```
// defaults to array(1, 2, 3)
JArrayHelper::toInteger($myArray, array(1, 2, 3));

// defaults to array(1, 0, 3)
JArrayHelper::toInteger($myArray, array('1', 'TWO', '3ish'));

// defaults to array(1)
JArrayHelper::toInteger($myArray, true);

// defaults to array(0)
JArrayHelper::toInteger($myArray, false);
```

This isn't quite as simple as it first appears! This is because the default value will also be used as an array, and it will be processed to ensure that all values within it are integers.

See also

It is, of course, not always appropriate to cast an entire array to integers. For information about retrieving and casting individual values, refer to the previous recipe, *Getting a value from an array*.

Sorting an array of objects

This recipe explains how to sort an array of objects based on a property and direction, that is, ascending and descending.

How to do it...

We will use the following array as an example:

```
// create objects
$anObject         = new stdClass();
$anotherObject    = new stdClass();
$yetAnotherObject = new stdClass();

// add ordering
$anObject->ordering         = '2';
$anotherObject->ordering    = '3';
$yetAnotherObject->ordering = '1';

// build array
$array = array($anObject, $anotherObject, $yetAnotherObject);
```

To sort this array, we use the static `JArrayHelper::sortObjects()` method. To this method we pass two parameters—the array we want to sort and the name of the instance variable by which we want to order the array.

```
$array = JArrayHelper::sortObjects($array, 'ordering'));
```

As one would expect, the result of this will be:

```
Array
(
    [0] => stdClass Object
        (
            [ordering] => 1
        )

    [1] => stdClass Object
        (
            [ordering] => 2
        )

    [2] => stdClass Object
        (
            [ordering] => 3
        )

)
```

How it works

The ordering is calculated using the normal PHP greater-than and less-than operators. For more information, refer to `http://php.net/manual/language.operators.comparison.php`.

Due to the way in which the greater-than and less-than operators function, it is always advisable to only sort based on values of the same type. That is to say, we should avoid sorting based on instance variables that may contain different types of value; for example, strings and objects.

There's more...

It is possible to sort in the opposite direction, that is, in a descending order. To achieve this, we must provide the third optional parameter. This parameter should be either 1 or -1.

```
// sort ascending
$asc  = JArrayHelper::sortObjects($array, 'ordering', 1));

// sort descending
$desc = JArrayHelper::sortObjects($array, 'ordering', -1));
```

Imploding an array

PHP provides us with the `implode()` function to which we can pass an array and, optionally, some glue. This gives us a string representation of an array. However, it is relatively basic. For example, it does not take any account of array keys. This recipe explains how we can use `JArrayHelper` to create more complex strings from arrays.

How to do it...

We will use the example array shown below. Notice that the third element does not have a name; instead, it is indexed at position `0`.

```
$array = array('x' => 34, 'y' => 28, 3);
```

The static `JArrayHelper::toString()` method uses two different pieces of glue. The *inner glue* is used to stick keys and values together. The *outer glue* is used to stick elements together. By default, the inner glue is an equals character and the outer glue is a space character. Here's how we use `JArrayHelper::toString()` in its most basic form:

```
$string = JArrayHelper::toString($array);
```

This gives us the following:

```
x="34" y="28" 0="3"
```

Notice that there are double quotation marks around the values. These are always added, *but be aware that the values are not escaped!* The quotation marks are a bit of a nuisance, as they prevent the method from being as flexible as we might like. For example, it is not possible to generate an INI string without additional processing.

We can specify alternative glue by providing the second and third optional parameters, for example:

```
$string = JArrayHelper::toString($array, ' is ', ' and ');
```

This gives us the following:

```
x is "34" and y is "28" and 0 is "3"
```

There's more...

When an element in the array is an array itself, this gets combined into the result, which can be confusing. Consider the following example:

```
$array = array(
   'a' => 34,
   'b' => array(
      'a' => 12,
      'b' => 9
   ),
   'c' => 28
);

$string = JArrayHelper::toString($array);
```

Notice how the inner array defines elements with the same names as the outer array. As a result, the value of $string is ambiguous.:

```
a="34" a="12" b="9" c="28"
```

Although it does not resolve the problem, we can opt to include the name of the key to which the inner array belongs. This does not resolve the ambiguity, because there are no delimiters around the strings generated by the inner arrays. For example,

```
$string = JArrayHelper::toString($array, '=', ' ', true);
```

results in

```
a="34" b a="12" b="9" c="28"
```

The JArrayHelper::toString() method works best with single dimension arrays and multidimensional arrays that define unique consecutive elements.

11
Error Handling and Reporting

This chapter contains the following recipes:

- ▸ Raising an error-level J!error
- ▸ Raising a warning-level J!error
- ▸ Raising a notice-level J!error
- ▸ Enqueuing a message
- ▸ Changing the default J!error handling
- ▸ Handling and raising a bespoke J!error
- ▸ Logging errors and events using JLog
- ▸ Throwing exceptions with PHP 5
- ▸ Catching exceptions with PHP 5

Introduction

Joomla! has its very own way of dealing with errors. Our gateway to this is the static `JError` class. There are three error levels defined by Joomla!—**Error, Warning**, and **Notice**. These should sound very familiar to PHP developers because they have the same names as the built-in PHP errors.

 In this chapter, we make the distinction between PHP errors and Joomla! errors by referring to Joomla! errors as **J!errors**.

Like their PHP counterparts, J!errors have a corresponding integer value that can be used to build bit masks. In fact, the J!error integers are the same as that for the three basic PHP errors. The following table shows different J!errors, their corresponding values, PHP constants, and a brief description of when each should be used.

Value	J!error	Constant	Description
1	Error	E_ERROR	Fatal error, which will gracefully stop the script
2	Warning	E_WARNING	Non-fatal error
8	Notice	E_NOTICE	Negligible problem which has not affected execution

For a complete description of PHP error constants, refer to the official PHP documentation at `http://php.net/manual/errorfunc.constants.php`.

What actually occurs when J!errors are raised is configurable. For this reason, we should never assume that certain things will happen when a J!error is raised. For example, we should take an action to ensure that fatal errors really are fatal! Changing the way in which J!errors are handled is discussed in the *Changing the default error handling* recipe later in this chapter.

In addition to the three core J!errors described in the above table, it is possible to define our own types of J!error. This can be especially useful in instances where we want to handle certain errors differently, but do not want to affect the handling of normal J!errors.

There is a handy function in Joomla! called `jexit()`. As the name suggests, this function is very similar to the PHP `exit()` and `die()` functions. This function will stop execution of the script immediately; no questions asked! We can pass this function an error message or an integer in the same way as we would when using the `exit()` or `die()` function. We should always use `jexit()` in preference to `exit()` and `die()`, because this function will give Joomla! the opportunity to complete the cleanup work prior to exiting, or in the case of unit tests, *tear-down* work.

PHP 5 introduces exceptions. Joomla! 1.5 is not written for PHP 5 and does not use exceptions. However, it does define the class, `JException`. This class is used to encapsulate information about J!errors. Indeed, when we raise any type of J!error, we will be rewarded with our very own `JException` object, which includes useful information such as a trace to the source of the problem.

In this chapter, we take a look at the PHP 5 technique of throwing and catching exceptions. Although Joomla! 1.5 does not use exceptions, it is perfectly acceptable if we are building Joomla! 1.5 extensions specifically for PHP 5 environments to incorporate exceptions.

Looking to the future, Joomla! 1.6 (in development at the time of writing) will use PHP 5 style exceptions. In Joomla! 1.6, the use of the `JException` class will become common place. In Joomla! 1.6, this class is a child of the built-in PHP 5 `Exception` class and thus can be thrown. For more information about PHP exceptions, refer to the last two recipes in this chapter, *Throwing exceptions with PHP 5* and *Catching exceptions with PHP 5*.

When dealing with errors of any kind in Joomla!, it can be useful to be aware of `JObject` error handling. The majority of the classes in Joomla! are descendents of the `JObject` class and, therefore, this applies to most of the Joomla! classes. These objects are capable of maintaining a history of errors. We can add errors to the history using the `JObject::setError()` method and retrieve errors using the `JObject::getError()` method. For a detailed description of dealing with errors in a `JObject`, refer to the previous chapter, *JObjects and Arrays*.

Raising an error-level J!error

This recipe explains how to raise a J!error of the level error. We should use this type of J!error when we encounter a *fatal* problem, that is, when the problem cannot be overcome and execution needs to stop. The nice thing about this approach is that although the J!error will be fatal, the termination of the script will be graceful and will provide the user with an understandable error page.

How to do it...

To raise a fatal J!error, we use the static `JError::raiseError()` method. This method requires two parameters, an error code and a message. For example:

```
// raise an internal server error
JError::raiseError(
    500,
    JText::_('INTERNAL SERVER ERROR')
);
```

Notice that the second parameter is translated using `JText`.

 The error code is used in the HTTP response headers and, therefore, must be a valid HTTP error code. For a complete guide to valid HTTP error codes, refer to `http://www.w3.org/Protocols/rfc2616/rfc2616-sec10.html`. Generally, we will use the following codes: `500` (internal server error), `404` (resource not found), `401` (access denied—unauthorized), and `403` (access denied—forbidden).

It is a good idea to use `jexit()` directly after raising a fatal J!error. It is possible to change the way errors are handled, thus placing a call to `jexit()` directly after raising an error will guarantee that the script stops executing.

```
// raise an internal server error
JError::raiseError(
    500,
    JText::_('INTERNAL SERVER ERROR')
);
// make sure the JError is fatal
jexit(JText::_('INTERNAL SERVER ERROR'));
```

Clean up after yourself

Prior to raising an error, it might be necessary to *clean up* any loose ends; for example, *undoing* what has already been completed during the execution of the script. Failure to do this could result in security weakness CWE-459.

How it works

Raising an error in Joomla! will terminate script execution. Unlike the `jexit()` function and the PHP `exit()` and `die()` functions, it will create a user-friendly error message. The following is an example of an error message a user might receive should he or she encounter a fatal error. This output is generated using the error template located in the `templates/system/error.php` file. *It is possible to override this template file in a site template extension.*

---

500 - Internal Server Error

You may not be able to visit this page because of:

1. an **out-of-date bookmark/favourite**
2. a search engine that has an **out-of-date listing for this site**
3. a **mistyped address**
4. you have **no access** to this page
5. The requested resource was not found.
6. An error has occurred while processing your request.

Please try one of the following pages:

- Home Page

If difficulties persist, please contact the System Administrator of this site.

Internal Server Error

It can be useful to enable site debugging when errors are encountered, as this will produce a trace showing the exact point of failure in the code. *Remember that debugging should never be enabled on live sites because of security considerations.*

There's more...

We can pass a third parameter to `JError::raiseError()` in which we can place data that will provide us, as a developer, with a more verbose response. *However, it should be noted that this extra information is not outputted by the default error templates for security reasons.*

```
JError::raiseError(
    500,
    JText::_('INTERNAL SERVER ERROR'),
    $someVerboseErrorInformation
);
```

See also

To learn how to raise a J!error of a lesser level, refer to the next two recipes, *Raising a warning-level J!error* and *Raising a notice-level J!error*.

Raising a warning-level J!error

In this recipe, we will explore how to raise a warning-level J!error. These J!errors are specifically for use when an error occurs that is not fatal, but alters the actions taken by the script.

How to do it...

To raise a warning, we use the static `JError::raiseWarning()` method. This method requires two parameters, an error code and a message. This type of J!error is often raised when input validation fails. For example, if a required form field is empty, we might do this:

```
JError::raiseWarning(
    500,
    JText::_('PLEASE SUPPLY A VALUE FOR FORM FIELD X')
);
```

Notice that the second parameter is translated using `JText`.

The purpose of the error code in the context of a warning is not entirely clear. Due to the way in which warnings are handled, the error code is not really put to good use. The de-facto standard is to use the HTTP-style error code `500`, which equates to *internal server error*.

Stick to HTTP error codes

It is best to stick to HTTP error codes when raising warnings. Remember that handling of J!errors can be altered and that for fatal errors, the code is used in the HTTP response. For a complete list of HTTP error codes, refer to `http://www.w3.org/Protocols/rfc2616/rfc2616-sec10.html`.

How it works

Warnings are displayed at the top, or near the top of the page. The exact location of the warning and the look and feel of the warning will depend on the site template. The following three examples are based on the templates that are bundled with Joomla! 1.5 (*rhuk_milkyway, beez,* and *ja_purity*):

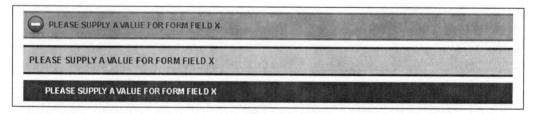

When we redirect the browser using the `JApplication::redirect()` method, all warnings are persisted. That is to say, if we raise a warning and then redirect to another page, the warning will be displayed on the next page.

There's more...

We can also opt to pass a third parameter in which we can place data that will provide us, as a developer, with a more verbose response. *It should, however, be noted that this extra information is not outputted by any of the default templates.*

```
JError::raiseWarning(
    500,
    JText::_('AN ERROR OCCURED'),
    $someVerboseErrorInformation
);
```

As warnings are not fatal, it can be useful to grab the return value of
`JError::raiseWarning()`. This value will be a `JException` object, which
includes handy debugging information about the error. It is common to add this
value to a `JObject`, typically the current object in which the error occurred:

```
// raise warning
$exception = JError::raiseWarning(
    500,
    JText::_('AN ERROR OCCURED'),
    $someVerboseErrorInformation
);
// assign warning to the current object
$this->setError($exception);
```

See also

To learn how to raise a fatal J!error, refer to the previous recipe, *Raising an error-level J!error*.

Alternatively, to raise a lesser J!error, refer to the next recipe, *Raising a notice-level J!error*.

Raising a notice-level J!error

In this recipe, we explore the least invasive of the J!error levels. A J!error notice is
informational. It should only indicate trivial problems that are expected to occur
periodically, but do not affect the flow of the script execution.

How to do it...

To raise a notice, we use the static `JError::raiseNotice()` method. This method requires
two parameters, the error code and a message. For example, if a form did not include a value
but a default is known, we might do the following:

```
JError::raiseNotice(
    500,
    JText::_('NO VALUE FOR FORM FIELD X, ASSUMED VALUE Y')
);
```

Notice that the second parameter is translated using `JText`. In practice, we would be more
likely to use the static `JText::sprintf()` method. This is because we can pass the
field name and the assumed value to this method separately, thus removing the need for
hardcoded values in the translations.

As with the J!error warnings, the purpose of the error code is not clear. The de-facto standard is to use the HTTP-style error code `500`, which equates to *internal server error*.

Stick to HTTP error codes

It is best to stick to HTTP error codes when raising warnings. Remember that handling of J!errors can be altered and for fatal errors, the code is used in the HTTP response. For a complete list of HTTP error codes, refer to `http://www.w3.org/Protocols/rfc2616/rfc2616-sec10.html`.

Notices are not success messages

It is tempting to think of notices as being suitable for success messages; for example, *Some items successfully saved*. But this is not the case. Anything that we raise through `JError` is an error by definition. To create a success message, refer to the next recipe, *Enqueuing a message*.

How it works

Notices are displayed at the top of the page, and are useful for informing users about minor problems. Unlike warnings, notices generally indicate an error that has had no discernable effect on the execution of the script; for example, failure to send an email notification. The exact look and feel of the notice will depend on the site template. The following three examples are based on the templates that are bundled with Joomla! 1.5 (*rhuk_milkyway*, *beez*, and *ja_purity*):

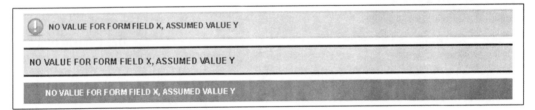

When we redirect the browser using the `Japplication::redirect()` method, all notices are persisted. That is to say, if we raise a notice and then redirect to another page, the notice will be displayed on the next page.

What actually occurs when a J!error is raised is determined by the J!error handling options. This can be changed at any time. For more information, refer to the *Changing the default error handling* recipe later in this chapter.

There's more...

For details about including extra information in the J!error and using the returned value of `JError::raiseNotice()`, refer to the *There's more...* section of the previous recipe. Note that `JError::raiseNotice()` works in the same way as `JError::raiseWarning()`. So, much of the recipe information is the same.

See also

To learn how to raise a J!error of a more prominent level, refer to the previous two recipes, *Raising a warning-level J!error* and *Raising an error-level fatal J!error*.

Enqueuing a message

It can be useful to pass informational messages to the user. For example, we might want to inform users that an action has been performed successfully, or that the page they are viewing is not up-to-date. This recipe explains how to use the application message queue to create information messages that will be displayed as a part of the site template.

How to do it...

To enqueue a message, we must first gain access to the global `JApplication` object.

```
// get the application
$app =& JFactory::getApplication();
```

 It is possible to use `global $mainframe` or even `$GLOBALS['mainframe']` instead of `JFactory::getApplication()`. Although this is acceptable, it is considered deprecated and should be avoided.

To enqueue a message, we use the `JApplication::enqueueMessage()` method to which we pass the message we want to enqueue.

```
// Add a message
$app->enqueueMessage(JText::_('AN ENQUEUED MESSAGE'));
```

> **Redirecting**
>
> If we want to display a message directly after a redirect, there is an easier way! We can use the (optional) second `JApplication::redirect()` parameter to enqueue a message.

How it works

The global `JApplication` object maintains a queue of messages. It is essential that the messages are stored in a queue: Queues are **FIFO (First-In-First-Out)** data structures. This means that when messages are outputted, they appear in the same order in which they were inserted into the queue.

The message queue is persistent. For this reason, when we redirect the browser using the `JApplication::redirect()` method, the message queue is retained. That is to say, if we enqueue a message and then redirect to another page, the message will be displayed on the next page.

Messages consist of two parts: the message itself and the type of message expressed as a string. The message type is usually a `message`, `notice`, or `error`. The type of the message affects its appearance; the exact look and feel of the messages will depend on the site template.

When we use the `JApplication::enqueueMessage()` method, the message that is created defaults to the `message` type. The following three example messages are of the `message` type as displayed by the templates that are bundled with Joomla! 1.5 (*rhuk_milkyway*, *beez*, and *ja_purity*):

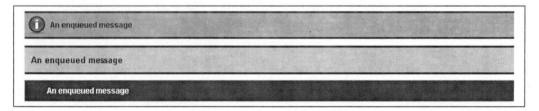

>
> The message type `notice` is used specifically for J!errors raised as notices. And, somewhat confusingly, a message type of `error` is used specifically for J!errors raised as warnings.

There's more...

When we enqueue a message, we are required to supply the first parameter, the message. We can also pass a second parameter, the message type. By default, this is `message`. For example, we could enqueue a message of the custom type `information`.

```
// Add an information message
$app->enqueueMessage(
    JText::_('AN INFORMATION MESSAGE'),
    'information'
);
```

In an HTML response, the message type normally equates directly to a CSS class name. We say *normally* because this is determined by the way in which the site template renders the message queue. If we wanted to use an alternative message type, we should create some corresponding CSS. For example, we could add some CSS to make an information message look like a Wikipedia message.

```
$style = "/* Informative Messages */
dl#system-message dt.information {
    display: none;
}
dl#system-message dd.information ul {
    background : #FBFBFB url(someimage.png) no-repeat scroll 4px
                                                        center;
    border     : 1px solid #AAAAAA;
    border-left: 10px solid #F28500;
    color      : #000000;
    padding    : 8px 8px 8px 25px;
}";
$doc =& JFactory::getDocument();
$doc->addStyleDeclaration($style);
```

This will create the following message:

 An enqueued informative message that looks like a Wikipedia message

Let's compare it to a Wikipedia citation message:

This article **does not cite any references or sources**. Please help improve this article by adding citations to reliable sources. Unverifiable material may be challenged and removed.

See also

To learn how to enqueue messages as the result of J!errors, refer to the *Raising a warning-level J!error* and *Raising a notice-level J!error* recipes.

For information about adding custom CSS to a page, refer to Chapter 6, *Interaction and Styling*.

Changing the default J!error handling

By default, J!error errors result in a fatal script termination that first displays a user-friendly error message. On the other hand, J!error warnings and J!error notices enqueue messages ready to be displayed at the top of the page when it is rendered. We can change the behavior of all of these.

How to do it...

To alter the handling of J!errors, we use the static `JError::setErrorHandling()` method. This requires two parameters—the error type for which we want to modify the handling, and the handler (also known as the mode) we want to use. *An explanation of the J!error types and the corresponding constants is provided in the chapter introduction.*

We will use J!error notices as an example. As J!error notices are informative but should not affect the script flow, we can safely change the mode to `Ignore`.

```
// ignore all notices from this point forward.
JError::setErrorHandling(E_NOTICE, 'Ignore');
```

Conversely, we could choose to output a more complete picture of the error. The `Verbose` mode outputs the error details, including the extra information that can be passed when the error is raised.

```
// output everything we know about the warning.
JError::setErrorHandling(E_WARNING, 'Verbose');
```

 The `Verbose` mode should be used with caution. It outputs information that could potentially allow a malicious user to glean an unprecedented level of understanding about our system, which could be used to form a basis for an attack, `CWE-209`.

It is generally assumed that `raiseError()` will stop the script. Therefore, it is not a good idea to change the handling of `E_ERROR` unless the alternative mode also stops the script execution.

How it works

When an error is raised with `JError`, one of the modes described in the following table will be used. *Each mode is technically a static method in the `JError` class, which can be invoked when an error is raised.*

Mode	Method	Description
Ignore	handleIgnore	Error is ignored
Echo	handleEcho	Prints the `JException` message to screen
Verbose	handleVerbose	Prints the `JException` message and back-trace the information to screen
Die	handleDie	Terminates the application and prints the `JException` message to screen
Message	handleMessage	Adds a message to the application queue
Log	handleLog	Adds a log entry to the application error log
Trigger	handleTrigger	Triggers a PHP error
Callback	handleCallback	Calls a static method in another class

Unfortunately, it is not possible to set the handling such that several handlers are used. For example, `Log` and then `Die`. However a solution to this can be achieved using the `Callback` mode, as described in the next section.

There's more...

The most flexible of all the modes is `Callback`. This mode allows us to use our own code to handle the J!error. In order to specify the function or method we want to handle the J!error, we must provide the optional third parameter when calling the static `JError::setErrorHandling()` method. The following example tells Joomla! to invoke the `myErrorHandler` function when a J!error error is raised:

```
// use the function myErrorHandler to deal with E_ERROR errors
JError::setErrorHandling(
    E_ERROR,
    'Callback',
    'myErrorHandler'
);
```

The third parameter is of the PHP pseudo type, `callback`. For more information, refer to `http://php.net/manual/language.pseudo-types.php`.

In order for this example to work, we must declare the `myErrorHandler()` function. In the following example, we take advantage of the J!error modes `Log` and `Die` by invoking the corresponding static methods in the `JError` class:

```
/**
 * Log error and die
 *
 * @param JException $error    Error that needs handling
 * @param array       $options Handling options
 */
function &myErrorHandler($error, $options) {
    // Log the error
    JError::handleLog($error, $options);

    // End the script
    JError::handleDie($error, $options);

    // all done
    return $error;
}
```

Take note of the function signature. When this function is called, it will be passed a `JException` object which encapsulates the error information, and in some instances, a variable containing options that can be used to change the way in which the function operates.

The `$options` parameter is used only by the `JError::handleCallback()` method. It is however good practice to pass this parameter to the other methods. Notice that we return the `$error` parameter. This is not really required in our example because the `JError::handleDie()` method will stop the script from executing anyway. *All functions and methods that handle an error should return the original `JException` object.*

See also

To avoid interfering with J!errors, it can be a good idea to define our own J!error levels. This is especially important if we want to use radically different modes to handle our J!errors. For more information, refer to the next recipe, *Handling and raising a bespoke J!error.*

Handling and raising a bespoke J!error

Sometimes we may want to handle our errors in a very different way from the normal J!error types—error, warning, and notice. We can separate our J!errors from the regular J!errors by defining bespoke J!error levels. This ensures we do not interfere with Joomla! and that we maintain a logical separation of the J!error types.

How to do it...

To register a new error level, we use the static `JError::registerErrorLevel()` method. This method accepts the following three parameters:

- The error level represented as an integer
- The human-readable name of the error level
- The error mode (optional)

For more information about error modes, refer to the previous recipe, *Changing the default error handling*. In the following example, we register a new error level using `JError::registerErrorLevel()`:

```
// declare the error level constant
define('BESPOKE_ERROR', 32768);

// register the error level with JError
$registerd = JError::registerErrorLevel(
    BESPOKE_ERROR,
    'Bespoke Error'
);
```

It is important to check the return value of `JError::registerErrorLevel()`. If the value is `false`, it indicates that registration of the error level was not successful because the error level has already been registered. Under these circumstances, it is generally best to stop the script.

```
if (!$registered) {
    JError::raiseError(
        500,
        JText::_('BESPOKE ERROR LEVEL ALREADY DEFINED')
    );
}
```

As we mentioned, there is an optional third parameter that defines the J!error mode. By default, the J!error mode is `Ignore`. To use a different J!error mode, we simply supply the name of the mode, as defined in the previous recipe, *Changing the default error handling*.

One problem exists with the static `JError::registerErrorLevel()` method. If we want to use a J!error mode that requires options—for example, the `Callback` mode—we cannot do this when we register the error level. Instead, we must change the mode afterwards, as described in the previous recipe.

To use our new J!error level, we must use the static `JError::raise()` method. However, because this method signature is quite complex, it is easiest to create a function or method that calls this for us, similar to the `raiseError()`, `raiseWarning()`, and `raiseNotice()` methods with which we are likely already familiar.

```
/**
 * Raise a bespoke error
 *
 * @param int    $code Error code
 * @param string $msg  Error message
 * @param mixed  $info Additional error information
 * @return JExcpetion
 */
function &raiseBespokeError($code, $msg, $info = null) {
    $exception =& JError::raise(
        BESPOKE_ERROR,
        $code,
        $msg,
        $info,
        true
    );
    return $exception;
}
```

This significantly reduces the effort required to actually raise a bespoke error. Notice that the `JError::raise()` method accepts five parameters, while our function only accepts three. Of these five parameters, only two are required.

How it works

As Joomla! purposely uses error-level codes that can be used in bit patterns, it is generally a good idea to stick to binary values. Joomla! uses three error-level codes. They are 1, 2, and 8. However, it shares these with the PHP equivalents. Therefore, instead of specifying a value of 16 for the next new error level, it is preferable to use the next available code, that is, 2^{15} or 32768.

All of the J!errors are ultimately raised using the static `JError::raise()` method. This method accepts five parameters, described in order in the following table. Note that `$info` and `$backtrace` are not required.

Parameter	Default	Description
`$level`		J!error level
`$code`		Error code specific to the error that is being raised, usually an HTTP error code; for example, `500` is an internal server error
`$msg`		Human-readable message that describes the error
`$info`	`null`	Additional information about the error
`$backtrace`	`false`	Option to include debug information, which can be used to trace the source of the error

See also

To modify the handling of J!errors, refer to the previous recipe, *Changing the default error handling*.

Logging errors and events using JLog

This recipe explains how to add entries to a log file. We can either add entries to the default Joomal! error log, or we can create our own log files in one easy step. Although `JLog` is a part of the `joomla.error` library namespace, this recipe is not suited only for logging errors. We can use `JLog` to create logs for anything!

Getting ready

Before we attempt to use the `JLog` class, we must import it.

```
// import JLog
jimport('joomla.error.log');
```

How to do it...

The first thing we need is an instance of the `JLog` class. To get this, we use the `JLog::getInstance()` method. In its most basic form, this method doesn't require a single parameter! *Notice that we use the `=&` assignment operator to ensure that we get a reference to the `JLog` object, and not a copy.*

```
// get an instance of JLog
$log =& JLog::getInstance();
```

Alternatively, if we want to create our own log file in the Joomla! `log` folder, we need to pass the name of the log file to the method. *If the error log file does not currently exist, it will be created when we log the first entry.*

```
// get an instance of JLog for myerrors log file
$log =& JLog::getInstance('myerrors.php');
```

Now to the good bit—adding entries to the log file. For this, we use the `JLog::addEntry()` method. Entries are expressed as arrays. By default, an entry should contain a **level, status,** and **comment**. The date, time, and client's IP address will be automatically added to the entry.

```
// create entry array
$entry = array(
    'LEVEL'   => '1',
    'STATUS'  => 'SOME ERROR:',
    'COMMENT' => 'Some error occurred'
);

// add entry to the log
$log->addEntry($entry);
```

 The purpose of `LEVEL` is unclear. There are no examples in Joomla! where this is used, nor is there any documentation explaining its purpose. It is acceptable to omit elements from a log entry. In these instances, a dash will occur in the log file.

And that's it! We're all done!

How it works

The `JLog` class wraps up the whole logging process for us. We don't need to create the log file, nor do we need to deal with dates, times, and IP addresses. When we add a new entry, a log file will be created if it does not exist. Log files include useful headers that describe the log file format and prevent direct access to the log file, as shown in the following example:

```
#<?php die('Direct Access To Log Files Not Permitted'); ?>
#Version: 1.0
#Date: 2009-07-02 10:46:10
#Fields: date    time    level   c-ip    status comment
#Software: Joomla! 1.5.11 Production/Stable [ Vea ] 03-June-2009 03:30
                                                                    GMT
```

Notice that the first line of the header includes some PHP. This prevents users from snooping through our error logs. *This is why it is important to make sure that our log file is a PHP file.*

There's more...

The `JLog::getInstance()` method accepts up to three parameters: the name of the log file, an options array, and a base path.

The options array only uses one option, a format string. Format strings are plain-text strings that include field names encapsulated in curly braces. The field names are ultimately substituted for the corresponding entry elements. By default, the format is:

```
{DATE}\t{TIME}\t{LEVEL}\t{C-IP}\t{STATUS}\t{COMMENT}
```

 The `{DATE}`, `{TIME}`, and `{C-IP}` fields are automatically generated when adding entries. Therefore, we can use these as we please in our format.

The final parameter is the base path, or rather the folder in which the error log is located. By default, this is the Joomla! `log` folder.

In the following example, we create a bespoke error log located in our component's `log` folder:

```
$file   = 'myerrors.php';
$format = "{DATE}\t{TIME}\t{C-IP}\t{USER}\t{DESCRIPTION}";
$path   = JPATH_COMPONENT . DS . 'logs';

// get JLog instance
$log = JLog::getInstance(
    $file,
    array('format' => $format),
    $path
);
```

We can now start adding entries to the log file as per the previous example. However, this time our entry should include the elements USER and DESCRIPTION, as expressed by the format string. The following is an example of the bespoke log file:

```
#<?php die('Direct Access To Log Files Not Permitted'); ?>
#Version: 1.0
#Date: 2009-07-02 10:46:10
#Fields: date    time    c-ip    user    description
#Software: Joomla! 1.5.11 Production/Stable [ Vea ] 03-June-2009 03:30
                                                                    GMT
2009-07-02       10:46:43      127.0.0.1      admin  Some error occurred
```

Throwing exceptions with PHP 5

In PHP 4, we are used to functions returning `false` or something similar on failure. The problem with this is that the failure is handled only if the invoking code bothers to check the returned value. Exceptions provide a more robust solution that forces the failure to be handled. This recipe looks at how we create, or rather how we *throw*, an exception in PHP 5. *This recipe applies only to extensions being built specifically for PHP 5.*

How to do it...

To throw an exception using PHP 5, we use the `throw` statement. In its most basic form, it will work like this:

```
throw new Exception();
```

Exceptions are represented as objects. In this instance, we have used the most basic of all exception classes, `Exception`. This class accepts two optional parameters, an error message and an error code.

```
throw new Exception(
    JText::_('SOMETHING HAS GONE AWRY'),
    500
);
```

We do not have to create the `Exception` object as part of the `throw` statement.

```
$myException = new Exception($message, $code);
throw $myException;
```

When we declare a function or a method that might throw an exception, it is a good idea to include a phpDoc `@throws` tag to this effect in the function or method DocBlock.

```
/**
 * My function that does something
 *
 * @todo implement method
 * @throws Exception Function might throw an exception
 */
function myFunction() {
}
```

The `@throws` tag is normally used in the following form:

```
@throws [classname [description]]
```

A `@throws` tag should be added for every type of exception the function or method can throw.

How it works

Exceptions stop the normal script flow. As soon as an exception is thrown, it must be handled. Failure to handle an exception will result in an ungraceful fatal error. To learn about handling exceptions in PHP, refer to the next recipe, _Catching exceptions with PHP 5_.

 Java programmers may be interested to know that PHP 5 does not support checked exceptions. For more information about checked exceptions, refer to http://java.sun.com/docs/books/tutorial/essential/exceptions/.

There's more...

It is common practice to extend the built-in Exception class to provide greater specialization for specific exceptions. For example, we could create an exception class that deals exclusively with verification failures:

```php
class VerificationException extends Exception {
    /**
     * Expected value
     */
    protected $expectedValue;

    /**
     * Actual value
     */
    protected $actualValue;

    /**
     * Overrides Exception constructor
     *
     * @param mixed  $expectedValue Expected value
     * @param mixed  $actualValue   Actual value
     */
    public function __construct($expectedValue, $actualValue) {
        $message = 'Actual value ' . $actualValue
                 . ' does not equal expected value '
                 . $expectedValue;
        parent::__construct($message, 500);
        $this->expectedValue = $expectedValue;
        $this->actualValue   = $actualValue;
    }
}
```

When defining additional class properties, it is best practice to define them as `protected` and to create suitable accessor methods; for example, `getActualValue()`. We have not done this in the example for ease of reading.

The Standard PHP Library includes a number of useful predefined `Exception` classes. It is worth noting these before creating our own `Exception` classes. For more information, refer to `http://php.net/manual/spl.exceptions.php`.

Another reason for extending the built-in `Exception` class is to provide greater control when it comes to handling exceptions. For example, it can be beneficial to create a new class that extends `Exception`, but does not add to it because the type of exception determines what can handle it.

As stated in the chapter introduction, looking into the future, in Joomla! 1.6 (in development at the time of writing), the `JException` class will be a child of the built-in PHP 5 `Exception` class, and thus will be throwable.

See also

This recipe is very much designed to be used in tandem with the next recipe, which describes how to handle an exception after it has been thrown.

Catching exceptions with PHP 5

Once an exception is thrown, it must be dealt with before normal script execution can continue. Continuing the throw analogy, handling an exception is known as **catching**. This recipe explains how to **catch** exceptions.

How to do it...

We use the `try` and `catch` blocks to catch PHP exceptions. Within the `try` block, we place the code that could potentially throw an exception. Within the `catch` block, we place the code that deals with an exception if it is thrown in the `try` block. The following is a basic example:

```
try {
    myFunction();
} catch (Exception $e) {
    echo $e;
}
```

Exceptions can be specialized from the built-in PHP `Exception` class. That is to say, as shown in the previous recipe, we can create subclasses from the PHP `Exception` class, and we can throw these.

We can create a `catch` block that deals specifically with specialized `Exception` objects by changing the `catch` statement. We could change our example to only catch `VerificationException` objects (as defined in the previous chapter).

```
try {
    myFunction();
} catch (VerificationException $e) {
    echo $e;
}
```

It is possible to define several `catch` blocks, each with a specific type of exception in mind.

```
try {
    myFunction();
} catch (VerificationException $e) {
    echo 'Verification Failed';
} catch (Exception $e) {
    echo $e;
}
```

> Unlike some languages, PHP 5 does not support the `finally` statement. In PHP, all exceptions must be derived from the built-in `Exception` class. Thus, the last `catch` statement shown in the above example will catch any exception that has not been handled by a prior `catch` block.

How it works

The `try` block is very simple: between the curly braces, there is some code that could cause an exception to be thrown. We can place as much or as little code in the `try` block as we like.

PHP 5 introduces **type hinting**. We see an example of this in `catch` statements, such as `catch (Exception $e)`. This equates to "Catch exceptions of type, `Exception` and assign the exception to `$e`."

When an exception occurs, PHP will work its way through the `catch` statements looking for a suitable `catch` block. Each `catch` statement is interrogated until a `catch` block that is capable of handling the exception is located. Therefore, the order of the `catch` blocks is important.

A `try` and `catch` block does not have to deal with all exceptions. If a suitable `catch` block is not found, the script will move up through the stack of `try` blocks until it finds a suitable `catch` statement, or until there are no options left, at which point the script will end fatally.

 Once an exception has been successfully handled, the script will resume after the `try` and `catch` block that successfully handled the exception. That is to say, the script will not continue where it left off. For this reason, it is generally considered bad practice to create `try` and `catch` blocks that encapsulate unnecessarily large blocks of code.

There's more...

The way in which the examples deal with the exceptions is not particularly tactful. Simply outputting an exception as a string does not overcome the error, nor does it produce user-friendly output. But perhaps more importantly, it poses a potential security weakness because it reveals a complete trace to the point of failure, including the full path to each file and the line on which code was invoked leading to the failure, CWE-209.

A more appropriate way of dealing with exceptions is to provide the user with a user-friendly error message and in extreme instances, end the script gracefully. We can get the basic gist of the exception from the exception message without giving away the details. We retrieve the message using the `JException::getMessage()` method. We can exit gracefully by raising a fatal HTTP 500 J!error message.

```
try {
    doSomething();
} catch (Exception $e) {
    // create a user friendly error message
    $message = 'An exception occurred: '.$e->getMessage();

    // exit Joomla! gracefully
    JError::raiseError(500, $message, $e);

    // for good luck, make sure we do actually stop now!
    jexit($message);
}
```

The following table describes some handy methods we can use to interrogate PHP `Exception` objects:

Method	Description
getMessage()	Human-readable exception message
getCode()	Code that describes the type of exception
getFile()	File in which the exception was thrown
getLine()	Line on which the exception was thrown
getTrace()	Array that describes the point of failure in the same way as the PHP function debug_backtrace()
getTraceAsString()	Human-readable equivalent of getTrace()

Clean up after yourself

We should always clean up after an exception occurs. For example, if we are halfway through a process, it may be necessary to *undo* the first part of the process. Failure to do this could result in a security weakness CWE-459.

For a good guide on how to use exceptions, you may want to refer to the book, *"Clean Code: A Handbook of Agile Software Craftsmanship,"* Robert C. Martin, Prentice Hall.

See also

To discover how to throw an exception in the first instance, refer to the previous recipe, *Throwing exceptions with PHP 5*.

12

Files and Folders

This chapter contains the following recipes:

- ▶ Checking whether a file or folder exists
- ▶ Reading a file
- ▶ Deleting a file or folder
- ▶ Copying a file or folder
- ▶ Moving and renaming files and folders
- ▶ Creating a folder
- ▶ Uploading files to Joomla!
- ▶ Reading a directory structure
- ▶ Changing file and folder permissions

Introduction

The recipes in this chapter discuss how to work with the local filesystem. When developing for Joomla!, it is good practice to take advantage of the static helper classes `JFile`, `JFolder`, and `JPath` when dealing with files and folders.

These classes provide a robust way of working with the filesystem. The key to the robust nature of these classes is the use of FTP. When FTP is available, many of the methods defined in these classes will attempt to use FTP instead of PHP filesystem functions. The advantage of this approach is the nature of the filesystem permissions. Using FTP means that we are not reliant on the web server user's filesystem permissions. Instead, we gain the same level of access offered by our normal FTP credentials.

Of course, FTP can only be used in installations where the FTP details have been configured. To configure your FTP settings for your installation, navigate to the installation global configuration and look for the **FTP Settings** field-set. *If FTP is not enabled, this will not prevent us from using the filesystem helper classes or prevent the classes from operating as expected.*

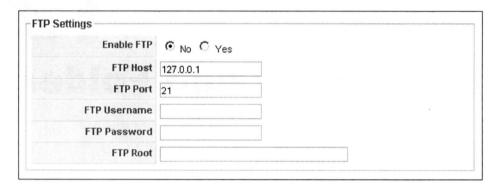

In order to use the `JFile`, `JFolder`, and `JPath` static classes, we need to import them. The following code snippet applies to all of the recipes in this chapter, and imports all three of the classes. *It is not uncommon to find that `JFolder` and `JPath` are already available; however, there is no harm in importing them a second time.*

```
// import JFile
jimport('joomla.filesystem.file');

// import JFolder
jimport('joomla.filesystem.folder');

// import JPath
jimport('joomla.filesystem.path');
```

Permissions are an important part of the modern filesystem. When we refer to permissions of users and user groups to files and folders, we are not discussing Joomla! users and Joomla! user groups. We are referring to users and user groups defined by the operating system.

Store files in the database for improved security

If we need to make our files secure, it is a good idea to store them in the database rather than the filesystem. This will prevent the web server from directly serving files without checking the necessary Joomla! permissions. Always remember to store the original filename and MIME type.

When we talk about permissions in this chapter, we use both *nix alpha notation (also referred to as *symbolic notation*) and *nix octal notation. As octal suggests, we have three bits, we can count from 0 to 7. The most significant bit (msb) represents **Read** access. The least significant bit (lsb) represents **Execute** access. The remaining bit represents **Write** access. This is summarised in the following table:

msb	lsb		Notation		
Read	**Write**	**Execute**	**Alpha**	**Octal**	**Binary**
NO	NO	NO	- - -	0	000
NO	NO	YES	- - x	1	001
NO	YES	NO	- w -	2	010
NO	YES	YES	- wx	3	011
YES	NO	NO	r - -	4	100
YES	NO	YES	r - x	5	101
YES	YES	NO	rw -	6	110
YES	YES	YES	rwx	7	111

There are three sets of these values when defining filesystem permissions. These sets represent the owner, the group, and everyone else. For example, the permissions rwxr-xr-- (or 754) allow the owner to read, write, and execute, allow the group to read and execute, and allow everyone else to read.

In some instances, we will find an additional part to the start of the permissions. This is used to indicate the file type. For example, d tells us that we are looking at a directory, where as a - (dash) tells us that we are looking at a regular file.

 Generally speaking, we should set folder permissions to 755, and file permissions to 644. Execute permissions are not required for PHP files; the server only needs read access to PHP files.

For information about security when dealing with the filesystem, refer to Chapter 2, *Keeping Extensions Secure*. It explains how to use some important static methods in JPath that can significantly reduce the risks associated with working with the filesystem; for example, path traversal.

Checking whether a file or folder exists

This recipe explains how to check whether or not a file or a folder exists within the filesystem. This can be useful in all sorts of situations; for example, making sure if a file is available to be read before attempting to read it, or making sure a folder exists before placing an uploaded file into it.

How to do it...

To determine if a file exists, we use the `JFile::exists()` method.

```
$fileExists = JFile::exists($filePath);
```

To determine if a folder exists, we use the `JFolder::exists()` method.

```
$folderExists = JFolder::exists($folderPath);
```

As you would expect, both of these methods return a Boolean value.

How it works

The `JFile::exists()` and `JFolder::exists()` methods differ very little from the PHP `is_file()` and `is_dir()` methods. The only important difference is the extra security. The path that is passed to the `JFile::exists()` and `JFolder::exists()` methods is cleaned prior to checking for the existence of the file or folder.

There's more...

A similarly useful method is, `JPath::find()`. This method can be used to locate a file that may reside in one of several folders. This is useful especially when implementing overriding, such as that which is often used for layouts.

```
$paths = array (
    JPATH_COMPONENT . DS . 'location',
    JPATH_COMPONENT . DS . 'anotherLocation',
);

$filePath = JPath::find($paths, 'myfile.php');
```

The paths in the `$paths` array appear in order of significance. For example, if both paths contained a file called `myfile.php`, the first path would take precedence.

This method returns a string, which is the full path to the found file. In instances where no file is successfully found, the method returns Boolean `false`.

See also

Files can be used as data sources, for example a CSV has obvious uses. The next recipe explains how to read the contents of a file.

For information about creating a folder if it does not exist, refer to the *Creating a folder* recipe, later in this chapter.

Reading a file

This recipe explains how to read the contents of a file.

How to do it...

To read a file, we must know where the file in question resides. Generally speaking, this should be a full path. In the following example, `$filePath` points to a file named `myfile.csv` in a folder called `files` in the root of the current component.

```
$fileName = JPATH_COMPONENT.DS.'files'.DS.'myfile.csv';
```

To read the contents of this file, we use the `JFile::read()` method. In its most basic form, this method reads the entire contents of the file and returns the contents as a string.

```
$fileContents = JFile::read($filePath));
```

How it works...

The `JFile::read()` method is surprisingly configurable, as described in the next section. It uses a file pointer resource created using the `fopen()` PHP function to read file contents. The contents of files are read in chunks; the advantage of this from our perspective is that we can read any given chunk of the file. This is handy, especially when dealing with large files from which we only want a small amount of data.

The only downside of this method is that it is not UTF-8 aware. Thus, chunk positions and lengths are measured in bytes rather than characters. Of course, it depends on the file contents as to whether or not this will pose a problem.

There's more...

We can set the second optional parameter to `true` if we want to look for the file, in which we want to read the contents, in the PHP `include_path`. *By and large, it is best to avoid this because it reduces our control over which file is read and can potentially introduce security vulnerabilities (the wrong file might be read).*

```
$fileContents = JFile::read('myfile.csv', true));
```

Sometimes, it can be useful to restrict the amount of contents from the file that we read. For example, we may only want the first line of a file; if we know the length or maximum length of the first line, we can safely restrict the file read. The following example reads the first `100` bytes of a file. Note that the length is expressed in bytes, not characters—this can be problematic when dealing with multi-byte character encodings such as UTF-8.

```
$fileContents = JFile::read($filePath, false, 100));
```

The next optional parameter is used to determine the size of the chunks in which to read the file. This is used only in instances where the size of the file cannot be determined, *something which only tends to occur when dealing with especially large files.* By default, this value is `8192` bytes.

```
$fileContents = JFile::read($filePath, false, 0, 4096));
```

Problems can arise when restricting the read length. Imagine we restrict the read length to `100` bytes and `JFile::read()` is unable to determine the size of the file. This will result in the chunk size being used to read the file contents. Instead of getting a string of `100` bytes, we may get a longer string. An easy way to combat this is to specify a chunk size equal to the read length or a divisor of the read length (for example 1, 2, and 5 are divisors of `10`).

```
$fileContents = JFile::read($filePath, false, 100, 100));
```

The final parameter allows us to specify an offset from which to start reading a file. This can be useful when processing a file a bit at a time. The following example will read from the 301st byte to the 400th byte:

```
$fileContents = JFile::read($filePath, false, 100, 100, 300));
```

Offset from the end of the file

We can use a negative offset value to specify an offset from the end of the file. For example an offset of `-100` will read the last 100 bytes of the file.

See also

Prior to reading a file, it can be useful to ensure that the file already exists. For more information, refer to the previous recipe, *Checking whether a file or folder exists.*

To add files to the filesystem, refer to the *Uploading files to Joomla!* recipe, later in this chapter.

Deleting a file or folder

This recipe explains how to delete a file or a folder from the filesystem. This recipe also explains how we can easily delete a group of files in one go.

How to do it...

To delete a file, we use the static `JFile::delete()` method. In its most basic form, this method takes a single parameter, that is, the full path to the file we want to delete. The method returns a Boolean value, which determines whether or not the file was deleted successfully.

```
// define path to file to delete
$filePath = JPATH_COMPONENT . DS . 'deleteme.txt';

// attempt to delete file
$fileDeleted = JFile::delete($filePath);
```

Similarly, to delete a folder, we use the static `JFolder::delete()` method. We pass it the full path of the folder we want to delete. This method also returns a Boolean value, which determines whether or not the folder was successfully deleted.

```
// define path to folder to delete
$folderPath = JPATH_COMPONENT . DS . 'deleteme';

// attempt to delete folder
$folderDeleted = JFolder::delete($folderPath);
```

 The static `JFolder::delete()` method does not care if the folder being deleted is not empty. If it does contain files or folders, these will be deleted recursively.

How it works...

To delete files and folders, the `JFile::delete()` and `JFolder::delete()` methods will attempt to use the simple PHP functions, `unlink()` and `rmdir()` respectively. In instances where these functions are not successful, and FTP is enabled, the methods will attempt to use an FTP connection to delete the files and folders.

There's more...

The static `JFile::delete()` method has a nifty trick up its sleeve: it is able to delete multiple files in one go. To achieve this, we must pass the method an array of paths instead of a single path.

```
// define paths to files
$filePaths = array (
    JPATH_COMPONENT . DS . 'deleteme.txt',
```

```
        JPATH_COMPONENT . DS . 'deletemetoo.txt'
    );

    // attempt to delete files
    $fileDeleted = JFile::delete($filePath);
```

Note that the same usage cannot be applied when dealing with the static folder delete method JFolder::delete()*.*

 The static JFile::delete() method always returns one Boolean value. If we attempt to delete several files in one go and one file fails to delete, the method will terminate at that point and return false.

Before deleting any file or folder, it can be useful to verify that the file or folder already exists. Attempting to delete a folder that does not exist will result in a return value of false and a slightly ambiguous warning message stating that the path is not a folder. Similarly, attempting to delete a file that does not exist will result in a return value of false and a warning message stating that the delete failed.

See also

To learn how to check for file and folder existence, refer to the *Checking whether a file or folder exists* recipe at the start of this chapter.

Copying a file or folder

This recipe explains how to create copies of files and folders.

How to do it...

To copy a file, we use the static JFile::copy() method. This method requires a minimum of two parameters be passed: the path to the source file and the path to the destination. This method returns a Boolean value that determines whether or not the copy was successful.

```
    // prepare paths
    $filePath = JPATH_COMPONENT . DS . 'copyme.txt';
    $fileCopyPath = JPATH_COMPONENT . DS . 'newcopy.txt';

    // attempt to copy file
    $fileCopied = JFile::copy($filePath, $fileCopyPath);
```

The static `JFile::copy()` method will overwrite existing files.

To copy a folder, we use the static `JFolder::copy()` method. This method is very similar to the static `JFile::copy()` method. It too requires a minimum of two parameters be passed: the path to the source folder and the path to the destination folder. This method returns a Boolean value that determines whether or not the copy was successful.

```
// prepare paths
$folderPath = JPATH_COMPONENT . DS . 'copyme';
$folderCopyPath = JPATH_COMPONENT . DS . 'newcopy';

// attempt to copy folder
$folderCopied = JFolder::copy($folderPath, $folderCopyPath);
```

Unlike `JFile::copy()`, the `JFolder::copy()` method does not overwrite existing folders. That is to say, the destination path must not currently exist. If it does, an error will be raised, terminating the script.

 If we attempt to copy a file to a folder that does not exist, the results may vary depending on the installation. If FTP is enabled, the method will attempt to create the destination folder. Otherwise, the method will fail. Therefore, it is best to use this method only when we know that the destination folder exists.

How it works...

The `JFile::copy()` and `JFolder::copy()` methods favor FTP over PHP filesystem functions. That is to say, if FTP is enabled, these methods will use FTP in preference to PHP filesystem functions. If for any reason, the methods fail when using FTP (for example, due to restricted permissions), they will not attempt to use their PHP counterparts.

There's more...

Both the `JFile::copy()` and `JFolder::copy()` methods accept a third optional parameter. This is a path prefix which is prepended to both the source and destination parameters. For example, we can rewrite our file copy example:

```
// prepare filenames
$file = 'copyme.txt';
$fileCopy = 'newcopy.txt';

// attempt to copy file
$fileCopied = JFile::copy($file, $fileCopy, JPATH_COMPONENT);
```

We mentioned that the `JFolder::copy()` method will raise a fatal error if the destination already exists. It is possible to prevent this using the fourth `JFolder::copy()` parameter, `force`. If we enable `force`, the method will continue even if the destination folder already exists. If the destination already contains files and folders, these will remain intact, but files may be overwritten.

See also

The next recipe describes two similar filesystem functions, *Moving and renaming files and folders*.

Moving and renaming files and folders

This recipe explains how to move a file or folder from one location to another. This process is technically the same as renaming a file or folder.

How to do it...

To relocate a file, we use the static `JFile::move()` method. This method requires two parameters: the source file and the destination path. The destination path includes the filename. Thus the `JFile::move()` method is as much about renaming files as it is about moving files. The method returns a Boolean value determining the success or failure of the method. Note that when the method fails, a Joomla! warning will be raised.

```
// prepare paths
$filePath = JPATH_COMPONENT . DS . 'moveme.txt';
$fileMovePath = JPATH_COMPONENT . DS . 'here.txt';

// attempt to move file
$fileMoved = JFile::move($filePath, $fileMovePath);
```

On the other hand, to move a folder, we use the static `JFolder::move()` method. This method also requires two parameters: the source folder and the destination path. The destination path includes the folder name. Thus the `JFolder::move()` method can be used to rename as well as move folders.

```
// prepare paths
$folderPath = JPATH_COMPONENT . DS . 'moveme';
$folderMovePath = JPATH_COMPONENT . DS . 'movemehere';

// attempt to move folder
$folderMoved = JFolder::move($folderPath, $folderMovePath);
```

Error handling is significantly different in the static `JFolder::move()` method. This method returns Boolean `true` on success and an error string on failure. Unlike the `JFile::move()` method, no Joomla! warning is raised on failure.

How it works...

The `JFile::move()` and `JFolder::move()` methods always use FTP rather than PHP filesystem functions if FTP is enabled. Despite the different error handling used by these two methods, their actual implementations are incredibly similar. When FTP is enabled, these methods use the FTP `RNFR` and `RNTO` service commands (accessed through the PHP function `ftp_rename()`). When FTP is not enabled, the methods use the PHP filesystem function `rename()`.

There's more...

Much like the `JFile::copy()` and `JFolder::copy()` methods, we can supply the `JFile::move()` and `JFolder::move()` methods with a base path. This is prepended to both the source and destination parameters. For example, we can rewrite our folder move example:

```
// prepare paths
$folderPath = 'moveme';
$folderMovePath = 'movemehere';

// attempt to move folder
$folderMoved = JFolder::move($folderPath, $folderMovePath,
                                        JPATH_COMPONENT);
```

See also

To copy a file or folder, see the previous recipe *Copying a file or folder*.

Creating a folder

This recipe describes how to create a new folder in the filesystem.

How to do it...

To create a new folder, we use the static `JFolder::create()` method. In its most basic form, we pass this method a single parameter, the full path of the new folder we want to create. The method returns a Boolean value, which determines whether or not the folder was successfully created.

```
$folderPath = JPATH_COMPONENT . DS . 'afolder';
$createdFolder = JFolder::create($folderPath);
```

Luckily for us, the static `JFolder::create()` method is intelligent enough to cope with paths in which several folders do not currently exist. For instance, if while executing the following example, the folder `afolder` does not exist, it will be created before creating the subfolder `anotherfolder`.

```
$folderPath = JPATH_COMPONENT . DS . 'afolder' . DS . 'anotherfolder';
$createdFolders = JFolder::create($folderPath);
```

The only downside of this is the simplistic nature of the return value. If the method were to fail, we would not know the point at which the failure occurred. To determine this, we would have to check the existence of each folder in the path.

For security reasons, it can be a good idea to use the static `JPath::check()` method on the path of the proposed new folder prior to executing `JFolder::create()`. The `JPath::check()` method checks for file snooping. That is to say, it makes sure that the path is in the current Joomla! installation part of the filesystem. For more information, refer to Chapter 2, *Keeping Extensions Secure*.

How it works

The static `JFolder::create()` method always attempts to create new folders using FTP in preference to PHP filesystem functions. Using FTP reduces the likelihood of encountering problems when dealing with folder permissions. *Obviously, FTP can be used only where the installation instance has the necessary credentials*.

In instances where there are no FTP credentials, the method will use the PHP `mkdir()` function. The problem with this function is that it is not recursive; however, the `JFolder::create()` method will deal with this issue for us. *Note that as of PHP 5.0.0, it is possible to use `mkdir()` recursively*.

There's more...

By default, all new folders are created with the permissions 0755, or rwxr-xr-x. It is possible to override this by providing the second JFolder::create() method parameter. For example, we can create a folder with the permissions 0644, or rw-r--r--.

```
$createdFolder = JFolder::create($folderPath, 0644);
```

This parameter is ignored in instances where the folder already exists. That is to say, if the folder we are trying to create already exists and has different permissions to those which we specify, the permissions will not be changed.

See also

To check if a folder already exists, refer to the first recipe in this chapter, *Checking whether a file or folder exists*.

For information about changing permissions on existing folders, refer to the last recipe in this chapter, *Changing file and folder permissions*.

Uploading files to Joomla!

This recipe describes how to deal with files uploaded via HTML forms.

Getting ready

To upload a file to Joomla!, we must first create a form in which the user can select a file to upload. This will usually be located in a tmpl layout file in a view. When we define the <form> element, we must set the enctype attribute to multipart/form-data. The enctype attribute defines the content-type of a POST payload; by default, it is application/x-www-form-urlencoded.

```
<form enctype="multipart/form-data"
      action="index.php"
      method="post"
      name="adminForm">
```

Nested within the <form> element, we need to add a file upload box. This is an <input> element of the type file.

```
<input class="input_box"
       name="uploadFile"
       type="file"/>
```

How to do it...

Information about uploaded files is accessed through `JRequest`. In the following example, we get the data about the file specified in the field `uploadFile`.

```
$uploadFile = JRequest::getVar('uploadFile', null, 'FILES', 'ARRAY');
```

The value of `$uploadFile` should be an array populated with data about the uploaded file. (It does not contain the file itself.) To make sure that a file was uploaded, we simply need to check that `$uploadFile` is an array:

```
if (!is_array($uploadFile)) {
    // @todo handle no upload present
}
```

The next step is to verify that the upload was indeed successful.

```
if ($uploadFile['error'] || $uploadFile['size'] < 1) {
    // @todo handle upload error
}
```

Now, for a bit of security. We should always verify that the file specified in the array is indeed an uploaded file, using the `is_uploaded_file()` PHP function.

```
if (!is_uploaded_file($uploadFile['tmp_name'])) {
    // @todo handle potential malicious attack
}
```

Once we have verified the integrity of the uploaded file, we can start working with it. It is best to move the file before we start working with it, either to its ultimate location or to the Joomla! temporary directory for inspection. We do this using the static `JFile::upload()` method.

The static `JFile::upload()` method accepts two parameters, the source file path and the destination path. The method returns a Boolean value we can use to determine if the method was successful.

```
// Prepare the temporary destination path
$config          = & JFactory::getConfig();
$fileDestination = $config->getValue('config.tmp_path') . DS
                        . JFile::getName($uploadFile['tmp_name']);

// Move uploaded file
$uploaded = JFile::upload($uploadFile['tmp_name'], $fileDestination);
```

In the example above we move the uploaded file to the Joomla! temporary folder. Notice that the filename we use is determined by using the static `JFile::getName()` method. It extracts the filename alone from the passed parameter, in this case the current complete path of the file.

Remove temporary files after use

It is always important to remove any temporary files after we have finished working with them.

How it works

In a normal situation, we would use the global `$_FILES` variable to access uploaded file data. However, in Joomla! we access this data through `JRequest`. For more information about `JRequest`, refer to the *Safely retrieving request data* recipe in Chapter 2, *Keeping Extensions Secure*. The array that is extracted should contain the following elements:

Element	Description
error	Error code expressed as an integer. A code of 0 means no error. For more information, refer to `http://php.net/manual/features.file-upload.errors.php`.
name	Original name of the file.
size	Size of the file in bytes.
tmp_name	Full path to the temporary location of the file uploaded to the server.
type	MIME encoding of the file—this is provided by the client and, therefore, should never be considered entirely reliable.

When we check the `error` element, we are looking for a value greater than 0 because an error code of 0 means that no errors occurred. We also make sure that the file is not empty and has a size of at least 1 byte. This is not required but is generally a good idea.

The `is_uploaded_file()` PHP function checks if the specified file is a file that was uploaded in the request. Without this malicious users could potentially trick us into working with the wrong file, as described in `CWE-616`.

There's more...

Upload file sizes are restricted by PHP and are set in the PHP configuration file. It is possible to set this value in the form data. To set this in the form data, add a hidden field with the name, `MAX_FILE_SIZE`. The value of `MAX_FILE_SIZE` is expressed in bytes, so in the following example the maximum file size is one megabyte.

```
<input type="hidden"
       name="MAX_FILE_SIZE"
       value="1048576" />
```

The MAX_FILE_SIZE field must appear before the file field.

This is not an entirely reliable mechanism, as it relies on the data sent by the client. We can also check the size of a file after it has been uploaded, using the size key in the file array. The value of the size key is also expressed in bytes.

```
if ($uploadFile['size'] > 1048576) {
    // @todo handle upload larger than 1MB
}
```

For an extra layer of user niceties, we can check if uploads are enabled in the PHP configuration file using the PHP ini_get() function.

```
// Check if uploads are allowed
if ((boolean)ini_get('file_uploads') == false) {
    // @todo handle PHP uploads disabled
}
```

We can also inform the user of any upload size restrictions.

```
$maxFileSize = ini_get('upload_max_filesize');
```

The value returned by this is not entirely consistent. This is because the value can be expressed in bytes, kilobytes, megabytes, and since PHP 5.1.0, gigabytes. To get this value in bytes we can use the following function, based on the function described at http://php.net/manual/function.ini-get.php.

```
/**
 * Gets the maximum size of file uploads
 * expressed in bytes
 *
 * @return int
 */
function getMaximumUploadSizeInBytes() {
    $uploadSize = trim(ini_get('upload_max_filesize'));
    $last = strtolower($uploadSize[strlen($uploadSize)-1]);
    switch($last) {
        // The 'G' modifier is available since PHP 5.1.0
        case 'g':
          $uploadSize *= 1024;
        case 'm':
          $uploadSize *= 1024;
        case 'k':
          $uploadSize *= 1024;
    }
    return $uploadSize;
}
```

To create a user-friendly value that always displays in megabytes, we can use the following function:

```
/**
 * Gets the maximum size of file uploads
 * expressed in megabytes
 *
 * @return int
 */
function getMaximumUploadSizeInMegaBytes() {
    $bytes = $this->getMaximumUploadSizeInBytes();
    return $bytes / 1048576;
}
```

For more information about the `upload_max_filesize` directive, refer to `http://php.net/manual/ini.core.php#ini.upload-max-filesize`.

Avoid dangerous file types

If we intend to store files in the filesystem, it is vital that we do not allow dangerous files (`CWE-434`). For example, we should not store uploaded PHP files in the filesystem because a malicious script could be uploaded and executed. *If we are storing files in a database, this is less of a problem.*

To check a file type, we can use the file extension as follows:

```
$extension = getExt($uploadFile['name']);
```

We can go further by checking the MIME type of the file. The MIME type is often included in the file array. However, this is determined by the client and is, therefore, vulnerable to spoofing. A more robust solution is to use the `mime_content_type()` PHP function, available as of PHP 4.3.0 or the more accurate PECL Fileinfo extension, enabled by default as of PHP 5.3.0.

```
if (function_exists('finfo_file')) {
    // use PECL Fileinfo
    $finfo    = finfo_open(FILEINFO_MIME);
    $mimeType = finfo_file($finfo, $uploadFile['tmp_name']);
    finfo_close($finfo);
} elseif (function_exists('mime_content_type')) {
    // use PHP mime_content_type() function
    $mimeType = mime_content_type($uploadFile['tmp_name']);
} else {
    // use the client data
    $mimeType = $uploadFile['type'];
}
```

For information about reading the contents of an uploaded file, refer to the second recipe in this chapter, *Reading a file*.

Reading a directory structure

This recipe explains how to read the structure of the filesystem from a given point. This includes recursive reading of folders and files.

How to do it...

To read a directory structure, or rather to get a list of folders and subfolders, we can use the static `JFolder::listFolderTree()` method. In its most basic form, this method requires two parameters: the path to the folder in which we want to know the directory structure and a filter. To get all folders, specify a filter value of . (single period character).

```
$folders = JFolder::listFolderTree($path, '.');
```

Check the folder exists before execution

It is a good idea to check that the path we point `JFolder::listFolderTree()` at does exist. If we pass the method a non-existent path, the method will not respond well; it will throw a Joomla! warning and a PHP warning.

How it works

The value returned by `JFolder::listFolderTree()` will always be an empty array or a two-dimensional array. An empty array indicates there are no subfolders. The array is not organized in a tree-like structure. In the case of a two-dimensional array, all folders, irrespective of their position in the directory layout, will be represented by an inner array in the returned array.

We can put this into context by using an example. The following is a sample directory structure:

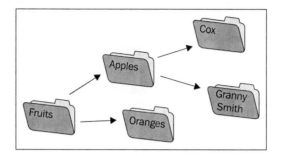

If we point `JFolder::listFolderTree()` at `Fruits`, the method will return an array containing four elements, each representing one of the folders. _Note that the root folder, in this instance_ `Fruits`, _is not included in the result._ The outer array does not use any special form of indexing; it is just a basic array. The inner arrays contain five elements, the keys of which are described in the following table:

Key	Description
id	Unique identifier in this array, used by `parent`
parent	Reference to the parent folder (this references the value of `id`, not the array index), if this is `0` the parent folder is that defined in the original path
name	Name of the folder, for example `Apples`
fullname	Full path to the folder
relname	Path to the folder relative to the root folder

There's more

There exist two similarly helpful static `JFolder` methods. The `JFolder::files()` method retrieves a list of files. The `JFolder::folders()` method retrieves a list of folders. Unlike the `JFolder::listFolderTree()` method these methods are not recursive. These methods require one parameter, the path to the folder in which to look for files or folders.

```
// prepare the path
$path = JPATH_COMPONENT . DS . 'somefolder';

// get the files and folders in somefolder
$files   = JFolder::files($path);
$folders = JFolder::folders($path);
```

Both of these methods return an array of strings with the names of the files or folders. We can change the behavior of these methods using the remaining four optional parameters, which are same for both the methods. The following table describes the parameters:

Parameter	Default	Description
path		Path to the folder in which to look
filter	.	Regular expression to filter by (must not include pattern delimiters)
recurse	false	Get files/folder in subfolders
fullpath	false	Return the full path of the files/folders or just the name
exclude	array('.svn', 'CVS')	Files and folders to exclude from the results

Changing file and folder permissions

This recipe explains how to modify the permissions of files and folders.

Getting ready

This recipe relies on the static JPath class. Therefore, we must import this class before continuing.

```
// import JPath class
jimport('joomla.filesystem.path');
```

How to do it...

Prior to changing permissions, it is a good idea to check the current permissions. We can do this using the static JPath::getPermissions() method. This method returns a string that represents the permissions in *nix alpha notation (described in the chapter introduction).

```
// get the current file permissions
$permissions = JPath::getPermissions($path);
```

If we want the file or folder to have specific permissions, we simply check the value returned by this method. For example, if we want to check for the permissions 644, normally applied to PHP files, we would do this:

```
// check for permissions 644
if ($permissions != 'rw-r--r--') {
    // @todo permissions are not 644!
}
```

Optionally, we can check if we have the necessary permissions to modify the permissions of the file or folder. We do this using the static `JPath::canChmod()` method.

```
// check if we can change the permissions
if(JPath::canChmod($path)) {
    // @todo change permissions
}
```

 Chmod, or Change Mode, is the act of changing the mode of an item in the filesystem.

Now for the bit we have been waiting for! To change the permissions, we use the static `JPath::setPermissions()` method. To this method, we pass three parameters: the path to the file or folder for which we want to change the permissions, the permissions we want to apply to the files, and the permissions we want to apply to the folders.

```
// change the permissions
JPath::setPermissions($path, '0644', '0755');
```

 We are not required to supply the second and third parameters. These parameters default to `'0644'` and `'0755'`, the most common permissions for files and folders when dealing with PHP applications.

How it works

Unlike many of the filesystem helper class methods, changing the permissions of files and folders is never attempted using FTP. Therefore, we can set permissions only for files and folders that the PHP/web server user has permissions to change.

The static `JPath::setPermissions()` method is recursive. This means that if we point it at a directory, all subfolders and files will also have their permissions altered. This is why the method provides two permissions parameters. We can easily apply different permissions to files and folders simultaneously.

When setting permissions on a folder, it is possible not to change the permissions of files held in the folder and other subfolders. We do this by supplying a value of `null` for the second parameter.

```
// change the folder permissions only
JPath::setPermissions($path, null, '0755');
```

In a similar fashion, we can use the `JPath::setPermissions()` method to only alter permissions of files held in a folder and its subfolders. We do this by supplying a value of `null` for the third parameter.

```
// change the file permissions only
JPath::setPermissions($path, '0644', null);
```

Index

Symbols

A

R

raiseError() 291
RAW document, outputting from MVC component
  steps 190, 191
  working 191
Read access 307
Really Simple Syndication. *See* **RSS feed**
record
  checking, JTable used 89-91
  creating, JTable used 84
  deleting, JTable used 88
  incrementing, JTable used 95
  modifying, JTable used 91, 93
  publishing, JTable used 93, 94
  reading, JTable used 88
  unpublishing, JTable used 93, 94
  updating, JTable used 87
record, updating
  JTable used 87
  starting with 87
recurse parameter 324
regular expression
  executing, on UTF-8 string 139
  unicode characters 140
  working 140
rel attribute 189
request data
  casting 60
  JRequest::getVar()method, using 59
  retrieving, safely 58-64
  starting 59
  strings, masking 62-64
responses
  client caching, controlling 182, 183
  client caching, working 182
  updation information, JDocument::setModified
    Date()method used 183
RSS feed 185
RSS feed creation, in MVC component
  <link> tag, adding 189, 190
  icon 188
  icon, displaying 189
  JDocumentFeed::set() method, using
    186-188
  starting with 185
  steps 186
  values, setting 188

S

SCIntilla based Text Editor 126
SciTE 126
SCM
  about 8
  need for 10
security weaknesses CWE-459 282
separator button 209
session
  data, adding to 99-101
  data addition, JSession::set() method used
    100
  data addition, starting with 100
  data setting, alternative way 101
  working 100, 101
session data
  checking for 104
  getting ready 102
  JSession::has() method, using 104
  JSession::get() method, using 102
  obtaining 102, 103
  obtaining, alternative way 103, 104
  working 102, 104
session handler
  JSession object, retrieving 98
  obtaining 98, 99
  starting 98
  working 98, 99
session token
  checking 105
  JSession::getToken() method 105
setError() method
  overiding 266
size element 319
Source Control Management. *See* **SCM**
spacers
  adding, example 210
  adding, to toolbar 210, 211
  JToolBarHelper::spacer() method, using 210
SQL-safe LIKE string comparison queries
  encapsulating process 46
  escaping process 46

[PACKT] Thank you for buying
PUBLISHING Joomla! 1.5 Development Cookbook

Packt Open Source Project Royalties

When we sell a book written on an Open Source project, we pay a royalty directly to that project. Therefore by purchasing Joomla! 1.5 Development Cookbook, Packt will have given some of the money received to the Joomla! Project.

In the long term, we see ourselves and you—customers and readers of our books—as part of the Open Source ecosystem, providing sustainable revenue for the projects we publish on. Our aim at Packt is to establish publishing royalties as an essential part of the service and support a business model that sustains Open Source.

If you're working with an Open Source project that you would like us to publish on, and subsequently pay royalties to, please get in touch with us.

Writing for Packt

We welcome all inquiries from people who are interested in authoring. Book proposals should be sent to authors@packtpub.com. If your book idea is still at an early stage and you would like to discuss it first before writing a formal book proposal, contact us; one of our commissioning editors will get in touch with you.

We're not just looking for published authors; if you have strong technical skills but no writing experience, our experienced editors can help you develop a writing career, or simply get some additional reward for your expertise.

About Packt Publishing

Packt, pronounced 'packed', published its first book "Mastering phpMyAdmin for Effective MySQL Management" in April 2004 and subsequently continued to specialize in publishing highly focused books on specific technologies and solutions.

Our books and publications share the experiences of your fellow IT professionals in adapting and customizing today's systems, applications, and frameworks. Our solution-based books give you the knowledge and power to customize the software and technologies you're using to get the job done. Packt books are more specific and less general than the IT books you have seen in the past. Our unique business model allows us to bring you more focused information, giving you more of what you need to know, and less of what you don't.

Packt is a modern, yet unique publishing company, which focuses on producing quality, cutting-edge books for communities of developers, administrators, and newbies alike. For more information, please visit our website: www.PacktPub.com.

Learning Joomla! 1.5 Extension Development

ISBN: 978-1-847191-30-4   Paperback: 200 pages

A practical tutorial for creating your first Joomla! 1.5 extensions with PHP

1. Program your own extensions to Joomla!

2. Create new, self-contained components with both back-end and front-end functionality

3. Create configurable site modules to show information on every page

4. Distribute your extensions to other Joomla! users

Joomla! Web Security

ISBN: 978-1-847194-88-6   Paperback: 264 pages

Secure your Joomla! website from common security threats with this easy-to-use gu

1. Learn how to secure your Joomla! websites

2. Real-world tools to protect against hacks on your site

3. Implement disaster recovery features

4. Set up SSL on your site

5. Covers Joomla! 1.0 as well as 1.5

Please check **www.PacktPub.com** for information on our titles

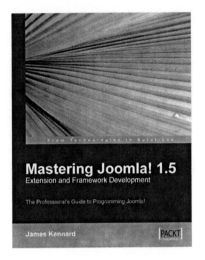

Joomla! 1.5 Template Design

Create your own professional-quality templates with this fast, friendly guide

Tessa Blakeley Silver

PACKT

Joomla! 1.5 Template Design

ISBN: 978-1-847197-16-0   Paperback: 284 pages

Create your own professional-quality templates with this fast, friendly guide

1. Create Joomla! 1.5 Templates for your sites

2. Debug, validate, and package your templates

3. Tips for tweaking existing templates with Flash, extensions and JavaScript libraries

Joomla! E-Commerce with VirtueMart

Build feature-rich online stores with Joomla! 1.0/1.5 and VirtueMart 1.1.x

Suhreed Sarkar

PACKT

Joomla! E-Commerce with VirtueMart

ISBN: 978-1-847196-74-3   Paperback: 476 pages

Build feature-rich online stores with Joomla! 1.0/1.5 and VirtueMart 1.1.x

1. Build your own e-commerce web site from scratch by adding features step-by-step to an example e-commerce web site

2. Configure the shop, build product catalogues, configure user registration settings for VirtueMart to take orders from around the world

3. Manage customers, orders, and a variety of currencies to provide the best customer service

4. Handle shipping in all situations and deal with sales tax rules

5. Covers customization of site look and feel and localization of VirtueMart

Please check **www.PacktPub.com** for information on our titles

Lightning Source UK Ltd.
Milton Keynes UK
03 November 2009

145753UK00001B/85/P